News on the Internet

OXFORD STUDIES IN DIGITAL POLITICS
Series editor: Andrew Chadwick, Royal Holloway, University of London

The Digital Origins of Dictatorship and Democracy: Information Technology and Political Islam
Philip N. Howard

NEWS ON THE INTERNET

Information and Citizenship in the
21st Century

David Tewksbury and Jason Rittenberg

OXFORD
UNIVERSITY PRESS

OXFORD
UNIVERSITY PRESS

Oxford University Press, Inc., publishes works that further
Oxford University's objective of excellence
in research, scholarship, and education.

Oxford   New York
Auckland   Cape Town   Dar es Salaam   Hong Kong   Karachi
Kuala Lumpur   Madrid   Melbourne   Mexico City   Nairobi
New Delhi   Shanghai   Taipei   Toronto

With offices in
Argentina   Austria   Brazil   Chile   Czech Republic   France   Greece
Guatemala   Hungary   Italy   Japan   Poland   Portugal   Singapore
South Korea   Switzerland   Thailand   Turkey   Ukraine   Vietnam

Published by Oxford University Press, Inc.
198 Madison Avenue, New York, New York 10016

www.oup.com

Oxford is a registered trademark of Oxford University Press

Library of Congress Cataloging-in-Publication Data
Tewksbury, David.
News on the internet : information and citizenship in the 21st century / David Tewksbury & Jason Rittenberg.
    p.   cm.—(Oxford studies in digital politics)
Includes bibliographical references and index.
ISBN 978-0-19-539196-1 (hardcover : alk. paper)—ISBN 978-0-19-539197-8 (pbk. : alk. paper)
1. Citizen journalism. 2. Online journalism. 3. Citizenship—Technological innovations.
4. Political participation—Technological innovations. I. Rittenberg, Jason. II. Title.
PN4784.C615T48   2012
070.4—dc23   2011032439

Printed in the United States of America
on acid-free paper

CONTENTS

ACKNOWLEDGMENTS

David thanks Risa, Neil, and Maggie for their patience and encouragement. They make everything possible.

Jason would like to thank his wife, Lori, for all of her support and patience while working on this book. He would also like to thank his children, parents, friends, and colleagues for their encouragement during the process.

News on the Internet

CHAPTER 1
Introduction

I magine, if you can or if you remember, the days before the internet. Most people received the bulk of their news from local and national television news broadcasts. The number of news stories contained in 30 or even 60 minutes of news was relatively small, and most stories ran for a minute or two at most. What is more, television news stories were programmed to run in a particular order. To get to information about sports or weather, people had to wait through lead stories on a variety of topics (mostly local, national, and international public affairs). There was a thriving newspaper industry in those days—even as the number of people reading daily newspapers had been steadily falling for decades. Listening to radio news and reading magazine news accounted for some news consumption, but broadcast television news and newspapers were king.

Much of the news that audiences received in the 20th century was based on a model of objective reporting. That model did not guarantee perfectly neutral or balanced news, as many critics and observers convincingly argued (e.g., Bennett 1996), but journalists and others in the business said that objectivity was both a format for news presentation and a goal for news content. Of course, the news business of the 20th century was largely built on profit incentives, and those incentives led to the production of a relatively homogeneous product much of the time (Bennett 1996).

The world of news that we are describing is very different from the one we now inhabit. Indeed, the news business of the recent past is already coming to seem a little fantastical. Today, audiences for broadcast television news and newspapers are experiencing steep and steady declines. The audience for news on the internet has grown from nothing in 1993 to second behind only television (Pew Research Center 2010). These and other changes in the media marketplace have been accompanied by a number of changes in the content and presentation of news. Cable television news has become segmented into topically and ideologically discrete channels, the number of print newspapers continues to dwindle, and the number of internet-based news sources has mushroomed.

Perhaps most important for the future of the news business, the very meaning of news is shifting. Large corporate news divisions based in New York and Washington still produce quite a bit of content about public affairs, but the nature of that content is rapidly changing. Pressures on the news business have led news providers to expand the commentary they produce as they shrink their newsroom staffs. Journalists cover more topical ground than they did before, and they often are expected to interact with audiences in online discussion environments. Increasingly, news consumers are also the creators. Online and mobile technologies allow them to feed information into the news stream and the public conversation. Almost anyone with internet access can break a story or even create the news, at least in principle.

Changes in the news business are challenging the old definitions of press and audience. On the one hand, the dividing line between journalist and citizen is becoming particularly fuzzy, as more people become involved in the creation of news. On the other hand, the current technologies have facilitated a change in the meaning of an audience. The dominant media of the 20th century operated within a system of centralized, largely one-way news dissemination. To consume the news was to ingest a diet of information selected by news professionals. What is more, the major media determined the flow of news. Even a newspaper, always the most customizable news format, contains a structure that largely organizes news for audiences. Today, the receivers of the news exert substantial control over their news diet. They can choose among numerous outlets, preselect specific topics, and focus their time and attention on the messages they prefer.

Twenty years ago, it would have been hard to predict the transformations that have passed through the news business. Things look very different today. Of course, some things remain the same. People are still people, wars are still wars, and much of what has reliably drawn audiences to the news continues to do so. Nonetheless, much about online news is novel and emergent. Researchers in communication and allied fields have been speculating about the political and social effects of all of the changes in the nature of news and audiences.

Our goal in this book is to organize and review what is known and said about news on the internet. We look at news and audiences online, describing how audiences approach the news and influence its content. We look at the kind of news that appears on the internet, compare it with what shows up elsewhere, and speculate about the meanings of these patterns.

We then return to the news audience, think about how people are getting and creating news online, and offer some conclusions about how current uses of the news may affect the quality of social and political life in modern democracies.

This introductory chapter serves two functions. First, it provides background information for much of what we discuss in the book. The evolution of the news business is directly related to the evolution of politics and public discourse in a democracy. Therefore, we start with a short discussion of information and its relationship with citizenship. Then we preview, in general terms, some of the attributes of the internet that are most relevant for the creation, presentation, and consumption of news. We also foreshadow the connections between these characteristics and some of the consequential potential effects of online news. Finally, we briefly describe the plan for the book and sketch the major emphases of each chapter.

NEWS AUDIENCES AND CITIZENS

In our review, we describe the content and presentation of news on the internet and how people are interacting with that news. Making up much of what is novel and important about online news are the developments that force us to think about the role of audiences. The shift from a top-down media system to one that features more horizontal interaction of people and news represents a change in the relationship that citizens and others in a nation have with information. For our discussion, it is useful to consider some of the ways that scholars have described the roles of citizens and information in democratic nations.

Information in the Political System

Political scientist Bruce Bimber argues that information and the technology of its control and dissemination form a central pillar of power in a democratic society. Indeed, he notes that information and its control are at the core of the relationship between citizen and state and the intermediaries between them. A relatively stable set of relationships between information flows and political institutions constitutes what he calls an "information regime." When the nature of information structures change, political relationships also change: "Information regimes in the United States have been interrupted by information revolutions, which involve changes in the structure or accessibility of information. These revolutions may be initiated by technological developments, institutional change, or economic outcomes. An information revolution disrupts a prior information regime by creating new opportunities for political communication and the organization of collective action" (Bimber 2003, p. 18).

Changes in information regimes are consequential because ". . . democratic power tends to be biased toward those with the best command of political information at any particular stage in history" (Bimber 2003, p. 18). The media system of the 20th century was very hierarchically organized. As we have noted, news and other information flowed downstream from centralized news organizations to audiences. Political and economic leaders had ready access to journalists and news providers, exercising power, in part, through their control of information.

Of course, centralized control of news and information is still the rule in much of the American political system, but things are changing. In part through harnessing the properties of the internet, audiences have more input into the news system and more control over the flow of news. As we note in this book, some people use their control to avoid news about public affairs entirely, but others use it to expand their knowledge of issues and other topics. Some members of the news audience prefer a one-way flow of news, but others are using the internet to expand the reach of their voices.

The Requirements of Citizenship

Most 20th-century interpretations of democratic theory have placed the active citizen at the center of democratic systems (Berelson 1952). Political power ultimately rests with citizens in a democracy. With that power, citizens have a responsibility to gather information about public affairs (e.g., government, politics, and international events) and to form reasoned judgments about political leaders and issues. In this framework, the citizen is essentially a consumer of information. In order to be such a consumer, the citizen must seek out public affairs information (Berelson 1952). He or she must be an active user of the media. Ultimately, the news helps citizens gather the information they need. In many respects, the news is a public service of journalists and other news producers.

Although this is the dominant interpretation of democratic theory, there are others. Perhaps chief among them is offered by Michael Schudson (1998). In a review of the history of citizenship in the United States, he suggests that the relationship between citizens and political activity has changed. Initially, the duty of citizenship featured the relationship between the individual and political leaders. Everyday-citizen involvement in politics was limited to evaluating the qualities of leaders who represented them in government. The subsequent bulk of the 19th century featured a "partisan" model of citizenship. Here the citizen was expected to participate in the political system through support of political parties. This pluralist system replaced leaders with parties as the object of important political decision making. The 20th century is the period that put information at the core of citizens' political activity. It also saw the rise of political activity built around the establishment and protection of citizens' rights in the political system.

The role of the news in each of these periods is tied to the needs of the citizen for political information. In all times, information matters. But the need for citizens to follow a range of events, issues, and people in public affairs certainly depends on the dominant model of citizenship at any one time. Schudson suggests that the role of citizens in a democratic system is a malleable one. Political, social, and legal circumstances can influence how people think about their civic responsibilities and their relationship to the news.

Detailed knowledge about issues and policies in government has not always been central to citizenship, although it appears to occupy an important role today. Ultimately, any changes in the relationships among people, information (i.e., news), and political authority will influence how a society functions and how its citizens fare. That is one of the chief reasons we all should care about the provision and consumption of news on the internet.

THE ROLE OF TECHNOLOGY IN THE RELATIONSHIP AMONG CITIZENS, NEWS, AND SOCIETY

A central premise of the theory and research discussed in this book is that the technology of information delivery matters. We will neither examine nor state that assumption very often, but it is the foundation for research on the form, use, and effects of news on the internet (just as it informed earlier work on the effects of television; see Williams 1974).

A little background on the role of technology in social change and in people's lives is useful here. To say that technology matters is rather simplistic, of course. Perhaps more to the point, most researchers in communication assume that information technologies both provide ways for people to do what they want to do and suggest new things to do (e.g., Hughes 1997). That is, new communication technologies continue some social practices, facilitate desired new ones, and inspire novel developments. They do these things simultaneously.

For example, when television was widely adopted in American households in the period after World War II, the industry in the United States largely moved successful content from radio programs to television (Sterling and Kittross 2002). The new technology let people do what they already did (e.g., enjoy drama and comedy programming). But television proved to be more than radio with pictures. It facilitated the development of a number of new kinds of programming (e.g., the "Spectacular" of the 1950s and 1960s; Sterling and Kittross 2002) that moved broadcast entertainment content beyond what had been popular on radio. Similarly, the internet was primarily a product of government researchers and other scientists seeking to improve computing power and efficiency (Margolis and Resnick 2000). It ably accomplished that mission for early users of the system in the 1970s. But, as we know, widespread diffusion of the internet in the 1990s and today has inspired a number of additional uses. These examples illustrate that communication technologies satisfy existing needs and help generate new ones at the same time.

Sometimes theory and research on new technologies can seem to imply that technologies cause change or even that people are helpless to resist inevitable effects of technology. Most researchers today try to avoid that perspective, often pejoratively labeled "technological determinism" (e.g., Williams 1974), because it does not grant people much agency in the creation and shaping of technologies. A number of researchers examining new technologies have advocated a perspective closer to social shaping of technology. They suggest that people get the technology they want (e.g., Williams 1974), shape how it is used (MacKenzie and Wajcman 1985), and help determine its effects (Winner 1985).

We come down pretty close to the social perspective. We do not assume that new technologies such as the internet impose changes on people and political systems. Rather, we assume that social, economic, and political changes happen in concert with technological change. They facilitate one another. Which factor exerts the greater influence likely evolves over the course of a process of change. So, it may appear at times that the internet is driving social and political revolution. We prefer to think—taking the long view—of transformation in the role of citizens in a democracy as a joint product of technological and other changes. We try to implement that perspective in our discussion of the relationship between news and audiences. We describe what audiences do with the news and how they select news outlets, choose stories, and process information. We will similarly describe how news outlets present information and build audiences. The relationship between information and people is necessarily interactive.

The central focus of this book is the study of the potential effects of internet presentation of news. It is worth considering the particular way we approach theory and research on this topic. There are many paths to knowledge; the longer one engages in research, the more confidence one develops in the notion that many paths may lead to truth. Nonetheless, researchers (and authors of books like this one) make choices about how they will approach concepts and their study. The theory and research we review in this book come from different traditions. For example, we rely on analyses from political economy and theory from a number of domains. Underlying the bulk of our discussion and analysis, though, is the tradition of media effects research.

The media effects approach is grounded in the idea that social phenomena—such as media content and audience reactions—are open to observation and measurement. What is more, the dominant social-scientific strain of media effects research suggests that the effects of exposure to media content are unknown until they can be measured and tested. The tradition is not wholly yoked to empirical research norms, but they certainly define the parameters of much of the research in this area.

The media effects approach is one of several ways to study social phenomena. The study of media is replete with research that focuses on the social context of messages and audiences, the linguistic power of words and images, and the sociology of power within societies and institutions (such as news organizations). Some of these research traditions suggest that media effects research is too closely wedded to linear (i.e., cause leads to effect), empirical research (McQuail 2010). Critical theory, for example, suggests that media, messages, and audiences are all situated within power hierarchies that circumscribe and define communication and its outcomes (McQuail 2010). An empirical cause-and-effect orientation toward media necessarily omits important, underlying elements of social communication.

The media effects approach, largely centered in social-scientific research, retains several advantages for the aims of this book. Among them is the muscle it provides analysts wishing to compare media and messages across topical, national, and cultural boundaries. Researchers studying the content of the media might claim that they can identify the core elements of news from across the globe and within the various strata and social groups found in any one society. Likewise, media effects research can build and test theory that helps researchers understand and predict the outcomes of exposure to specific and general classes of media content. It is the generalizability of the findings of media effects research that makes them most useful for studying the potential personal and social role of the media.

Taking the media effects perspective, our efforts to describe the content of news online involve empirical analyses of sites and messages. Likewise, we summarize what theorists and other observers have predicted about the effects of exposure to news online and subject their expectations to empirical scrutiny. Anecdotal evidence is useful, to be sure, and we appreciate the heuristic power of exemplars and focused case studies. Nonetheless, we foreground empirical research when it is available. When it is not, we rely on theory, the available evidence we have, and a skeptical brand of common sense. We also willingly conclude that many research questions are still unanswered. That is what makes research fun.

ONLINE NEWS AND ITS EFFECTS

In many ways, the internet is the sum of all other media. When trying to describe it, its uses, and its effects, one must set parameters. There are a few primary features of news on the internet that take center stage in this book. They represent some of the most exciting developments with the technology and its use, and they have implications for how information and citizenship operate in advanced democracies. We briefly preview them here, noting how these characteristics generate certain themes that run through this book.

The Internet has a Wealth of News

Among the defining features of the contemporary internet is its information storage capacity. The internet is a big place. There are few practical limitations on the amount of news and information that can be stored and accessed online. This characteristic has two dimensions relevant to the presentation of news.

First, audiences can find a greater variety of news online than they can find in other media. It is hard to imagine that there is a topic or perspective under the sun that is not covered in some way online. Chris Anderson (2004) popularized this characteristic as the "long tail" of the internet. This phrase relates to a hypothetical distribution graph where the majority of users are clustered among a few popular sources at one end, but there continues to be at least some audience for many more outlets as the number of sites continues to rise. The "long tail" is shorthand for the fact that the size of the internet allows for niche content and audiences. Users not only may find substantial diversity in news opinion and topics, but they also may find substantial depth on a single news topic. News outlets can maintain links to dated material on their own sites and links to related content on other sites. Thus, people looking for depth of information on a topic can readily find it.

Among the originators of content online are professional new organizations. Many of these outlets also produce news for television, radio, magazines, and newspapers. Others are internet-only outfits, although they operate in a fashion that parallels the offline media. Perhaps more interesting is that the majority of people creating content for the internet are people who may have been called mere audiences in the time of the old media. These people are posting information and commentary to Web logs (blogs), reaching their own audiences with mass tweets over Twitter, or joining discussion boards on news sites. These typically are not paid news professionals, but they are adding to the volume and diversity of news online.

The second factor, then, is that private citizens creating content online and in other technologies are redefining the nature of news. They are adding to the flow of information online—be it opinion, links to related concepts, images, or other content—and they are contributing to the social and political lives of nations. They are sometimes called "citizen journalists" (Witt 2004). Their presence is often welcomed and facilitated by professional news organizations, but citizen journalists implicitly and explicitly challenge the authority of the major news media. The force of that challenge and what it means for the news and citizenship form one of the most compelling stories being played out online.

The trend of information control shifting away from a few powerful entities toward smaller outlets and even citizens is a type of information democratization. This concept, which is the focus of chapter 8 in this book, emphasizes the social transformation that has been made possible by digital media. It may seem trivial that your friend publishes a news-opinion blog that is read by ten people, but just a few generations ago, this person would likely not have had the inclination, means, or even knowledge to share his or her views through the media. Of course, this is not to say that any given blog makes a significant contribution to society. Information democratization is an aggregate-level concept marking the greater overall involvement of common citizens with the news and other political information.

Audiences are Changing

The technology of the internet allows individuals to post their own content and repurpose what has been posted by others. The concept of citizen journalism illustrates the fragility of the distinction between audience and journalist online. The composition and meaning of audiences on the internet are changing in other ways, too. The adoption of subscription media—such as cable or satellite television, in the past—naturally raises questions about how people think about the audience for a medium and its messages.

Internet access and use are costly, on a number of dimensions. To use the internet, people need a device (such as a computer or a smartphone) and a way to connect it to the network. This may be done very cheaply, such as by using workstations at a public library or accessing a free Wi-Fi signal at a public location, but the inconvenience of those methods limits the medium's accessibility. The costs in time and money for easy internet access are not small. Some people can afford the costs, but others cannot. The distance between these two kinds of people is called the digital divide. There are additional divisions between people who have facility with the internet and those who do not.

Gaps in internet access and skill prompt questions about the effective audience of news online. If the medium can empower people to control and parse the flow of news, some parts of the audience have access to that power, and others do not. It could be that younger people in a society have the upper hand with the internet. As a result, their relatively low offline political power—represented in low voter-turnout rates for young voters in the United States—could be partially offset by their ability to receive and influence online news.

The Internet Could Steal Audiences from Other Media

As the audience for online news has evolved since news started going online in the mid-1990s, so have audiences for the traditional media (newspapers, magazines, and broadcast radio and television). An ongoing topic for study has been the effect of internet news adoption on use of traditional news media. Audiences have been moving away from newspapers and broadcast television for some years, so it is not clear how much the internet is responsible for their declines. Nonetheless, there is clear evidence that use of new media is tied to use of the older ones. There are several ways to conceptualize that relationship, from replacement to complementary use. We will discuss their relevance in this context.

A key point with respect to news exposure in one or several media is that much exposure happens as a function of audience habit (Diddi and LaRose 2006). As a general rule of thumb, people develop their media-exposure patterns as they reach early adulthood—although they are influenced by factors experienced earlier in life—and tend to retain them over time (Diddi and LaRose 2006). When people adopt a new media habit after that time, they often add it to what they already do. They could drop their older habits, but established patterns can be quite resilient. One of the ways that media habits are most likely to change is through cohort replacement over time, the tendency for successive waves of people in a population to develop distinct habits as they enter adulthood and hold on to them later in life. Social-level change happens when new cohorts—with new habits—eventually replace the old ones.

Learning from the News Online may be Different

Some news that appears online is no different in form and content from what one might find in the traditional media. But some news organizations and news providers take advantage of the technologies of the World Wide Web to present information in novel ways. Journalists and citizens can link concepts and stories through hyperlinks, embedded computer language that allows for easy user navigation from one set of information to another.

A central question for news providers, audiences, and researchers is whether consuming news online is better than consuming it through other media. A dominant frame for that question is to ask whether people learn more from the news online than from the news offline. Hyperlinks can serve as a way for audience members to explore the many dimensions of a topic, but they can also confuse a news reader, essentially offering more information than can be easily consumed. It is hard to imagine the internet without hyperlinks, but it is not clear how much they help people learn.

People can Control their News Consumption

The internet allows and even forces people to make choices. With the news, this has meant that audiences can choose the sites, topics, stories, posts, and images they prefer. Consuming news online is often far from a passive experience. People do not need to be active in their selection and consumption of the news, but scholars and observers often assume that they are. Indeed, an active audience orientation to news consumption runs through much of the literature in this area.

Researchers often assume that people will take advantage of the capacity for choice that the internet provides. Audiences will be selective with what they choose and will focus on the topics and stories that suit their tastes and predispositions. Indeed, online news providers offer a number of ways for people to limit their exposure to unwanted information and ideas. This sort of selective exposure can limit the variety of information that people receive.

People who are exposed to a narrow range of information about public affairs might develop topical blind spots. With a great many news topics and entertainment options from which to choose, people might not be exposed to the important public affairs news of the day. Such a fragmented state of affairs, many observers say (e.g., Katz 1996; Webster and Phalen 1997), can affect how well people can function as citizens. They might not know enough about things in the political realm to function effectively. As we have noted, "functioning effectively" is a loaded concept, but at the very least, a fragmented citizenry has fewer things to talk about and perhaps fewer things in common (Sunstein 2001).

Not everyone assumes that people will naturally initiate processes of fragmentation by being highly selective. Regarding the lure of selectivity in cable television, Neuman wrote: "Some amount of filtering and skipping of news will continue to take place, but such filtering is balanced against the convenience and habitual reliance of the half-attentive audience member on the editorial judgment of news professionals. The average citizens want to review headlines to make sure they are at least aware of the basic events and issues everyone else is likely to know about" (1986, p. 156).

News Providers and Audiences Interact Online

The offline media changed substantially over the course of the 20th century. They once were largely mass media, which is what we call media when many or most of the outlets in an industry seek to attract large heterogeneous audiences (McQuail 1997). When pressured by other media and other forces, all except newspapers became specialized. That is, the majority of outlets in media industries defined their target audience in terms of stable characteristics such as demographic features (e.g., age, sex, race, ethnicity) or predispositions (e.g., political party or issue interest). They created content for the target and benefited from efficiencies of delivering well-defined, segmented audiences to advertisers.

The internet did not go through an evolution from mass to specialized medium. The specialized media environment into which the internet grew and its ability to support many content producers and consumers made it particularly suitable for news segmentation from the start of its public phase in 1993 (Margolis and Resnick 2000). Some news outlets provide content constructed for specific segments of the audience, and most others support technologies (e.g., customizable news portals, RSS feeds, blogs) that allow audiences to focus their consumption on specific content areas.

The more people look to the medium for segmented news, either located at specific sites or delivered through customized news technologies, the more they come to resemble other people in their segment. Naturally, they also come to be less like people in other segments. Ultimately, social segments grow apart from one another when what they know about politics becomes increasingly separate. Some researchers and observers have expressed concern that this sort of polarization will degrade the quality of democratic discourse and participation (e.g., Sunstein 2001; Webster and Phalen 1997).

Not all is bad, though. The internet allows news media to be very responsive to their audiences. News organizations allow people to leave comments attached to specific news stories, they encourage them to send messages to their reporters, and they provide places for people to upload their own stories and bits of information. What is more, news outlets can monitor activity on their sites and discern (from patterns of selection of specific stories) what their audiences want to see. Thus, sites can increase the efficiency with which audiences consume the news.

THE PLAN OF THIS BOOK

The internet is increasingly becoming the place where people in contemporary democracies go to get and leave information. This book discusses the dual role of the internet as a source of authoritative news and a vehicle for citizen creation and sharing of information. The fact that anyone with internet access can upload and consume information in thousands or millions of locations gives the medium a multidimensional character. The internet embodies the centralized ownership that characterizes the traditional media (McChesney 2004) and suffers from many of the biases that have plagued the press in the past (Bennett 1996), yet it features widespread popular creation of content and discussion of public affairs. In many ways, the internet is all media: mass and interpersonal, political and apolitical, wise and vacuous. We will attempt to discuss these attributes in a way that will illuminate their origin and point to the future of the news and politics.

In this book, we focus on the interaction of audiences and the internet. Indeed, whereas it is possible—though perhaps unwise—to talk about television or another of the older media without direct reference to its audience, this is not possible when talking about the internet. Everyone contributes to what is on the internet.

We start in chapter 2 with a look at how people use media and become an audience. We note that people can be passive or active members of an audience and that the internet forces us to think about audience activity in a new way. A primary focus of the chapter is on the identification of how audience activities influence the content and operation of media. We turn next, in chapter 3, to describe how news is generated and presented online. We compare content created for the offline media with that created for the internet—and the diminishing meaning of such distinctions. In chapter 4, we continue with a focus on online content, looking at how media conceive of content breadth and audience segments and how the two interact. We look at the extent to which online news sites tailor their content to specific audience characteristics and interests.

We return to a central focus on audience activity in chapter 5, where we examine the concept of audience selectivity. How much news audiences focus their internet time on the news and on specific topics might affect news outlets and the content they provide. From a normative perspective, the primary function of the news is informing people about political affairs. What people learn from the online news and how are the topics of chapter 6. We review what researchers have discovered about how people learn from the news, and we observe that consuming the news online might offer new ways for people to think about politics.

We next consider some of the substantial normative implications of online news provision and consumption. In chapter 7, we review two much-prophesied outcomes of online news consumption: fragmentation and polarization. We discuss the conditions under which they may occur, and we note that there is some evidence, though not yet a lot, that they are developing. Chapter 8 turns the table on the previous chapter a bit; we look at the normatively positive implications of how news appears and is consumed online. If more people feed information into the news stream and if this level of activity increases broad public engagement with politics, the internet is a democratizing force. It helps shed light on dark corners of public affairs. Once again, the internet has many faces. We conclude in chapter 9 with a brief summary and discussion of the ideas and evidence we have presented, looking ahead to news in the future.

CONCLUSIONS

Widespread adoption and use of the internet for news dissemination and consumption has prompted some questions about the meaning of citizenship and its relationship to information. Some conceptions of democracy suggest that people need to consume information and make informed decisions about public affairs. This approach is not universal, but information is certainly an important component of the relationship between citizens and political power.

When people talk about new communication technologies, they typically assume that technologies affect what people do. We would do well to remember that people determine what technologies do, certainly more often than the reverse. Our aim in this book is to eschew easy claims about the effects of the internet on people, processes, and institutions. The relationship between users and the internet is certainly a balance, in terms of both the flow of information and the power to effect change.

Despite the seemingly constant change one sees on the internet, it has some relatively stable attributes that form the core of the descriptions we offer in this book. Running throughout our discussion is the understanding that the medium carries an enormous quantity of information, some of it generated by organizations but much of it by individuals. The volume and diversity of news online, the convenience that many people experience when accessing it, and the control it provides users are all attractive features that may be pulling audiences away from the traditional media. What people do with the news online will affect what individuals know about politics, how knowledge is distributed in societies, and how democratic systems function.

We have talked quite a bit here about change, and we will continue to do so. Throughout this book, though, we need to bear in mind that new technologies do not always usher in social and political change. Bimber notes that information technology ". . . may increase opportunities for superficial, thoughtless, democratically hollow speech as well as opportunities for meaningful deliberation and public speech" (2003, p. 30). We cannot say, in the end, whether the internet is good or bad for publics and politics, but we can say a few things about how people and the medium work together. We offer predictions for how the news business—online and offline—will continue to evolve as a result of its interaction with audiences.

CHAPTER 2

Shifting Audiences

The audience is not a unified, static concept. Instead, the audience for any given type of content, or even any single program, is really a collection of smaller audiences and individuals who have banded together through a common interest. Audiences coalesce because of some combination of content, motivation, actors, hype, or social pressure. Media outlets are constantly challenged to find—and then maintain—a larger audience, and this is understandably difficult. Although the audience has always been an important consideration of media studies, the availability of choices through cable television and the internet has granted audiences an even more important role in this area. As a handful of media options have become 20, 100, and now millions, the fact that any given audience is made up of many smaller interests has become ever more apparent.

The reality of the compiled audience has provided a particular challenge to the news media. The availability of choices has enabled audiences to move away from broadcast news to new formats or nonnews topics altogether (Prior 2007). On the internet, we see many people choosing to get their news from partisan blogs, news aggregators, or even their friends. Many people do continue to watch the evening news, or at least visit the websites of major news organizations, but there is no denying that the overall audience for news content has shifted. In the current media system, the total news audience is divided into thousands of smaller audiences receiving content from thousands of sources. This compounds the challenge of compiling large audiences for media organizations and makes profiting from audiences particularly difficult.

Shifting audiences is the key factor for understanding online news. This chapter addresses the broader points of why audiences move between media and how these shifts affect the business of media. Specifically, the chapter begins with a discussion of how to define audiences and then explains how media selection works and how it affects media content. Finally, we specifically address the internet audience in terms of both the digital divide and how the audience will affect the news industry as a whole. Through this wide-ranging discussion, we hope to illuminate the relationship between contemporary audiences and the challenges facing the news industry.

DIFFERING CONCEPTUALIZATIONS OF THE AUDIENCE

Conceptualizing audiences is not a straightforward task, because there are many possible ways to do this. Because the internet is unique in its ability to facilitate user activity, we find behavior-based approaches to defining current news audiences the most interesting. One definitional method is to focus on normative expectations for the audience, which is to focus on how audiences should behave. A second method is to look at profiles of audiences, defining an audience from the ground up, as it were. This approach works best when a profile is based on long-term interests and tendencies, rather than on simple demographics.

Normative Conceptualizations of Audiences

The most common approach to thinking of audiences in terms of what they should do is democratic theory. Democratic theory might be best understood as a particular branch of philosophy that focuses on popularly elected government, its institutions, and its people. It would be impossible and unnecessary to cover all of it here. We can limit ourselves to just three of the more common forms of democratic theory—republicanism, liberal pluralism, and complex democracy—and even then, we can restrict our conversation to just the role of the people.

Republicanism (Baker 2002) may be the concept of government with which most people are familiar. This form of democratic theory argues for a democracy reliant on individual involvement to drive government decisions. This is made possible by a media system that is expected to provide useful information; this requires the mass media's journalistic norms of objectivity. Republicanism also has a lofty concept of what the public (i.e., the audience) should do. Individuals are expected not only to be able and willing to consider political phenomena and societal well-being above self-interest (Baker 2002) but also to participate regularly in public debates on government and policy. This form of democratic theory has dominated discussions of media and audiences over the course of the last century, but it is not the only possibility.

Liberal pluralism, our second form of democratic theory, is a group-centric model of democracy. In terms of media, this means that news outlets are more oriented to specific interests than the population as a whole (Baker 2002). Liberal pluralism also defines audience behaviors in terms of groups. Instead of needing to participate directly, individuals are expected to affiliate with organizations, which are themselves capable of expressing members' needs to government. The expectation for individual citizens is therefore much lower than under republicanism, because liberal pluralism does not require nearly the same degree of information or involvement.

Complex democracy is essentially a combination of the first two models. Complex democracy envisions vocal groups operating within a governmental system that is largely geared toward individuals (Baker 2002). This duality helps protect potentially marginalized concerns while still expecting most citizens to participate actively in government. The media for a complex democracy need to provide both a level of information that is sufficient for individual participation and information sources that can cater to special interests. Audiences are also more complicated under this model, because multiple norms of viewing behavior will exist. For example, strongly committed members of political groups will consume most of their media from related, trusted sources. Weak members may lean on supportive media but spend some time with broader content, and non-members may use a wide variety of media. The simultaneous presence of these political—and media—tendencies is the defining characteristic of the aptly named complex democracy.

These three normative definitions of audiences may seem abstract, but they can be practically applied. The mass-media system of newspapers and network television largely provides objective information aimed at individuals, which maps closely to the republican ideal. The alternative media today tend to provide content that is primarily aimed at particular interests (as we discuss later), which suits the liberal-pluralism form of democracy. Because both of these media exist today, it could be easily argued that the current media system is that of a complex democracy. This would seem to suggest that we should anticipate that citizens will match these expectations, which are to be individually informed and capable of participating in government if possible. If they do not participate, they must at least be informed and involved on some specific, important subject. However, even though our current media seem to fit this description, it is still possible to argue for other normative expectations. As we will see (particularly in chapters 6 and 7), it is still common for social observers to evaluate the role of audiences with the lofty standards of republicanism.

Profiling Conceptualizations of Audiences

There are many ways to define audiences in terms of who they are or what they do (instead of what we think they should do). These forms do not help us create expectations about how people, journalists, or media organizations should behave, but they can do more to reveal the media and audience as they actually are than can be achieved by applying normative expectations. There is an almost overwhelming number of profile-based categorizations available. We focus here on some of the more informative.

Diffusion-based Profiles

These profiles take their general name from diffusion research (Rogers 2003), which developed an early taxonomy categorizing people on the basis of their propensity to adopt certain behaviors, ideas, or technologies. Diffusion-based profiles, whether tied to the theory directly or indirectly, focus on categorizing people based on their tendency to use one news platform versus another. Such profiles are useful in that they help reveal not only what type of people are likely to use a given news format but also when or if nonusers are likely to adopt the technology in question.

Diffusion research has largely focused on an S-shaped curve to describe the spread of concepts and technologies (Rogers 2003). The curve, which is based on the percentage of people using a technology at any given time, defines early adopters as the people who enjoy getting to a new product first so they can be the ones to test and review it. Next come the opinion leaders, who learn about the product from early adopters and decide whether it is worthy of adoption. If so, then the product goes out to the early and late majorities. The final group, which may never even use the technology, includes the laggards. These profiling categories can be applied to specific news formats, facilitating predictions of whether and when the format is likely to reach acceptance from the masses.

One of the more recent and useful diffusion-based profiles was presented by the Pew Research Center for the People and the Press (2008b). This scheme categorized people based on their adoption of internet news. Pew essentially applied a sliding scale of traditional-media and new-media use, labeling exclusive users of old media as "traditionalists" (46 percent of American respondents), blended users as "integrators" (23 percent), and exclusive users of the internet as "net-newsers" (13 percent; the remaining percentage either could not be defined or did not use news at all). Taken together, diffusion-based profiles reveal the life cycle of the adoption of a technology and can also highlight which specific groups are making full or partial use of internet services.

Marketing-based Profiles

The marketing-based profile is a particularly useful way for content creators or advertisers to conceptualize audiences. This approach revolves around categorizing individuals into discrete audiences, in order to determine what content or products will appeal to each audience. When done successfully, marketing-based profiles help a media organization provide users with content that they want and help advertisers achieve better click-through rates. These objectives are somewhat synergistic, as more successful sites will also be better for advertising, and vice versa. Although scholars do not regularly investigate marketing-based profiles, they are very important to the financial development of internet media.

Marketing-based profiles can be created based on a number of factors, but demographics, interests, and behaviors will all typically play a role. For example, the *Washington Post* is the paper of record in America's capital. The paper's website is likely to be read by government officials, contractors, and their staffs. This information helps reveal the demographics and interests of the audience, which can be supplemented through other means. The *Washington Post* website often features content about government policies and advertisements from government (particularly defense) contractors. The orientation of content and advertising is clearly based on the marketing profile of the audience. A second example of these profiles in action can be seen in *Wired* magazine. This publication features technology news, and its users are presumably people who are both interested in and users of technology. *Wired* therefore became one of the most prominent early creators of an iPad magazine application. The company knew that the behavior of its audience leaned toward reading content through internet-capable mobile devices and accordingly created a service to suit this profile. In short, marketing-based profiles are based on a definition of audiences as consumers, and they use available information to refine this conceptualization.

How Profiles help us Understand Audiences

This discussion focused on some important conceptual schemes for defining audiences; we did not explore categorizations based on browsing habits or content creation. Normative perspectives on audiences are important, because we must decide what people should know if we are going to say anything constructive about news media and its effects. Putting them together, we see that audiences are commercial targets, adopting services at different speeds and, it is hoped, browsing with an eye toward becoming better-informed political participants. This broad conceptualization provides a foundation as we take a more critical look at the individuals who make up audiences.

AUDIENCE ACTIVITY AND SELECTIVITY AS CONCEPTS

Research on the actions and reactions of audiences falls within the research tradition often called media effects. It is concerned with the content of media messages and the study of how they affect audiences. Using the media involves making choices—many of them. Today, we take it as given that people are purposive and active in their selection of media and content. When they make decisions about what to see or hear, people are also determining what they will come to believe, feel, and do about the world. A central tenet of media effects research is that media selection decisions help determine the effects of messages on audiences. Despite the fact that work conducted as early as the 1950s connected individual content choices with effects (e.g., Delia 1987), this assumption has not always been a focus of media research. Rather, media effects scholars often consider the selection and the effects of media to be largely separate issues, and separate research usually deals with each. Fortunately, the new media systems have finally encouraged more widespread, simultaneous attention to both aspects of media.

Most broadly focused research today will consider media exposure as a circular process. Such an approach may start (although, as with all circular process, the starting point is relatively arbitrary) with forces that determine what content is available to audiences and the way people think about what they want from the media and the choices they have. The processes include how people sort through their options in order to select the medium, outlet, and content they want. The model may then consider how the goals people bring to the consumption of media influence how they experience a message. The exposure may ultimately lead to some set of effects that are partially attributable to the features of the message, the way people process the message, and the beliefs, feelings, and experiences they bring to the exposure. One likely outcome of most media exposure is a set of perceptions about the message and the experience that will influence future decisions about media. This may, in turn, influence both the media options people will face in the future and how they will respond to those options.

In this circular process, a prime figure is the active audience member, sorting through stable predispositions, externally supplied options, and more ephemeral considerations to make decisions about what to hear, watch, and read. Audience activity plays a central role in the consumption and effects of online news by largely defining the diet of news that people receive. Given the abundance of content online, an active audience can exert substantial control over what news it consumes and—most important—what it comes to believe and feel about the world.

Uses and Gratifications

How people select media and messages is rarely random. People base their exposure decisions on things they want from the media. The uses and gratifications approach pays substantial attention to the concept of audience activity, which emphasizes the "voluntaristic and selective nature of the interaction between audience and mass media" (Levy and Windahl 1984, p. 51). By considering the exposure process as an interaction, the concept of audience activity encompasses both the sequence of media consumption (content selection, message exposure, and postexposure reactions) and the levels of audience involvement in the process.

The uses and gratifications approach suggests that social and psychological forces combine with the availability of media options to affect how people select news content (Katz, Gurevitch, and Haas 1973). Social forces (e.g., demands from other people) and psychological forces (e.g., beliefs, likes, and dislikes) continue to act on audiences as they consume messages, affecting the level of attention they pay to messages, how existing sets of knowledge and attitudes (often called schemas in the research literature) help them interpret messages, and, finally, how they store information, impressions, and feelings in long-term memory. People are also active in interpreting the outcomes of their media use. They decide whether the media supplied what they wanted, and they form impressions about what particular media, outlets, and messages can do for them.

"Activity" is a very broad term that can be applied to multiple locations in the interaction of media and audiences. The primary concept we will employ in this book is selectivity. Rubin and Perse describe selectivity as "an individual's initiative in linking perceived needs and communication choices" (1987, p. 62). We will consider a number of needs that can influence how people choose media, outlets, and messages. The most common use of the term is in the context of selective exposure to messages (Klapper 1960), the desire to consume messages that will be consistent with our preconceptions (e.g., our political opinions). We return to selective exposure and how it is affecting online news exposure in chapter 5.

The models defined above demonstrate that media choices do not occur in a vacuum. This is particularly true when considering a new medium, which involves (usually) both acquiring new equipment and adjusting extant media habits. Before addressing how audiences responded to the introduction of the internet, we should first turn to the history of American media adoption. Not too surprisingly, several consistent patterns have emerged around each medium, and these patterns will inform our expectations for internet adoption. This section, therefore, offers a much-abbreviated media history, with an emphasis on audience responses to the introduction of new media, dating to the first American newspaper.

An Overview of American Media History

The extent to which new communication media displace existing media has been a concern of media researchers for some time. The history of media development is characterized by the accumulation of media and the evolution of content. In the United States, the first newspaper appeared in 1690, and the first magazines were published some 50 years after that (Schramm 1960). Through the 18th and 19th centuries, the evolution of the media was marked by internal changes in these print media and substantial audience growth in both (Schramm 1960). Media-history scholars have argued that both the newspaper industry and the magazine industry shifted their primary target audiences in the middle of the 19th century from economic and political elites to a mass audience (e.g., DeFleur and Ball-Rokeach 1989; Hamilton 2004). This shift allowed them to appeal to a much larger base of readers and was achieved by focusing on content that would appeal to relatively uneducated readers (DeFleur and Ball-Rokeach 1989; McGerr 1986).

The media landscape shifted dramatically in the transition to the 20th century. First film (introduced in America in 1894; Ramsaye 1960) and then radio (the first radio stations in America appeared in the early 1920s; White 1960) technologies were introduced and improved, leading to widespread consumer acceptance of these media. By 1930, nearly 90 million movie tickets were sold each week, and 30 million households owned radios (DeFleur and Ball-Rokeach 1989).

Neither of the new media immediately replaced use of newspapers and magazines, but the early 20th century saw the beginning of a long slide, essentially unchecked through today, in the proportion of American homes subscribing to a newspaper. The industry peaked in 1910, with approximately 1.36 newspaper subscriptions per household (DeFleur and Ball-Rokeach 1989). This level had fallen to 1.24 per household by 1950, the beginning of the television era (DeFleur and Ball-Rokeach 1989). By 1970, the proportion was close to one newspaper for each household and has continued to decline steadily (DeFleur and Ball-Rokeach 1989). In 2006, about 52 million daily newspapers were bought by 114 million American households (46 percent; Project for Excellence in Journalism 2008; U.S. Census Bureau 2006). The overall picture these data present is that of a gradual shift in audience attention away from newspapers and toward other media. Radio, from the early 1920s through the early 1940s and television, through the end of the 20th century, have steadily eroded the audience for newspapers.

In contrast, the magazine industry has remained relatively robust over the past century (Campbell, Martin, and Fabos 2010). Subscriptions have been relatively stable for several decades. However, the success of television affected a number of prominent magazines in the United States, largely by drawing away their major advertisers. Magazines such as *Life* and *Look* folded in the 1970s as advertisers seeking large, broad audiences saw television as the more efficient medium (Campbell, Martin, and Fabos 2010). Perhaps surprisingly, the collapse of general magazines after the coming of television did not result from a dearth of readers (e.g., *Life* magazine had more than 5 million subscribers when it folded in 1972). It was the loss of advertising revenue that did them in. Specialty magazines were less affected by television, which was less efficient at reaching the smaller, more segmented audiences that specialized advertisers sought (Campbell, Martin, and Fabos 2010).

The success of television also affected the radio and film industries. While the penetration of televisions was rising from less than 1 percent of American households in 1946 to more than 87 percent in 1960, weekly film attendance was falling from 2.37 tickets sold per household to 0.53 per household over that period and has remained close to 0.25 since 1970 (DeFleur and Ball-Rokeach 1989). Television was not the only reason film attendance fell in the 1950s (Gomery 1991), but, at minimum, it appears to have drawn some of the people who abandoned movie theaters.

The case for television's impact on radio is less dramatic but more clear-cut. Three of the largest radio networks of the 1940s (CBS, NBC, and ABC) moved much of their programming to television (or other television networks stole it; Sterling and Kittross 2002). National advertisers moved their financial support, and audiences shifted their use from radio to television. In an average home in 1950, radio was used for four hours and 19 minutes a day, and television was used for 35 minutes; in 1959, radio use was 1:54 per day, and television was 5:29 (Schramm 1960).

Thus, there is ample evidence that radio listening was supplanted by the use of the new medium. However, radio survived by focusing on local advertising and programming. Listening recovered such that radio use in the average home was back up to 2:52 per day by 1971 (Sterling and Kittross 2002). When combined with television use of 6:02 in 1971, the average American household was using almost nine hours of broadcasting daily. With the coming of television, use of broadcast media had almost doubled in 20 years.

Choosing Media Replacement

This swift review of media development suggests a few possible effects of emerging technologies. The first is that the introduction of major new media (we have ignored some technological changes, such as FM radio, that have failed to remake a medium dramatically or did so only gradually) brings pressure to bear on existing media. In some cases, the new medium has diverted audiences from existing media. This is a case of media replacement.

McCombs is credited with developing the most influential theory of media replacement: the principle of relative constancy (McCombs 1972; Son and McCombs 1993). Based on an analysis of U.S. Commerce Department data from 1928 to 1968, McCombs concluded that American spending on mass-communication products tended to remain about 3 percent of consumer spending, regardless of the mix of media outlets (McCombs 1972; McCombs and Nolan 1992). Because audiences have limited resources of money and time, they must reallocate these resources to support new media. In other words, they reslice the media pie. If that is not sufficient, audiences must divert resources from other goods and services outside the marketplace for mass media (Son and McCombs 1993).

Some media researchers have therefore approached medium and outlet selectivity as a zero-sum situation. New media use comes at the expense of older media use. The history of American media contains many examples of apparent replacement. The evidence certainly suggests that film and radio audiences were drawn away by television, at least in part, and many national advertisers left radio and general-interest magazines for television when it rose in prominence. Nonetheless, replacement is not the complete story. Taken together, radio use and television use occupy more time today than radio alone did in its heyday. Similarly, the magazine industry largely avoided the ravages of replacement by radio and television.

Son and McCombs (1993) note that the diffusion of videocassette recorders in the United States failed to follow the relative-constancy principle. Spending on VCRs appears to have largely been in addition to existing patterns of media spending. Noh and Grant (1997) explain this apparent aberration through an analysis of media functions. They argue that the extra income devoted to the VCR would otherwise have been spent on non-media-related communication and interaction. Their analysis suggests that the zero-sum situation described by the principle of relative constancy needs to be placed in the overall context of consumer activity.

Choosing Nonreplacement

Sometimes when audiences go beyond their standard media activity, it is because they are adopting a pattern of media use that is not replacement. Different needs are met by different resources. If a new medium meets needs that were previously satisfied by existing media, then consumption of that medium may replace standing media uses. However, when the new medium appears to meet different needs, people can expand their expenditures of time and money (although obviously not without limit) to accommodate more media use. The accommodation of overall media use to the appearance of attractive new media is, in some ways, a more compelling characterization of media development than straight replacement.

People often appear willing to retain their existing media-use habits— or, perhaps more accurately, they are unwilling to change their habits—as they acquire the use of new media. The patterns of use that can result can be characterized as either supplementary or complementary. The differences between them are not large, but they can have implications for how specific content, such as news, is consumed.

When people supplement their existing use with new media, they likely see the new options as providing gratifications that are sufficiently different from those of the older media that they will seek to retain both the old and the new gratifications. Thus, the concept of supplementation suggests that people expand the total of what they receive (e.g., entertainment, information, or diversion) from the media when they acquire new media. In this situation, overall media use increases with the acquisition of new exposure patterns. Supplementation can certainly co-occur with replacement, when people see a new medium as meeting both existing needs and desires and new ones. For example, the co-occurrence of the two patterns nicely accounts for changes in radio and television use from 1950 through 1971. Initially, television largely replicated radio programming, luring most people to replace much of their radio listening with television viewing. Radio in the 1960s rebounded through a focus on local programming of music and talk, content that was harder to find on network television (DeFleur and Ball-Rokeach 1989). This change appears to have led to supplementation and an overall increase in media consumption.

In addition to supplementing current media use, new media can complement preexisting media. Although it is often hard to distinguish empirically from supplementation, it may be useful to conceive of the use of one medium being prompted by the use of another. That is, it is possible—even likely—that some people use one medium because of what they have encountered in some other medium or outlet. In that case, the use of one medium complements the use of the other. For example, suppose that audiences acquire basic information about a topic from news in one medium and use another medium to discover more about the topic. In some ways, bulletin news reports on radio and newspaper reports have functioned that way for many years.

Media outlets can work to create or adapt to complementarity among media. By assessing how people use existing media, new media or outlets can create content that builds on existing content such that one enhances the other. Imagine, for example, a radio station with a well-known meteorologist. On the basis of audience data, perhaps a marketing survey, the station decides to create a short segment featuring the meteorologist on a local television station. In this case, the radio station is hoping that audience use of one medium will enhance the use of the other such that the radio program gains in popularity. The television station may have a similar hope. In this example, both the radio station and the television station benefit from increased attention to content on the other medium.

De Facto Replacement

Sometimes new media are not chosen by current audiences at all, but they nonetheless replace the previous media over time. Witnessing this pattern requires moving from the individual level, where our conversation has focused thus far, to the societal level. Instead of looking at what happens when an individual faces options, the emphasis becomes what happens when the entire society faces options. At this macro level, one can discern patterns of media use among (usually age-based) segments of society to determine how the adoption of some new medium affects use of older media.

At this level of analysis, focusing on the differences between the people entering society and the existing members reveals how replacement happens over time. As groups, or cohorts, enter society and mature, it becomes possible to see both how the cohorts differ from one another and how the new cohorts change society as a whole. Applying this principle to media adoption suggests that even if individuals do not immediately choose a new medium, replacement may still be observed in the use patterns of new cohorts entering the overall American media audience (Basil 1990). The crucial point for understanding media development is the fact that the constellation of media choices available to any one cohort (e.g., everyone born from 1980 to 1990 might be considered as a members of a cohort) is unique. There are particular options available to that cohort that will influence how it develops its media-use patterns, and each cohort faces a slightly different constellation of choices.

The cohort process is evident in the overall adoption of television. Peiser (2000) studied cohort trends in the exposure to television and newspapers. He observed that Americans who developed their media habits when television was common in the household (the vast majority of American households after 1955) held more positive attitudes toward television over time than did older cohorts who had adopted the medium into their households. Furthermore, his analysis showed that newspaper reading was declining in a way that reflected a cohort process. After the adoption of television in America, fewer people in succeeding cohorts developed newspaper-reading habits. This resulted in a substantial overall decline in newspaper reading in America. The evidence suggests that the decline was not caused primarily by people dropping newspapers as they spent more time watching television. Rather, it was a gradual process of fewer people developing newspaper-reading patterns as they matured.

A cohort perspective suggests that changes in media use in a society can occur even if the habits of individuals (or within cohorts) remain unchanged throughout their lifetimes (i.e., as long as people are making media-consumption choices). Even if each cohort remains perfectly stable, which seems unlikely, change can come to society as new cohorts enter adult society and older ones exit. Obviously, the cohort-replacement process can be very slow, but its impact on how media are used can be substantial.

A Mix of Media and Content

Understanding the impact of one medium on another is best accomplished by looking at what audiences want and need. People rarely simply abandon one medium for another on a wholesale basis. Rather, they tend to adopt the elements of one medium that provided valued gratifications and drop parts of old media that no longer seem useful or necessary. This suggests a simple principle: media have multiple attributes, and people choose among them (Eveland 2003). People construct for themselves a mix of outlets and content that provides what they want from media, sometimes replacing one medium with another but often not. Indeed, as the media multiply, it is probably inevitable that people stop thinking about them as distinct entities or industries. More often, they may come to think about specific content options, at least partially divorced from medium.

CHOOSING A NEW MEDIUM, THE INTERNET

With the introduction of a public, graphical browser in 1993 (December 2002), audiences were again faced with a new medium. Historically, a new medium has been accepted through replacement, supplementation/com-plementation, or de facto replacement. We know that the internet has been widely adopted, but how that adoption occurred is not as evident. This is a point of vital importance for media producers (and a point of interest for many others), because the method of adoption goes hand-in-hand with the treatment of existing media. In this section, we review the accumu-lated evidence about the effect of internet news adoption on older media.

Evidence for Replacement

An initial look at Pew Research Center (2008b) data on media-use trends from 1995 (when access to the internet stood at about 14 percent of the American population) through 2008 (when access reached 67 percent) reveals substantial changes. The percentage of Americans who reported that they read a newspaper regularly dropped from 71 percent to 54 per-cent, the percentage who reported that they watched television news reg-ularly dropped from 82 percent to 75 percent, and the percentage who reported that they listened to radio news regularly dropped from 50 per-cent to 46 percent. Over that period, the percentage of internet users who reported that they got news online at least three days a week rose from 15 percent to 47 percent. On the face of it, there seems to be ample evidence of a restructuring of the news audience. And the internet appears to be at the center of the change.

Studies of electronic news delivery over videotex—a forerunner of internet services—in the 1980s and early 1990s suggest that people might give up print newspapers when they are able to read them on a computer (e.g., Butler and Kent 1983). Similar results have been observed in surveys of American internet users (e.g., Kaynay and Yelsma 2000; Dimmick, Chen, and Li 2004). For example, from 1995 through 2004, Pew Research Center (2004) asked national samples of internet users whether their adoption of online news had prompted them to use "other sources of news more often, less, often, or about the same." Although a large majority of people in each of seven surveys over that period reported that their use of the other media was unchanged, in almost every survey, slightly more people reported using other sources less often than more often (e.g., 15 percent versus 9 percent in 2004). When combined with substantial evidence that local and network television and newspaper audiences have been falling (Pew Research Center 2004), it is not hard to conclude that internet adoption is driving audiences away from other media.

Reality turns out to be more complicated. Some studies of internet news have found that users and nonusers differ little in their exposure to newspapers and television news (e.g., Ahlers 2006; Stempel, Hargrove, and Bernt 2000). An analysis of news audiences (Online Publishers Association 2004) identified four basic categories: people who receive news from online sources only (12.2 percent of Americans), those who use offline sources only (42.7 percent), those who get news consistently from both online and offline sources (21.5 percent), and "dabblers" who receive news infrequently from either source (23.6 percent). These data suggest that there are few people who have completely given up on newspapers, television news, and radio news for the internet. What is more, some studies have observed positive correlations between self-reports of online news use and newspaper-reading frequency (e.g., Althaus and Tewksbury 2000). This finding seems to be describing the multichannel users in the Online Publishers Association analysis and suggests that replacement might not (yet) be the best way to think about the effect of online news adoption.

Evidence for Nonreplacement

In a study of the media-adoption process, Ahlers observes that "the media are additive, and the dominant consumer strategy is to use multiple media to get news information" (2006, p. 36). Studies of internet use have shown how it is often used in conjunction with other media (e.g., Nguyen and Western 2006). Pew Research Center (2006) found in a national survey that half of Americans used more than one news medium in a day (the most popular combination was television and newspapers) and about a third used only one (television was most popular). One analysis of the integration of the internet with other media found that a substantial number of people are using the internet simultaneously with television (Nielsen 2010a).

The relationship between online and offline news use represents not just the allocation of time between two media. There is also a potential relationship between what people watch on one medium and what they watch on another. One analysis of Pew data from 2000 demonstrated consistent correlations between the categories of news that audiences were following online and in the traditional media (Dutta-Bergman 2004). For example, people who were particularly prone to attending to news about politics and government in newspapers and on television news were also likely to report attending to it online (Dutta-Bergman 2004). So, not only are many people using multiple media, but they may also be getting the same types of news across those media.

Whereas there is substantial evidence that online news use may be supplementing exposure to traditional news media, there is less bearing on whether online and offline exposure complement each other. An example of complementary use of news media may lie in people using one news medium to pursue news they heard on another medium. In 1998, 41 percent of internet news users in a national survey said that they sometimes went to online news to follow up on a story they initially heard in the traditional media (Pew Research Center 1998). Anecdotally, there are many examples of people following news topics from one medium to another or of media organizations encouraging people to go from one medium to another. Researchers have also found that visitors to online newspaper sites are also frequent readers of the organizations' print versions (Chyi and Lasorsa 2002). However, there are few systematic studies of how use of one medium may increase the potential audience of another, an implication of the complementation process.

A similar story can be told about cohort processes. To date, no analyses have examined whether new cohorts entering the adult population are bringing in news exposure habits that will gradually change the overall news audience. Single-shot surveys do tend to indicate that online media habits vary by age—a likely indicator of a cohort phenomenon. Specifically designed studies are necessary to confirm this evolutionary adoption. It does seem likely that such a cohort-replacement process is occurring, and a shift to online news may be at the heart of it.

WHAT HAPPENS TO NEWS MEDIA WHEN THE AUDIENCE CHANGES

The question of new media adoption is certainly an important one for a book about the internet, but we need to take a moment to consider what happens to the older media. Newspapers and broadcast media are struggling for relevancy, but their absolute demise is not imminent. These media will continue to exert an influence on—and adjust in response to—the internet. This section focuses on how older media are likely to adjust their content and economics, both of which will, in turn, affect online news.

Old Media and Content

Although most people prefer to think about entertainment or information as the most important parts of media content, the reality is that advertising is what counts. This is an unfortunate reality for traditional media, as advertisers are moving their content (and dollars) away from print and broadcast and toward other media. Changes in the industry caught up to print in 2007, which saw zero revenue gains without a corresponding recession (Project for Excellence in Journalism 2007). The following years were affected by recession, and revenues decreased by roughly a billion dollars for the newspaper industry (Project for Excellence in Journalism 2010c). Smaller papers, which traditionally relied heavily on beefy classified sections, have been feeling the effects of lost advertising for even longer. Sites such as Craigslist and eBay enable users to circumvent the printed classifieds, and those presses have not been able to match that lost revenue with new sources (Project for Excellence in Journalism 2010c). The advertising story is not limited to newspapers; magazines and network news have also suffered from a significant loss of advertising (Project for Excellence in Journalism 2010c).

These economic realities have forced traditional media to make significant changes to their news content. More specifically, organizations have largely responded by making cuts to the costs of news gathering, and this direct action has unavoidably influenced the content. For a news organization, cutting costs means limiting the amount of news covered and downsizing reporting staff (Project for Excellence in Journalism 2010c). Foreign affairs and science bureaus have been notably cut (Brainard 2008; McChesney 2008). Papers have had to rely more on the wire services, such as the Associated Press, for stories instead of generating original reporting. With fewer available reporters, editors have to rely more than ever on their own production biases to dictate the flow of the news (see Bennett 2009; Tuchman 1978). While factors such as a reliance on institutions and public-relations messages have always influenced reporting, the problem is exacerbated when there are not enough writers to devote to unprompted—or even investigative—reporting. The end result of the financial changes is likely a news product that is of lower quality than in the past.

Quantity and quality are not the only factors that constitute content, however, and the nature of the news also appears to be changing. The shift is particularly evident on cable television. Whereas a newspaper can cut costs by reducing its physical size, the 24-hour news network cannot. Less reporting means (1) more repetition and (2) cheaper content. Opinion- and analysis-based formats are on the rise among cable networks. These programs require fewer employees than a straight news program, and they have certainly proven popular. *The O'Reilly Factor* dominates cable ratings, although *Countdown with Keith Olbermann* held its own during the 2008 general election campaign (Seidman 2008). In addition to fea- turing the viewpoints of the host, these programs also tend to provide a fairly open (or entirely closed, if the guest is from the other party) plat- form for politicians and their surrogates. As a replacement for news con- tent, such programs are inadequate, but they are certainly successful vehicles for attracting viewers to political information of some sort.

The trend toward partisan formats is only part of the shift in the nature of news, which is more broadly a shift toward relatively narrow content. Over the past decades, media organizations have largely concentrated on providing content that would appeal to the largest audience possible. This has almost always been interpreted as neutral, objective, and safe report- ing. Seen in this light, the change that we are seeing is not simply that older media are moving from the middle toward an end on the political spectrum. Instead, what we are seeing is that the news media are willing to abandon the mass audience in favor of a more specific (but, they hope, still sizable) audience. We can see that this is the case more clearly if we go outside the news. Television programs, magazines, and movies are all increasingly designed with a particular group in mind. For example, most CBS programs target seniors (Bauder 2010). Targeting for specific audi- ences has a long history, but the example of the internet and economic necessity have helped make this tactic standard operating procedure for old media.

Old Media and Economics

It may not be obvious why content producers and advertisers are willing to make the transition to niche content. The answer lies in traditional economic theory. Hotelling's Law tells us that companies perform best in the long run when they position themselves close together near the cen- ter of their customers (Hotelling 1929). In other words, when there are few media organizations, they will all provide content that is of interest to the largest group (Mangani 2003). As more companies enter the media market, it becomes more difficult for any given outlet to succeed by competing for the attention of the largest group. Companies become increasingly likely to differentiate themselves from the mainstream and begin serving increasingly specialized interests. The notion that there is economic value in reaching niche audiences is popularly known as "the long tail" (Anderson 2004).

This economic explanation neatly describes the changes within the current media market. It is primarily the smaller, newer outlets that are willing to target niche audiences. With less overhead to consider, Web logs (i.e., blogs) and cable programs can be successful without the same level of revenue required by expensive newspapers and broadcast networks. The lower financial imperatives mean that it is less risky to target a smaller overall audience. When successful, the result is an audience that is more homogeneous and more interested in the media product, which, in turn, has its own financial benefits.

A close match between audience interests and content means that advertisers can also do a better job of targeting their products. This is known as advertising relevancy (Baker and Lutz 2000). The relevancy of niche-content advertising is a clear improvement over broad content, where a company may need to reach only part of the audience for a given program. In this case, the company is essentially wasting money by advertising to the remainder of the viewers, and audience members are also more likely to be annoyed by the commercials in this case. Content matching means that advertisements are more likely to be successful (Whitney 2008), and companies can use the internet (or cable boxes) to track effectiveness far better than before. Narrow content, therefore, means more effective advertisements and higher advertising rates.

The way forward for news media is clearly perilous. Journalism has been largely conducted by traditional media organizations. It is not yet clear whether the fall of old media will mean the death of traditional reporting or if it can be resurrected in some new form or venue. As we discuss in later chapters, new media organizations are not yet ready to fill the possible void, given that they are also largely reliant on the reporting of old media. In any event, moving all news content online will contribute to another set of social and democratic problems.

INTERNET ACCESS AND THE DIGITAL DIVIDE

A key factor working against the internet as a savior of political information and other news is that the availability of content is far from equitable. In fact, the digital divide between those with and those without internet access has long been a problem. A U.S. government report (National Tele-communications Information Administration 1995) revealed that people without access, which was primarily dial-up at the time, were more likely to be living in rural areas or city centers and were more likely to be minor-ities (particularly Latinos) than were those with access. Today, the majority (77 percent) of Americans have some form of internet access at home. Glob-ally, 103 nations have less than 25 percent internet penetration (Miniwatts Marketing Group 2010)—a sign of both inter- and intranational disparity. These gaps in access not only hinder the diffusion of the medium, but they may also hinder the ability of the unconnected to participate effectively in society.

Whether such divisions are a problem can be a matter of debate. Michael Powell, a former Federal Communications Commission chair-man, disliked the phrase "digital divide," saying, "I think there is a Mer-cedes divide. I'd like to have one; I can't afford one" (Labaton 2001). This sort of unconcerned elitism ignores the problems for democracy that arise when only specific segments of society have limited access to domi-nant media. With uneven access to the internet, there is also uneven access to democracy. This is because as a major provider of news, a key channel for campaign contributions, and a hub for activist organization, the internet is one of the most dominant sources—and arguably the most dominant source—for political communication. From this perspective, access should be given far more consideration as a necessity, rather than as a luxury.

Even in relatively high-access nations, there is a second-wave digital divide that should worry us. The primary question of access noted above concerns whether users can at least use dial-up on a telephone line to go online. In reality, however, the internet has moved far beyond these 56-kilobits-per-second connections. High-quality images and video, along with instant peer-to-peer communication, are the new norm for both personal and political content online. These more sophisticated forms require users to have faster connections. Broadband access is defined by the FCC as being at least 4 megabits (or 4,000 kilobits) per second, which is a significant upgrade in speed over dial-up. As of 2010, American broadband penetration stood at 66 percent nationally (Smith 2010). This percentage is an average, of course, and the rate among low-income groups can be much lower (45 percent). The gap poses a problem in light of findings such as the 2008 Pew survey showing that people with home broadband access are more likely to get the news, visit government websites, and look for campaign information than are people with dial-up access (Horrigan 2008). This second-level digital divide poses another challenge to society.

Unfortunately, the problem of equitable internet access is likely to worsen in the foreseeable future. Technology experts expect mobile devices soon to become the primary means of access for the majority of Americans (Anderson and Rainie 2008). Mobile devices are already used to make contributions (10 percent of mobile data users), post to Twitter (20 percent), and watch videos (40 percent). An advantage of mobile access in this context is that up-front costs can be lower (e.g., a subsidized smartphone may cost $99 versus a basic $399 desktop computer), potentially allowing low-income citizens access to the internet. However, mobile internet plans are necessarily tied to voice plans in the United States (and also conventionally tied to texting plans), and the costs of mobile access per bit are particularly high. For example, AT&T's cheapest wireless plan currently charges $15 per month (on top of a minimum $40 voice plan) for just 200 megabytes of data, while the cheapest high-speed access plan is $35 per month for 250,000 megabytes. If we wanted to step into consumer theory, we would argue that despite the promise of the up-front costs, the pricing model (higher cost for a quantitatively worse product) suggests that mobile internet access is a luxury good (demand is particularly high as income increases), rather than a normal (demand increases in step with income) or inferior (demand is higher as income decreases) good. Perhaps we finally draw the line and say that mobile access is in that "Mercedes" category. Nonetheless, there should be a concern if affluent members of society are better able to increase their political knowledge and engagement while other citizens are left behind.

Another form of the digital divide occurs between the skill levels of established and new or infrequent users. Web browsing is a computer skill, and research (e.g., Hargittai 2002) has found that even basic actions such as typing a Web address or using the back button challenge some users. For people who struggle to stay on top of page links and other interactive features, the internet can quickly become disorienting (Eveland and Dunwoody 2001b) and frustrating (Sundar, Kalyanaraman, and Brown 2003), rather than informative and useful. Such experiences may create a cycle in which less frequent users become unwilling to experiment with the more valuable content available online. Indeed, users from higher socioeconomic backgrounds are more likely to use the internet to build social capital (Hargittai and Hinnant, 2008), leaving users already on the short end increasingly far behind.

It is worth noting that any serious attempt to correct one of the various digital divides will have to be led by public policy. Internet service providers (ISPs) have consistently demonstrated that improvements in the scope or quality of internet access and infrastructure do not have a place in their business models. America has fallen considerably in the global rankings of broadband access (Schatz 2007), and this does not seem likely to change. ISPs are reluctant to wire remote areas without incentives, and whereas some cities are experimenting with open wireless access (Farivar 2008), even the commitments in the 2009 American economic stimulus package (Baker and Broder 2008) did not generate significant change in access rates. ISPs are also increasingly looking to restrict how much of the internet is available for those who do have access. Many service providers are turning to download limits (Adegoke 2008), which restrict the amount of content that customers can access each month. More significantly, ISPs are beginning to push for permission to restrict user access to certain sites or services (e.g., Gross 2008), which would mean an end to network neutrality. These types of changes could result in anything from restricted access to videos to internet service options that resemble the choices for cable television. In short, the interests on the private side of internet access are demonstrating a commitment to a more restrictive and more stratified medium, rather than a more open or equitable medium.

The digital divide is an important problem for news-media scholars to address. The quality of a democracy is arguably questionable if a significant portion of the citizenry cannot participate in the dominant media of their society. To be certain, the digital divide is a complex problem. Not only are there three tiers to this gap (access versus none, broadband versus dial-up, mobile versus not), but there is also an underlying skill gap that will be difficult to surmount. Deciding on the best approach to correct these divides is a topic of some debate, except for the fact that solutions will have to be driven by public policy rather than private investment. On a more practical level, this discussion of digital divides offers a key caveat to understanding the media effects that will be reported in the chapters below. That caveat is that the internet audience is not the least bit simple, and we should simultaneously be particularly impressed by any effects that are evident in digital media research and be especially contemplative about how those effects may account for—or be tempered by—one or more digital divides in the real world.

CONCLUSIONS

Audiences are frequently discussed as passive recipients of the news. This tendency is partly a lingering result of the mass media tradition and partly an unintended product of the media effects perspective. In reality, there are many ways in which the public exerts an influence on the form and content of the news. This chapter articulated several modes of audience participation, ranging in kind from relatively conceptual to quite concrete.

Models of audience activity focus on individuals and how their experiences and attitudes influence their media choices. Such choices are critical to understanding contemporary media and their effects. Democratic theory looks at audiences as public citizens and considers what individuals need to do and what they need from media in order to participate in government. These perspectives help establish standards for what society should expect from news media. The more concrete perspectives on audiences look at how different groups use media in different ways, which helps to identify which types of people are active users of various services. Regardless of the form of conceptualization, media scholars seek to define audiences at least partly according to their relationships with media.

Such relationships are particularly important during the introduction of a new medium. Typically, American audiences have chosen either to replace the old media with the new or to use both side-by-side. Sometimes that replacement occurs only as older audiences die off, taking their media use habits with them. How the internet fits these patterns remains unclear, as evidence points to both replacement and simultaneous use. Nonetheless, the effects of the introduction of the internet on print and broadcast are clear: those media are experiencing declines in both advertising revenue and content quality. The next few decades will tell us whether this is the start of a cohort-replacement process or simply growing pains.

All of this information sets the stage for the discussion of online news in the following chapters. Without this background, it would be much harder to appreciate that—particularly as far as news content is concerned—the internet is far more an integrated and evolutionary medium than an autonomous and revolutionary system. The continuing challenges of quality reporting and equitable access (the digital divide) are just two signs of the internet's codependency with other media. The next chapter further develops these relationships by focusing on the form of news as it goes from old media to the internet (and back again).

CHAPTER 3

Offline and Online News Content

I n some ways, it is difficult to overstate the level of change that the news industry has experienced in the last 20 years. The content media shift from print or broadcast to the internet is only one, relatively small aspect of this transition. The industry's patterns of ownership, modes of operation, customer bases, employees, and products have all shifted. Faced with new competitors and a shrinking advertising base, the news industry appears to be in the midst of radical changes in the way it reports and presents the news.

Appearances can be deceiving, of course, and highly visible changes in the news business may obscure a number of stable features. How journalists interact with sources and think about their audiences may be changing only gradually, and audience demand for new ways to consume information is still split. Certainly, some members of the audience appear to be demanding features such as automated news feeds, social media connections, and breaking news from blogs. But there may be just as many people comfortable with the traditional ways of producing and presenting the news. This split means that the news industry is not a uniform entity. New components of the business and large traditional players are competing for the future of the industry, but often they are working together. Indeed, the news that audiences receive today is a clear mixture of old and new approaches.

In this chapter, we look at the news as it appears online. We look at how (and how often) news produced for the offline media makes its way to the internet. We also examine news and news sites that don't have a component offline, considering whether the distinction between offline and internet-based news remains a meaningful one. Of note here are two-way flows of influence concerning the content and form of news. We then turn to the form of news that appears online. The issue there is with the extent that news online mirrors traditional notions of the importance of issues and events. The technologies of the internet appear to offer a number of novel ways that news content can be communicated to audiences. The chapter, as a whole, suggests that how news is created and presented online could have far-reaching effects on how citizens come to understand events, issues, and public policy.

CONTENT AND APPEARANCE OF TRADITIONAL NEWS WHEN IT GOES ONLINE

Many people solely consider content when evaluating news organizations. The appearance of any news medium is important, though, because of the relationship between design and audience effects. Tracking changes in the form of traditional news, in particular, can help reveal which styles or features of the ever-evolving internet have reached (relatively) mainstream audiences and which are still in the realm of early adopters. When observing the style or content of the websites of traditional media organizations, it is important to remain cognizant of the organization's original format. A quick browsing of the websites of print versus television outlets will reveal that, on average, these sites tend to appear rather different. This separation makes sense theoretically, because factors such as effective news cycle, interactivity potential, and aesthetic success vary significantly across media (Dessauer 2004; Eveland 2003). We can also expect that as print and television news outlets become more accustomed to the internet, each type will adopt features relatively uniquely. Here we examine print-internet and then television-internet relationships separately before discussing the combined evolution of news formats.

The Relationship Between Newspaper and Online News

On the surface, the transition from print news to the internet seems natural. After all, these media require a particularly careful consideration of layout, and early websites were primarily text- and image-based. However, similarity does not always guarantee effectiveness. Scholars assessing the visual success of news organizations moving online have found that print sites are likely to develop text-dominated sites (Li 1998; Cooke 2005). More specifically, the websites of newspapers have tended toward large blocks of text with a limited amount of additional information or features pushed to the margins of the page. This is an effective layout for focusing attention on the story and for maintaining visual clarity. Because of the nature of a user's gaze (see chapter 5), however, this formatting limits the reach of internet-only features, such as topic maps, photo slide shows, or even the related-article menus. The limited presentation style was probably ineffective as a means of attracting and retaining readers. In this sense, the familiarity of print media with planning layouts may be problematic.

These descriptions of newspaper websites do not entirely reflect the changes that have occurred since 2006. Around this time, with the rising penetration of broadband access and the concurrent increase in audience skill and application complexity, news websites began more fully incorporating interactive features. Whereas the sites may be relatively plain compared with television sites, embedded video, RSS feeds, photo slide shows, and interactive graphics have all become increasingly popular (see, e.g., washingtonpost.com or nytimes.com). Some of these items even find their way into the main portion of site content, rather than just off to the side. On the whole, it appears that newspapers are adopting, albeit slowly, comprehensive web layouts.

The slow evolution of online papers' appearances is reflected in the development of news content. Early work researching these sites found that newspaper sites rarely added stories beyond those available in print (e.g., Houston 1999; Singer 2003). Because additional features were still rare at this time, researchers essentially found that online papers were simply expanding access, rather than content. These early findings have largely held up over time. Of course, a few notable exceptions do exist. Boczkowski (2004) offers several examples of high-quality investigations led by the internet sectors of papers. These rare cases aside, scholars have largely continued to find few additional stories available online (e.g., Seelig 2008; Singer 2006).

Media outlets frequently outpace academic research, and news organizations might have begun posting more original content in the last few years. However, there are at least two reasons for newspapers to be largely unwilling to provide much additional content to their websites. Perhaps the most important of these is that the internet divisions within news organizations are unlikely to have sufficient resources to develop new content (Singer 2006). The underfunded, small staffs are unable to accomplish much more. Another reason that papers do not develop additional stories online is that, as discussed in chapter 2, a substantial portion of news outlets are not developing many of their own stories at all. As news staffs are cut and their dependence on wire services increases, there is a dwindling chance that these organizations will allow their online versions to host the original content. To the extent that "additional" content appears, it may be from wire and other news services. These structural biases seem to be reflected in the thoughts of internet editors, who have reported that investigative journalism is less important to them than it is to print editors (Cassidy 2005).

There are two noteworthy exceptions to the "internet content replicates print content" rule. The first is that online news does, at times, incorporate more local content than the paper includes (Singer 2001). However, the nature of these additions might be limited to additional wire copy (Gasher and Gabrielle 2004) and articles, such as event announcements, that are not entirely news. Some papers also add locally produced videos to support reposted wire service stories (Thurman and Lupton 2008). In other words, although this is material not available in print, the value of this original online content may be limited. These minor adjustments may nevertheless suit the readers, who tend to be predominantly local and may therefore appreciate the stronger emphasis on their area (Chyi and Sylvie 2001).

The second exception to the content replication rule occurs with editorial content. As early as 2001, observers (e.g., Macht 2001) were already finding more opinion pieces online. This trend continued, apparently modestly, for several more years (Singer 2006). Although specific analyses of more recent online papers have not specifically tested the observation, it seems that the addition of opinion content online has expanded. Beyond the number of professionally produced items, the growing popularity of user comments and other forums expands the traditional "letters to the editor" space (Boczkowski 2004). Furthermore, the widespread adoption of journalist blogs provides a mix of news and opinion that is not typically paralleled in print. As with the relatively recent acceptance of layout alternatives, the online versions of newspapers seem to be finally adapting to the benefits of the newer media.

The Relationship Between Television and Radio News and Online News

Although television news outlets may not have been wedded to a linear layout style, this does not mean that these organizations have produced comparatively better websites. The online presence of television stations tends to take a more chaotic approach to design (Siapara 2004), which might be overwhelming to many users (Eveland and Dunwoody 2001b). Part of the explanation for television organizations' general inability to produce effective websites might be the pressures that journalists face when adapting to a converged newsroom. Managers and editors have to adopt new styles (e.g., Aviles and Carvajal 2008), and the end product thus far has tended toward limited quality and creativity (e.g., Huang et al. 2004). Although converging newspaper organizations face similar challenges, the common reliance on text and layout may have inherently benefited print-internet mergers. Television-internet combinations often seem to have more trouble, perhaps because of the difficulties of translating video to text or making new videos. After all, cable news already faces criticism for airing too little original content on the networks themselves. The transition to the web may therefore present a substantial burden.

The most obvious point of visual convergence between television news and the internet is video. Before 2004, most news websites were not making use of video (Singer and Gonzalez-Velez 2003). Broadband penetration was lower during this period, and video was generally less common, which was probably why the primary media features were photo slides and audience polls. As high speed connections have become more common, so has the spread of news video. The Nielsen Company reported that more than 10 billion videos were streamed over the internet in one month in 2010 (this includes more than news video, of course; Nielsen Company 2010b). These changing norms of internet video partially explain why news outlets would add their own videos to wire content (Thurman and Lupton 2008). Indeed, research has confirmed this growth, finding that sites are increasingly incorporating streaming video and audio on a regular basis (Seelig 2008).

There is a less obvious, but perhaps even more important, form of visual convergence between television and internet news: the headline ticker. This bar across the bottom of the screen on most cable news shows displays information that is typically irrelevant to the material on the main portion of the screen. Many channels employ at least one ticker plus multiple boxes displaying information such as time, weather, or stock prices. This carving up of the screen is best described by the term "hypermedia," which essentially describes a layout that is divided so that multiple messages or even media are displayed simultaneously (Manovich 2001). In the case of cable news, the content (message A) on the main screen is some type of video that is not directly related to the information in the boxes (messages B, C, etc.), which is actually a text feed.

The hypermedia concept is useful for two main reasons. When used to describe the appearance of an interface, such as a television screen or a website layout, the term helps explain user reactions to media design. An outlet employing a limitedly hypermediated format might give users quick access to information, but too many boxes can lead audiences to become confused by (Sundar, Kalyanaraman, and Brown 2003)—or even to ignore (Adam, Quinn, and Edmunds 2007)—the display. Recognizing hypermedia design elements also makes it easier to identify and track the cross-development of different media, which is also known as remediation (Bolter and Grusin 2000).

The origin of the news ticker on a television screen has been traced to the modular design of most websites (Cooke 2005). Networks that were worried about declining news audiences hoped that even if viewers did not find the main story compelling, the presence of stock prices or scrolling headlines would keep eyes on the screen. The use of tickers in cable news is a remediation of the web. Furthermore, the automated news feeds (particularly RSS, Really Simple Syndication) and widgets remediate the appearance and content of news tickers back to the computer. These concepts help us see that while newspapers have largely limited the influence of internet advances to their online versions, television outlets seem to be more engaged in a give-and-take with the medium.

Evolving Relationship among Print, Audio, and Video Content Online

The sharing of news formats has affected not only tickers and RSS but also graphic incorporation and photo size (Cooke 2005). The accelerating effects of digital media are similarly increasing the pace of this visual convergence, and the internet is increasingly taking the lead. This is true partly because of special features that are really only available online. The other reason for the internet's dominance of news formats is that advances in digital technology mean that the internet can even do old media (i.e., print and broadcast) content better than the old media.

The growing leadership of internet news sources can be seen in the growth of the online news audience. The use of the medium as a primary— or at least secondary—source of news is growing. As of May 2010, 43 percent of internet users—a large majority of respondents—reported getting political news online *daily* (Pew Internet and American Life Project 2010b). This increasing popularity at a time of smaller traditional news audiences alone helps guarantee that print and television news will at least pay attention to advances in online formats. Relatively recent studies (e.g., Tewksbury 2006) have also found that people now go to the internet first when a big event happens. The September 11, 2001, attacks were one of the first such events (Althaus 2002; Salaverria 2005), but similar spikes in traffic have been witnessed during the 2008 election night and the 2010 World Cup. Some may argue that the internet's fast response (Dessauer 2004) leads to problematic content errors (Cohen 2002), and these might scare off the relatively conservative traditional media (e.g., McChesney 2008). However, the presence of features that can attract and maintain audiences seems sufficient to win the replication of mainstream media (e.g., CNN's social-media slot in its afternoon programming).

The expansion of broadband services has allowed internet content providers to make better use of embedded video (Singer 2006; Thurman and Lupton 2008). The expansion of this feature finally allows the internet to become more comparable to television, which, of course, is predominantly presented through video. There are clear advantages to internet video when compared with broadcast. The first is flexibility of access, in terms of both time and location. While online entertainment video may struggle to compete with digital cable-DVR combinations, online news videos provide a more flexible form of access. These videos also demonstrate the second advantage, which is the ability to control which, and how much of each, video is viewed. Cable news will certainly remain popular as a background provider of news video, but the technological advantage arguably lies with online news video.

The internet's dominance in applying news formats may be most apparent if we consider podcasting. Podcasts are gaining in popularity, in part because they offer an efficient way to get users video or audio news that can then be accessed at the recipients' leisure. Two factors have combined to help push podcasting to the mass public (Pew internet and American Life Project 2010a). The first factor is the increasing ease of access. The iPod and iTunes help the general public find and utilize podcasts with relative ease (Cook 2008). The second factor is the mainstream appeal of new podcasters. Most mainstream news agencies produce at least one podcast, and celebrities and politicians also are now regularly podcasting. Easier access and mainstream producers led podcasting to a breakout year in 2005 (Palser 2006), and the number of podcasts and subscribers continues to rise. This success is all the more impressive in the face of flagging interest in the traditional news, which is often the same content but in different media. As access and capabilities continue to grow, the internet's importance in news video's dominance should only increase.

INTERNET-ONLY NEWS

There are several original and significant formats for delivering the news online. Blogs are the best known. Frequent internet news readers, and perhaps more general users, too, will probably also be familiar with RSS feeds, news aggregators, and even news wikis. Earlier, we noted that much of the content available online is similar to, or even a mere replica of, offline content. What is interesting about these formats is that audiences use each type of source in a manner that is quite different from how they use traditional news. In looking at the connections between the original formats and traditional media, along with the features of the new styles, the significance of original internet news becomes apparent.

Online-only News Providers and the Mainstream

The initial reaction of most media sectors has been to ignore or attack online activity. The music industry allowed Napster to become a major phenomenon before initiating a legal battle. Television studios ignored the internet's ability to deliver on-demand content, instead allowing cable and satellite companies to provide these services. Traditional news outlets have followed a similar path, taking years to allow user comments and journalist blogs, while frequently questioning (although not without merit) the veracity of internet-originated news. The times are changing, however, and mainstream news media have become more open to online formats, as can be seen in the blossoming relationships between the formats.

HTML Links to Mainstream Sites

A hyperlink connection directly ties one story or idea to another and may be the most significant difference between the Web and print.[1] Links represent a physical point of connection between news organizations and therefore serve as a point of analysis for intermedia relations. In this case, we are considering the connections between blogs and traditional news media online.

Linking is a particularly important attribute of the blogosphere. Hyperlinks provide a form of citation that is more immediately useful to readers than a standard reference. A print journalist can only say, "according to this source," but an online writer can use links to direct readers to the reference material, which essentially allows readers to re-create the writer's train of thought (Manovich 2001). Links also help generate a sense of community among different blogs, and different groups of bloggers can develop distinct norms for linking standards. For example, even among political blogs, conservative blogs are more likely to link to one another than are liberal blogs (Adamic and Glance 2006). This translates into a tighter community on the right side of the spectrum than on the left, but linking practices suggest that bloggers of any ideology are more connected than are mainstream writers.

On the new media side of the relationship, popular political blogs link to the mainstream news more than to any other category of website (Reese et al. 2007). Even if smaller blogs are somewhat less likely to link to the traditional news with this same frequency, it is safe to say that blogs are more generous than their counterparts. Singer (2005) analyzed the websites of news outlets and found that the majority of links went to other mainstream sites, rather than to bloggers. Once again, this practice may be shifting, as the *New York Times* reports mainstream sites beginning to link back to blogs (Stelter 2008). Reciprocal linking between major outlets and blogs will foster audiences for both types of sources and may even lead to a better appreciation by each source for the work of the other.

Economic Connections to Mainstream Sites

The second form of a relationship between traditional and online news outlets is commercial linkage. Such connections typically occur either when a mainstream outlet purchases at least a portion of a Web news service or when traditional news stories claim space on one of these sites. In both cases, the website benefits financially, from payments themselves or from increased readership that promotes advertisement sales. The financial benefits for traditional media might be less clear, but such actions should lead to a larger audience and stronger reader communities.

The ownership-style commercial relationship typically exists so that the larger, purchasing company uses the online holding to diversify and segment the larger audience (see chapter 5 below). The original online news service receives relatively stable financial support. Many examples of this type of relationship exist. Some of the more notable ones are between the *Washington Post* and Slate, the *New York Times* and About.com, and CBS and CNET. Ownership can be risky for the smaller company, because it is likely to be high on the list for the chopping block when its parent company starts losing money. When times are good, this relationship can be advantageous for both parties.

The other type of commercial relationship could be described as hosting-style, by which we mean that the larger news organization claims a share (usually for a fee) of a broad Web service's space. For example, many news outlets, such as NPR and *the Washington Post*, appear on Facebook; Reuters purchased a news office with the briefly popular Second Life; many companies give a slice of their revenue to Apple in order to appear in the app store. The hosting-style relationship is certainly the most common form of commercial connection between traditional and new organizations. Business connections in either form demonstrate a commitment from the traditional media to investigate and channel what is good about original online news forms.

Blogs and Audience Creation of the News

Most of us probably have a general sense of what people mean by "blogs" or "the blogosphere." Nevertheless, we should establish a clear definition to help in the discussion of how to understand their role in the news environment.

BlogPulse, a blog tracking site, has identified more than 154 million blogs in existence, with another 91,000 created every day. These numbers include blogs by professionals, groups, and individuals; blogs can be hosted independently or as part of a corporate portal. Technorati provides a useful categorization of blogs. The site assigns a credibility rating to each blog, largely on the basis of the number of other sites linking back to it. Along these lines, when we speak of blogs, we are referring to sites that are fairly well read and linked to by other publishers. Furthermore, unless otherwise noted, we are discussing political or news blogs that are not part of mainstream-media sites.

This explanation does little to clarify what makes a blog unique from other online presentations of news media. Structure is typically the factor that jumps into people's minds. Reverse chronological ordering is the trademark ordering of a blog. Individual authorship used to be a key characteristic, but this is no longer necessarily the case (e.g., FiveThirtyEight and the Monkey Cage are group-authored). The relative speed of blog-based news is another intriguing characteristic, although typical blogs no longer seem much, if any, faster than mainstream sites. In fact, mobile devices and micro-blogging services such as Twitter are now the fast providers of information on emerging situations. These tools have been shown to be particularly effective at facilitating citizen journalism during crises (Thelwall and Stuart 2007), because the format encourages brief posts from people in the area. Again, multimedia styles have become more popular on both mainstream sites and citizen blogs (*PC Magazine* 2006). In short, few of the original characteristics of blogging still apply with any clarity.

The natural question, then, is what does separate news "blogs" from "sites"? Structurally, one of the most distinguishing facets of contemporary blogs may be the use of links. On the whole, blogs tend to link to news stories, other outlets, and internal content differently from mainstream news sites. For example, topic tags, which some scholars have described as a grassroots organization system (Hayes and Avesani 2007), provide more useful access to related articles than either archives or search alone can provide. Analyses of the cross-site linking practices of blogs indicate that a substantial portion of posts use mainstream news as a starting point (Project for Excellence in Journalism 2010b).

The natures of the content creators are also likely to be different. Mainstream sites are more likely to feature professional journalists, while "regular" citizens are more likely to be creating independent blogs. More specifically, bloggers tend to represent younger, more urban areas than do typical reporters (Lin and Halavais 2006) and are more likely (along with creators in other internet formats) to reach groups whose interests are not served by mainstream media (e.g., Lynch 2005). Given these different sources of authors, it does appear that blogs can address stories that receive less attention in the mainstream media (Lowrey 2006). However, such a conclusion can only be drawn cautiously, as the abundance of linkages with mainstream news indicates that blogs are far from independent operators.

Also worth noting is the migration of commenting from blog sites to mainstream news outlets. Few newspaper sites made this possible until the internet era was well under way (Imfeld and Scott 2005), but commenting is now a standard feature of news sites. The influence of comments on journalism appears to vary greatly. On the one hand, journalists tend to self-report that they find little value in much of the discussion occurring in postarticle comments (e.g., Boczkowski 2004). On the other hand, at least one study has shown that online forums—in this case, that of a major Chinese newspaper—can push local stories into the national news (Zhou and Moy 2007). Given the rapidity with which many discussion threads descend into hyperbole, incivility, or spam, it seems likely that if comments matter to the subsequent production of news it is the number of comments that would matter more than the content.

We might also consider the potential individual effects of online discussion threads. Walker (2006) argues that discussions are not very ideologically diverse, which is typically seen as a negative. However, Shah and colleagues (2005) demonstrate that online discussions produce more reader mobilization than offline news media. This is a net positive. These results are not necessarily mutually exclusive; some research suggests that discussion with like-minded others is associated with higher voter turnout (Mutz 2006). The normative value of comment forums may therefore be a matter of perspective. At this point, the clearest conclusion is that user comments have potential influences on both readers and journalism, but further research is necessary the better to tease out any effects.

Alternative Forms for Audience Creation of the News

When citizens who are not professional journalists create and publish original news content, this is generically called citizen journalism. As discussed above, news blogs can be a source of citizen journalism, although they often trend toward providing little more than opinions or links to mainstream news. In addition to blogs, citizens can contribute news to specific citizen journalism sites (e.g., chicagotalks.org) or to content mills (e.g., examiner.com, ehow.com).

An effects-based perspective on these types of news content has yet to emerge. Citizen journalism and content mills may affect news agendas by covering topics not typically addressed by professional journalists. However, it may be at least equally likely that mainstream news would not be affected by these sources. Some citizen platforms are heavily influenced by political perspective—something that most mainstream journalism has deliberately refused. In the case of content mills, the content frequently lacks news value (instead focusing on reviews or instructions) and is often of comparatively poor quality. The fact that Google began deliberately adjusting its search algorithm to limit the profile of content mills does not bode well for the future of these sources. In any event, very little hard evidence exists for effects by nonblog audience-created news.

News Feeds

News feeds are another format that is unique to the internet. The main type of feed is Really Simple Syndication, or RSS (which is actually RSS2; Atom feeds operate too similarly to distinguish here). RSS provides a flexible code capable of taking the posts or stories from a website and synchronizing them on another website or device (Kennedy 2004). This development allows individuals to create personal pages or "readers" loaded with several selected feeds. The primary benefit of this format for users is the convenience of access to the headlines of many stories on one simple page.

RSS-style news feeds bear many functional similarities to Facebook, Twitter, and other social-networking services. These services allow users to follow the postings of liked others. When those others are news services, or at least people posting news, the result is rather like an RSS feed. Social media are far more popular than RSS feeds, however, and Facebook was even driving more traffic to news websites than any other single service, including Google, in 2009 (Hopkins 2010). When users receive their news from social-media feeds, the end product is particularly filtered: first through editors, second through citizens, and third through the following process, described below. This structure has significant implications for both fragmentation (chapter 7) and information democratization (chapter 8).

News Aggregators

A news aggregator is a service that combines many different news outlets into a single, condensed source. Whereas news feeds are based on sources (e.g., a user chooses to follow CNN's feed), aggregators tend to be organized around topics. The offline equivalent of an aggregator would be one newspaper created from the clippings of the most popular articles in the country. Google News is the leader in the aggregator category, although there are many alternatives, including Yahoo! News. Wire content tends to dominate the results (Dover 2007), and blogs have also tended to be overrepresented by aggregators (Elmer, Devereaux, and Skinner 2006).

The way news is captured from the vast array of sources and then presented on the aggregator's site is a matter of critical importance. An illustration of why occurred in September 2008. On September 7, a Tribune Company paper added a link to an old—but undated—article about United Airlines filing for bankruptcy protection. Google News captured the article and included it in its news-headline section. An employee at Bloomberg, a financial information service, put the story on the wire, and United suffered a one-day 11 percent drop in stock price (Zetter 2008). Who is to blame here? Much of the problem lies with the original paper for not having a date on its article. What this story shows, perhaps overly dramatically, though, is that whereas traditional news, online papers, and blogs all risk human error, the automated processes involved with aggregators are not necessarily more secure.

Collaborative news-filtering systems, such as Reddit or Digg, have much in common with news aggregators. The key difference is that most news aggregators pull content based on a mix of search algorithms and preset user preferences, but collaborative news filtering systems determine leading content based on the recommendations of fellow users. For example, Reddit users can submit links to articles, questions, videos, or other content. Fellow users can then vote on whether the link is "good" or "junk," and content rises higher on a list of links as the net score trends toward "good." At the end of the day, readers of either type of service see a boiled-down set of stories from a much larger potential pool of content. Collaborative news filters are not widely used, but they offer one of the clearest examples of citizens serving as editors of content that can be found on the Web. However, the content that rises to the top of these services is frequently not relevant to public affairs, and collaborative news filters, therefore, likely detract from attention to—or knowledge about—traditional news content.

THE ONLINE NEWS AGENDA

We have been describing content and layout in online news. In part, what we have been describing is the agenda for news on the Web. A news agenda is a news producer's representation of the relative importance of events and issues in the news. A central part of the job of journalists and editors is sifting through everything that could be in the news. In that process, they decide, in essence, what stories should be in the news and how prominently they should be displayed (White 1964). When cable television and the internet began changing how people consumed the news, researchers and observers started speculating that the process by which audiences learn about important issues was also changing (McCombs 2004).

In this section, we describe how agenda setting works and whether the process operates differently online from how it operates offline. We start with a brief description of how print newspapers, television news programs, and other traditional media communicate story importance. We move to an exploration of how online news outlets present the media agenda and whether that presentation is markedly different from the case in the traditional media. Ultimately, the evidence is going to point to both continuity and change in the news agenda online. Some attributes of the online news environment inhibit uniformity in online agendas, while others seem to encourage its perpetuation.

News Agendas

Media researchers have assumed that the relative prominence that journalists and editors assign to a story reflects their judgment of the importance of the issue or event it concerns. Taken in the aggregate, the stories that are most prominent in the media are those that are highest on the "media agenda." A long line of research in communication and political science has documented how the media agenda can influence the agenda of news audiences (McCombs 2004). Citizens use importance cues from the media agenda to infer the relative importance of issues (Iyengar and Kinder 1987). These inferences can influence a number of perceptions and judgments, including evaluations of how well political leaders do their jobs (Krosnick and Kinder 1990).

Researchers and observers often talk about the media agenda in aggregate terms, assuming the presence of general agreement among journalists about what is important. Journalists go through a socialization process in journalism schools and newsrooms that tends to produce a shared set of standards for evaluating newsworthiness (Shoemaker and Reese 1996). As a result, what reporters and editors at a large city newspaper consider important issues may closely jibe with what their counterparts at a network television news program believe. There is a fair amount of evidence for such an assumption. For example, looking at newsmagazine and network-news journalistic practices in the 1970s, Gans (1979) was able to identify a number of story types that journalists thought deserved prominent attention (e.g., presidential election campaigns are perennial top stories).

Media observers have started to question the operation of a general news agenda today and in the near future (Chaffee and Metzger 2001; Katz 1996). They argue that increases in the diversity of news outlets on cable television and the internet have fractured any general agreement among news providers. There are two possible ways that technological change in news delivery might be affecting the agenda-setting process (undoubtedly, they are interactive, but we will try to identify them separately here). One factor involves shifts in how news is produced and presented in the news media today. As we have seen, news is an expanding concept online, and news outlets are drawing information and ideas from more places than just their in-house reporters and editors. The second mechanism, discussed in chapter 5, involves how audiences react to the flood of news content available online. If audiences react to increases in the amount of news and information they receive by changing their news selection processes, this could disrupt or alter the agenda setting process.

The Traditional (offline) Definition of the News Agenda

Researchers analyzing the traditional news media have identified a number of ways in which news providers create story prominence. The first is the number of individual stories devoted to an issue or event. As is relatively obvious, greater attention to a topic through story repetition is taken to represent a judgment of the topic's importance. This relationship is not always perfect, of course. For example, some events unfold very gradually, and multiple stories about such an event could reflect the pace of development, rather than the importance of the circumstances. An extended criminal investigation often works this way. All else being equal, however, journalists and editors pay more attention to the issues and stories they consider consequential, and so story repetition is a common metric of issue importance.

Issue or event importance can also be inferred from the prominence assigned to a story in news presentation (Iyengar and Kinder 1987). In a print newspaper, the stories on the front page (the higher on the page the better) are the more important stories of the day. Similarly, stories early in a television news broadcast are typically more important—most people assume—than stories later in the program. Prominence of news is also embodied in attributes of individual stories (e.g., story length or headline size in a print medium). Of course, prominence is not a perfect measure of topic importance. Some critics have argued that local television news, in particular, has given greater prominence to sensational stories (e.g., graphic murders, sex scandals) than to public-affairs stories. In that way, they have eschewed their agenda-setting roles.

Research has suggested that people are willing and able to use story repetition, placement, and attributes in their decisions about what to consume. In a groundbreaking study of newspaper audiences, Graber (1988) asked print-newspaper readers why they read what they did. Their responses suggest that people use the importance cues that editors provide with their own intrinsic interests when deciding whether to read a story. Graber observed that her respondents "were more likely to notice a story that appeared on prominent pages of the paper, was characterized by large headlines or pictures, and was given lengthy and repeated exposure" (p. 97). Scores of studies of agenda setting have confirmed these observations (McCombs 2004). People exposed to the news acquire at least part of the media agenda. They perceive problems that receive prominent coverage to be pressing issues. They also typically rank-order the issues similarly to how stories about them appear in the news.

Online and Offline Processes of Communicating an Agenda

There are several ways to compare the online and offline agendas. The various approaches can be grouped into two camps. The first asks whether the number and type of news providers in a medium and the volume of content they supply might affect how agendas are presented. The second asks whether an audience's experience of the news might affect how agendas are encountered. If either or both of these approaches demonstrate that the reception of news differs substantially across media, it would suggest that the aggregate operation of agenda setting is changing with adoption of online news.

The Internet and the Media Agenda

The first approach to thinking about agendas examines the intersection of technology and content. As we have seen, the range of what constitutes news seems to be much broader online than with the traditional media. Information from blogs and user-originated content is part of the online news stream. There are a few ways this could influence online agendas, and they operate at different levels of analysis.

At the level of individual news organizations, the question is whether there are technological and sociological factors that can influence how each outlet presents the news. The most basic level of this comparison looks at the offline and online agendas of individual outlets. The question here is whether one organization, such as CNN, maintains a different agenda online than it does on its traditional media outlet. Earlier in this chapter, we noted how news production and display can differ from one medium to another. It seems sensible to expect that these differences can affect an organization's agenda in different media. However, the primary finding thus far has been minimal changes to the content offered within a single organization. The exceptions to this, as noted earlier, are with local and opinion content.

Still another approach to comparing online and offline news is examining the agendas of selected categories of online and offline news providers. The most common approach is to look at the agendas of political blogs and mainstream news outlets. This is a popular topic among news commentators, because people want to see whether blogs can supplant traditional media as the gatekeeper. The relatively conservative nature of corporate news entities (McChesney 2008) suggests that there is some room for alternative media to originate and then transfer stories that would otherwise never appear in print or on the air. There have already been several high profile examples of this agenda pattern—both for good and for bad. Senator Trent Lott was criticized in the traditional media for remarks made to honor controversial Senator Strom Thurmond only after weeks of complaints circulating in the blogosphere. Dan Rather's removal from CBS over falsified Air National Guard documents in the 2004 presidential campaign was driven by blog-based investigations. A U.S. Department of Agriculture employee was fired in 2010 after an interview that was misleadingly edited by a blogger was picked up by cable networks. Thus, purely within the realm of one medium (the internet, in this case), agenda development can depend on the technology and how it is used.

The other major implication of the proliferation of content options online is a potential difference in agenda homogeneity. A basic tenet of theory in agenda setting is that the news agenda is relatively uniform across traditional news outlets. This homogeneity means that audiences of different news outlets would emerge from exposure with roughly similar impressions of issue importance. Rather uniformly, researchers have assumed that the aggregate online agenda is not homogeneous (Chaffee and Metzger 2001). With thousands of news sites of various types and millions of blogs online, agenda heterogeneity on the internet seems very likely. A few studies have attempted to assess agenda heterogeneity (e.g., Lee 2007), but more work is needed.

The Internet and the Audience Agenda

The experience of consuming news online differs from that in newspapers, television, and radio in a number of ways. Most of the differences lie in the presentation and selection options that newer technologies offer.

The result of audiences having more options is that they receive either fewer importance cues or a different set of them.

Many of the most basic importance cues that are characteristic of traditional news presentation migrate directly to the internet. Story selection and repetition, for example, should be just as operative on Google News as they are on the Fox News Channel on cable television. Other importance cues are less likely to make the transition. Researchers have argued that the presentation of news on many sites seems to offer fewer signals about the relative importance of stories (e.g., Althaus and Tewksbury 2002). For example, the most important two or three stories in a print newspaper appear on the top half of the front page. On a typical news site, on the other hand, as many as a dozen stories might have links near the top of the home page. As a result, online audiences are given less information about the relative importance of the stories. Similarly, news websites typically use a small number of headline font sizes on their sites. If many stories start on the home page, quite a few might share a headline font size. Again, readers have less information about which stories are more important than others. Grouping stories by subject, as some sites do, rather than by their ultimate importance, could have a similar effect.

One possible outcome of the muting of some traditional importance cues is that audiences might increase their reliance on the cues that do operate online or on cues unique to the internet. Indeed, the internet introduces a number of new ways to think about such cues. One fundamental characteristic of many online news stories is the inclusion of hyperlinks. News stories that focus on common topics might carry hyperlinks to previous reporting on the issue or to third-party (e.g., government or interest-group) information on the topic. Readers could use the number of links in a story as a cue about its importance. That is, readers could assume that an issue with a deep background (one with many links) is connected to many sectors of society or government. If so, such a story must be important, they may assume. This potential audience inference has not been explored empirically, and little is known about its possible operation.

Many prominent news sites provide information about how other users have reacted to stories, and it seems very likely that this information can guide audience perceptions. Research has demonstrated that people can use news popularity rankings in their story-selection decisions (Knobloch-Westerwick et al. 2005). It may also be that they will use those ratings in judgments about importance. Most members of the news audience know that they select stories, in part, because they are important (Graber 1988). If audience members believe that other people do the same, then popularity rankings provide a possible proxy for how other people have assessed the importance of the available news. This seems unlikely for stories devoid of issue information, but popular public-affairs stories (if there are such things) could work this way.

If news audiences search for news, the characteristics of how search results are prioritized and presented can provide information about potential story importance. Each search engine, at both aggregator and focused provider sites, has a unique algorithm for identifying and prioritizing stories (Hurley, Sangalang, and Muddiman 2009). Inasmuch as a search may be wide enough to identify stories about different issues—which may not be too often, in fact—the results could provide a unique importance ranking for the issues it captures.

The characteristic unique to news delivery over the internet with potentially the largest impact on the agenda that audiences receive is user filtering. The interactivity and selectivity that the medium provides allow news readers to improve dramatically the fit between their preexisting interests and the stories they encounter. News organization tied to menus, specialized news sites, social media, preset filters at sites and email servers, and a number of other technologies allow audiences to select the topics that best match their interests. They might never see stories about other issues or topics, thus missing many of the importance cues and enticements that editors use. In this way, existing personal agendas are reinforced at the possible expense of professionally determined agendas.

This discussion has focused on the characteristics of the online news agenda. Next, we turn to a comparison of the online agenda with that presented in the traditional media. Much of what researchers have studied about the online news agenda focuses on content differences, largely questions of issue inclusion, exclusion, and frequency. The research community has not yet turned in force to the study of how the agenda is presented online. This might be a result of the inherent difficulty of generalizing about agenda presentation in the face of great variety in where news appears online. It might also stem from some inertia in how researchers have conceptualized the news agenda. It might take some time for them to incorporate the new ways in which importance is communicated online into existing models of the agenda setting process.

Comparing the Online Agenda and the Offline Agenda

The source of the news agenda is an enduring concern for researchers and other observers. Ideas about what the news media should cover do not spring out of the heads of journalists, of course. Reporters and editors rely on people as sources of information about issues and their importance. Therefore, part of agenda setting research has examined how journalists' sources influence the news agenda (e.g., Salwen 1995). Perhaps not surprisingly, government officials and fellow media outlets appear to exert considerable influence over how journalists cover issues and policy debates. For much of the latter half of the 20th century, it appeared that major news outlets such as the *New York Times*, the *Washington Post*, and CBS News substantially affected the news agenda in other outlets (Graber 1997). In the 1990s and the first part of the 21st century, cable-television news outlets such as CNN appeared to exert some influence. As the first decade of the century turns into the second, the question is whether those older media and outlets will continue to influence others' agendas.

Some researchers have looked at how online news outlets use sources. In a content analysis of six popular political blogs (e.g., Daily Kos, Instapundit), Leccese (2009) found that links to mainstream news sites accounted for almost half (46.5 percent) of all links; links to other pages within a blog or to other blogs accounted for 38 percent. A recent Project for Excellence in Journalism (2010b) study found a rate of blog-to-mainstream linkage closer to 100 percent. The news-media sites most frequently linked were nytimes.com, msnbc.com, washingtonpost. com, and cnn.com. These results suggest that political blogs were relying on other media, rather than primary sources, for information. These results belie the picture of an online environment in which original idea generation is the norm.

Considering the increasing prominence of political blogs, McCombs (2005) speculated, "If blogs have an agenda setting role, it is likely to be an influence on the media agenda" (p. 549). Empirical research in this area has tested this perspective against one that claims that blogs reflect the values and content of the traditional press. Studies that compare mainstream (offline) agendas with blog agendas show rather mixed results. One study examined the content of popular political blogs with topical coverage in the print *New York Times* in late 2004 (Wallsten 2007). For many of the topics in the news, there seemed to be little relationship between the agenda of the *Times* agenda and that of the blogs. For other topics, some of the cross-lagged correlations indicated that the agenda moved from the blogs to the *Times*, and some indicated the reverse (Wallsten 2007). A more recent analysis by the Project for Excellence in Journalism (PEJ) (2010b) suggests that there are vast differences in coverage, at least at the broad topic level. The PEJ found that blogs covered technology and international (non-U.S.) news far more than traditional media did, but blogs gave less attention to the U.S. economy. It is certainly true that the economic and access pressures on the mainstream press often force it down a different (usually slower and more conservative) coverage path from other organizations (McChesney 2008). The extent to which traditional news will maintain such distinctions is currently unclear.

Some people have argued that the placement of more news on internet-based outlets encourages journalists to be more homogeneous. Boczkowski (2009) suggests that contemporary technologies provide journalists with ever more information about their competitors' judgments. They rely on that information when deciding what to cover and how to cover it. Boczkowski argues, "This is not new to journalistic practice, but the increasing reliance on technology and the decreasing face-to-face relationships with colleagues in other media suggest important transformations in how journalists gather information and make meaning out of it" (p. 51). Some empirical analyses have supported these speculations. A study of news coverage of the 2004 U.S. presidential election noted substantial continuity between online and offline news agendas (Lee 2007). In this case, the agendas of the *New York Times*, CNN, the Associated Press, and *Time* magazine were highly correlated with those of a number of popular liberal and conservative blogs. The findings in this study, however, might be tied to the relatively narrow and intense focus of the campaign season. Lim (2006) observed that online newspapers and news services in South Korea appear to drive each other's news agendas. What is still to be determined is the extent to which the proliferation of online news extends well-worn intermedia agenda-setting processes or has encouraged greater homogeneity than existed before.

The second clear indicator of continuing homogeneity involves the nature of news as a commodity. As long as the news business is an industry that treats news as a means to a profit-making end, there are forces that will constrain agenda heterogeneity. The major news providers online and offline continue to be owned by relatively few media companies. The most popular news sites are owned by Yahoo!, Microsoft, Time Warner, Google, and NBC Universal. These are sites that merely repackage others' news or are affiliated with a host of other news outlets. Therefore, when researchers look at major online sources to assess news agendas, they must be very careful to avoid comparing holdings of a single entity. Even emerging news sites online are often linked with existing large players or are merged with them in time. Beyond the *Washington Post*-Slate and CBS-CNET relationships, the recent purchase of fivethirtyeight.com by the *New York Times* is a clear example of this trend. These mergers mean that news audiences often encounter one of a relatively small number of news providers online.

CONCLUSIONS

The online news industry is not the news business of old. New and emerging online news sources have already changed the aggregate-level content and form of news online. There is certainly a broader definition of news today than was used in the years before the internet. And in many ways, the news business is using the internet to test new formats of news creation and presentation. Interestingly, though, some of that change is aimed at extending the livelihood of the traditional media. This might reflect the split in the news audience. For all of the citizens who prefer to get their news and information online, there are others who stay with the traditional media (and there are many people, as we shall see, who use both). So, the news industry appears to be struggling to find a way to incorporate new technologies into how they do business and maintain their connection with the largest audiences they can find.

Observers and critics have suggested that online news will present audiences with a new agenda of issues and policies. In some cases, people have speculated that the diffuse and diverse nature of news online will increase the diversity of the national agenda. As a result, there may be substantial heterogeneity in the agenda that audiences encounter online. Similarly, some features of news presentation online may mute the agenda that is constructed by journalists. The result of both features of online news could be substantially reduced public agreement about the most importance issues facing the nation. If so, widespread reliance on the internet for news could fundamentally change the relationship between citizens and their political leadership.

The evidence thus far suggests that news on the internet might bring a number of changes to how audiences receive the news and the overall agenda of issues. The organization and technology of online news are certainly different from parallel technologies in the traditional media. News feeds and hyperlinks for organizing content represent substantially different ways to present the news. At the same time, however, research has demonstrated substantial continuity between the traditional news agendas and those found online. Audiences might not be exposed to diverse and novel agendas online. As a result, the future of the agenda-communication process is unclear.

CHAPTER 4

News Specialization and Segmentation

From the vantage point of today's media environment, we can say that the old news media were built largely on a model of providing general news content to general audiences. To be sure, ethnic newspapers, specialized magazines, and format radio stations have targeted focused audiences for many years. But the bulk of the news business has relied on a model of news for everyone. In contrast, the news environment today is one that increasingly is based on the provision of specialized content for focused audiences. The change has come in part from a perception by many in the media industries that audiences want to make choices about what they receive from the media, and it comes in part as a reaction to the capabilities of the underlying media technologies today. The shift in the underlying model of the press to specialized delivery of the news might prolong the lives of news outlets and larger media companies—at least, that is what they hope. It might also change the way people learn about public affairs and other topics.

In chapter 2, we talked about the concepts of audience activity and selectivity. We noted that people are often quite intentional in their selection of news outlets and stories. In chapter 3, we described the many forms of news on the internet. Now we bring the themes from those chapters into a discussion of how online news providers are taking advantage of technological interactivity and audience selectivity. We begin with a review of how media tend to evolve; in the process of doing that, we introduce an organizing structure of media evolution. The structure suggests that content and audience specialization (i.e., segmentation) are an almost inevitable result of media competition and development. Inevitable is a strong word, of course, so we note some forces that will tend to restrain the segmentation of online news content and audiences into discrete units. We turn next to a discussion of online news structures and define specialization a bit more precisely. It turns out that there are different kinds of specialization, and there are structures in the online news environment that support them. Among the ways that news can be separated into categories is through the production of hard and soft news. We suggest that this is one way to examine online news, but we supplement that with analyses of content and audience segmentation along more specific topical lines. Ultimately, not much data are available for examining segmentation. What we do have suggests that some people may be selecting news and sites in ways that may facilitate the development of news and audience segments.

HISTORY OF MEDIUM SPECIALIZATION

We are fortunate to have tools for analyzing how news operates online and how it will evolve. These tools are derived from observation of how older media have evolved. As is typically the case with the internet, the new medium seems to break some of the rules set by its predecessors. Nonetheless, the patterns set by the older media provide considerable insight into some elements of the internet and the news outlets that operate there.

Media-system Evolution from Elite to Specialized Audiences

Media historians have noted that national media systems and individual media appear to pass through a fairly standard three-part—elite, popular, specialized (EPS)—cycle of development (Maisel 1973; Merrill and Lowenstein 1979; Wilson and Wilson 2001). Within each stage, typical outlets of a medium offer content geared toward a particular type of audience. Members of the audience, in turn, appear to choose media and outlets on the basis of their content and availability. Not all media in the United States and other developed countries follow the EPS cycle, but most do so relatively closely.

In their initial stage, media often appeal to elite audiences. Typically, because of barriers of medium cost or audience characteristics, media usually attract small audiences of people who have some elite position in society. For example, most newspapers in the United States attracted primarily wealthy, educated social elites in the 18th and early 19th centuries (Campbell, Martin, and Fabos 2010). Similarly, only some government, corporate, and academic researchers had access to the internet in the

1970s and 1980s (Margolis and Resnick 2000). People who had access to the medium in this stage were elite in terms of their levels of education and technical skill.

Major media typically move from the elite stage to a popular stage in which the medium becomes much more widely used. Typical outlets of the medium appeal to large portions of the audience. This is the point at which people refer to something as a mass medium. Television, for example, was in its popular stage in the United States from the late 1950s through the 1980s. Televisions could be found in almost every household in America, and the broadcast networks (ABC, CBS, and NBC) together were watched by as much as 90 percent of the television audience (Sterling and Kittross 2002). Content on television in this period was relatively homogeneous and was designed to appeal to wide, heterogeneous audiences.

The final stage in the EPS cycle is the specialized stage. Aggregate use of the medium remains at the level of the popular stage, but the number of outlets increases so that individual outlets draw smaller audiences. The outlets within the medium shift from a financing structure built on the attraction of large, heterogeneous audiences to one based on more homogeneous—and, therefore, smaller—audiences. For advertising-supported media, homogeneous audiences are more efficient for advertisers seeking to reach focused consumers. The advertisers do not need to pay for access to other segments of the population. Radio provides a good example of the transition from the popular to the specialized stage. When television's growth in the 1950s drew audiences, content, and advertisers away from national network radio, most local radio stations narrowed the focus of their programming (Sterling and Kittross 2002). Radio's broad entertainment programming (e.g., dramas, comedies, quiz shows, and soap operas) of the 1930s and 1940s was replaced by focused music and talk formats. Narrow radio formats are used today to assemble focused audience segments with shared attributes and interests. Advertisers seeking specific segments of the populace are willing to pay a premium to target their messages to those segments.

The example of radio illustrates the connection between audience appetite for specialized content and the development of specialized media outlets. Specialized outlets can thrive within a medium when audiences are willing to spend their time and/or money on narrow, relatively homogeneous content. To be sure, not every medium fits this pattern perfectly (e.g., with its financing structure traditionally based on ticket or video/DVD sales, film does not fit the pattern particularly well; there has been little advertiser-based incentive to segment film audiences), but the EPS cycle has been a useful tool for observers considering how newer media will develop over time.

The Internet and the EPS Cycle

The internet does not seem to have followed the EPS cycle as closely as other media have. The initial years of internet development—from 1969 through the early 1990s—certainly fit the pattern of an elite stage. Its adherence to the popular stage is more questionable. When Web browsers made access to the internet easier and more rewarding, popular use of the medium rose dramatically (Margolis and Resnick 2000). According to survey data from the Pew Internet and American Life Project (2010a), about 14 percent of the American population used the internet in 1995, and about 67 percent did so 10 years later. So, the size of the potential audience for a website certainly increased dramatically after the end of the elite stage.

The definition of the popular stage of the cycle, though, includes the requirement that a typical outlet in a medium carries content for a broad audience and is used by such an audience. There is not much evidence to support that description for the internet. From early in its public phase, there have been relatively general-interest sites that have tried to attract a large audience. America Online (AOL), Yahoo! and a host of other portal sites in the late 1990s sought to be the entry points for audiences' use of the Web. They offered a range of content, including email services, news headlines, weather, shopping, and chat, all designed for a general audience. These sites have been successful in attracting broad audiences. For example, in August 1999, AOL websites were visited at least once by 55 percent of home users of the internet (Nielsen//NetRatings 1999). That level of centralized use of some sites continues today. Google, for instance, is visited by about 70 percent of home and work users in a typical month (Nielsenwire 2010).

What prevents Web use in the 1990s or today from being termed popular in character is the division of audience attention across multiple sites, most of which are not general in focus. The average American internet user visits dozens of websites in a typical month (Nielsenwire 2010). If some of the sites he or she visits are general-interest sites such as Google or Yahoo! this still leaves quite a bit of internet activity spent at smaller, potentially more specialized sites. Since the mid-1990s, the vast majority of websites have been focused on particular topics. These sites fit the definition of specialized outlets. In sum, the evidence suggests that the internet simultaneously contains elements of both the popular and specialized stages of the EPS cycle.

How news fits into the site-specialization process is multidimensional. The EPS cycle suggests that in the specialized stage, most outlets will try to attract focused, internally homogeneous audiences. A website will do this in order to deliver an identifiable segment of the populace to advertisers seeking that segment. For example, a news site that covers government events in a state capital would draw government officials, lobbyists, and similar readers. Some advertisers might be very interested in reaching such an audience. Naturally, some news sites might deviate from a focused approach. They may seek a general audience for general advertisers. After all, not every advertiser will want to reach a small segment of the population. News sites might also seek a general audience that they can direct to an offline news outlet such as a newspaper or television news program, perhaps in a complementary fashion.

Decisions by news outlets regarding the types of content they carry depend primarily on the costs of news gathering and distribution and the gains to be had from attracting audience members. On the internet, the costs of distribution do not vary much across news and audience categories. Thus, the costs of gathering and presenting content play a significant role in determining the news. If a certain type of information is costly to gather, the rewards for supplying it to specific audience members need to be relatively high. For online news sites, this can mean that small audiences spread across many sites can have the effect of either increasing the breadth of content on the site or decreasing the amount of content on a site. For example, the MSNBC site can carry a wide array of information because it attracts a relatively large audience. General advertisers may be willing to pay for such an audience. A smaller news site—a local newspaper site, for example—would likely limit its offerings to what a smaller audience could support. Often, this has been news about local business, entertainment, sports, or government (Singer 2001).

FRAMEWORK OF MEDIUM SPECIALIZATION

Specialization simultaneously refers to two things. First, it refers to the way news providers create and format content for a desired audience. Second, it can refer to the way news audiences can tailor their news consumption to limit their exposure to a specific set of news topics. If sites successfully create targeted news and audiences successfully pursue their topics of interest, the result can be a highly functional fit between content and audiences. It also can divide parts of the audience from one another, an effect called segmentation. Segmented sites are those with relatively distinct audiences. Audiences of one segmented site may be visitors to other such sites, of course, but the key feature of a segmented site is the homogeneity of its users relative to some larger body of citizens.

Consider, for example, a news site such as cnn.com. If its audience were entirely unsegmented, we would expect that the average visitor from a general population (such as internet users in the United States) would match the demographic profile of the average member of the site's audience. The average visitor would be the same age, sex, race, and so on, as the typical member of the population. If, on the other hand, the average visitor to the site were substantially younger or better educated than the typical member of the population, we could say that cnn.com had an audience base in a particular segment or set of segments in the population.

Commercial online news organizations of different types share a common goal: to create audience segments that advertisers will be interested in reaching. News sites can employ any of the three main forms of specialization—unit, internal, or distribution—when targeting an audience segment. Unit specialization, which occurs when an outlet is entirely focused on a relatively narrow slice of content, is the form that people consider most often. However, this option is ill suited to news organizations that want to reach large audience segments. These outlets, therefore, turn to internal specialization, which simply requires creating distinct sections of the news site to deliver particular areas of content. Distribution specialization, by which an outlet creates a slightly different version of its product for different audiences, is also possible online—although in limited use among news organizations. Each form of specialization requires a unique approach to how a news site creates its content.

Unit Specialization: News Blogs

Among online news sites, unit specialization is best exemplified within the blogosphere. News blogs are almost always divided along lines of political ideology, which is a broad form of audience segmentation, and often further focused on a type of news. There are blogs focused on education, technology, religion, foreign affairs, and politics (to name a few). These categories can be split even further. For example, the blog techPresident covers technology in politics, while the blog FiveThirtyEight primarily covers polling within political elections. Each is a blog for political junkies, but they provide very different content.

Unit specialization that occurs in the final stage of the EPS cycle is rooted in fundamental economic principles. In chapter 2, we discussed Hotelling's (1929) positioning concept. Hotelling begins with the assumption that businesses want to reach as many people as possible. When there are few businesses, positioning in the middle (i.e., being a generalized news outlet) is the most effective way to reach customers. Each additional business will find it increasingly productive to position its product nearer to the end points (i.e., focusing on particular content or viewpoints), because this allows the business to reach people who are poorly served by the central organizations. What makes the positioning principle crucial for understanding internet news is that when the audience can be national, or even global, even very small portions of the total audience can mean thousands of viewers (see Anderson 2004). To put it another way, the vast reach of the World Wide Web gives outlets with even finely unit-specialized content potential financial viability.

Internal Specialization: Large News Sites

Large news sites have to take a different approach to segmenting audiences. These organizations want to attract a large overall audience, but they also likely want to create segments so that advertisers can reach readers with specific interests. Careful attention to website design allows news sites to balance these competing objectives. Consider the standard structure of many large news sites: a front page displays news stories falling into many different categories, with links connecting to pages that will display stories of only one type (e.g., politics, entertainment, sports, etc.). This design encourages a broad audience to view the front page, but subsequent pages appeal to an increasingly specialized group of readers. The site is therefore able to segment its broad audience through this use of internal specialization.

Website-design research suggests that manipulating site structure can have interesting implications for how readers experience the site. On the one hand, an effective design can improve agreement with content (Sundar, Kalyanaraman, and Brown 2003) and even encourage people to spend more time with it (Richard 2004). Of course, news outlets want audiences to spend as much time with the site as possible, because this means more advertisement exposures. On the other hand, requiring readers to click too many times to find the news they want can cause frustration (Benoit and Benoit 2005; Sundar, Kalyanaraman, and Brown 2003). The research indicates that online news sites hoping to employ internal specialization effectively need to consider audience experience as part of their design strategy. Traffic ratings suggest that many organizations are able to walk this line with some success (comScore 2011a).

Distribution Specialization: Mobile Platforms

Distribution specialization occurs when an outlet creates different versions of its main product for different audiences. The bulk of the product remains static, but there is a different cover or emphasis for each desired segment. This form of specialization is relatively new to the internet. Although the norm is to think about websites in terms of national or global distribution, it is increasingly possible for outlets to deliver particular content based on geography. Browsers (particularly on mobile devices) regularly deliver global-positioning information to the websites or services being accessed, allowing an organization to recognize the location of the individual and deliver specialized content. By knowing the location of the user, a news site can display articles about local news and events. This process has been popular for several years among political-issue movements (Howard 2006), but its use is expanding into other areas. News organizations will most likely follow suit in the near future.

It might be useful to provide a more detailed background for how distribution specialization actually works online. When a browser accesses a website, it gives that site's server information about the user's computer. Under basic conditions, this information is typically the computer's operating software, browser type, and internet protocol (IP) address. If the user is a return visitor and the website uses cookies, then the site may have additional information about the type of content that computer has accessed in the past. This can be used by the website to show, for example, links to similar articles instead of general articles on the home page. More advanced browsers (such as Firefox after version 3.5) might also give websites a geographic location for the user that is more accurate than what sites can learn from the IP address. Armed with this knowledge, a news organization's servers can automatically deliver a slightly different mix of stories (and advertisements) to readers from different geographic areas. This ability is increasingly important as location-based advertising becomes a standard feature of online advertising.

As we have suggested, when trying to create an audience segment, news organizations typically turn to a form of specialization, whether distribution, internal, or unit. Distribution specialization is relatively new and is currently more popular for mobile news applications. Regardless of the format, the objective is the same: to allow the organization to define clearly the interests of its readers to advertisers or other patrons.

EVIDENCE OF SITE SPECIALIZATION

Site specialization is fairly evident from a historical review of past media or from casual observation of current media. Our purpose here is to discuss the evidence for different forms of specialization from a different perspective. Content analyses of different news media and outlets can identify segmentation efforts based on unit specialization, and survey reports can reveal the extent to which audiences separate and reach out to distinct outlets. This section discusses research findings regarding topical, stylistic, and geographic segmentation strategies.

Evidence of Topic-based Segmentation

The tendency of news sites to tailor their content to a specific segment of the online news audience provides a direct link between what online audiences select and what news editors provide. That is, the editors of a news site with a focus on a particular audience should react to what desired members of that audience choose to read. If they consistently read one type of news, editors will be motivated to provide a good supply of that news. This raises the question of whether news sites pay attention to what audiences choose. There is some evidence that they do. MacGregor (2007) interviewed a sample of online journalists about their use of audience-activity data. The journalists reported that news organizations make extensive use of data about audience selection of news on their sites. Some journalists received reports from site editors about hits on individual stories, and journalists believed that the number of hits reflect audience preferences. News-site editors appear to make use of past data on audience preferences in determining what news to post and how to present it (MacGregor 2007). The journalists MacGregor interviewed stopped short of saying that site server logs drove news-production decisions, but the evidence suggests that journalists respond to some extent to what online audiences choose.

It is not hard to imagine how site segmentation could develop in such an environment. Audience selection of specific categories of news and editorial responses to their selection could develop in a spiral fashion. If people select news of a particular genre, the editors of a site might respond by providing more news in that genre—not a lot more, to be sure, but perhaps a little. The provision of more news in a particular area could attract audiences in search of that content (perhaps through word of mouth, link sharing in blogs and other social media, or links from news aggregators). As more people visit the site for that content, the website receives story-hit data that reinforce the perception that the audience wants that content. The editors will likely respond by providing more news of that type, continuing the cycle of audience-editorial interaction.

Unfortunately, we do not have a lot of specific evidence bearing on whether that sort of cycle operates in the development of news sites. Nonetheless, one study of audience traffic on a sample of news sites did find that the news selected on the various sites showed distinct patterns (Tewksbury 2005). This study examined two months of visits by a national sample of internet users to news sites in March and May 2000.[1] Each page hit was categorized into one of 14 news topics (see Tewksbury 2005 for more information). These hits were then aggregated across the two months. Table 4.1 shows that the news that audiences select varies substantially across these sites. Among the marked differences visible here are the distribution of page views of sports, arts and entertainment, business and money, politics, and opinion and editorial. For example, visitors to *USA Today* online selected sports, arts, and entertainment proportionally more often than did visitors to the other sites. CNN online users were particularly unlikely to view arts and entertainment but very likely to view business and money pages. *New York Times* online readers viewed very little sports news but proportionally quite a bit of politics and opinion and editorial content.

These data suggest a few tentative conclusions. The news that people select is not uniform across news sites. Audiences appear to encounter and select specific constellations of news topics that differ by the site. Of course, these data do not show how the content offered by each site over the studied two-month period varied. It is likely that the selection of news can be considered as relatively constrained by what is offered. Perhaps the amount of content in each topic and the way it was presented determined the observed differences among sites. To take a fully constrained example, it could be that 41.9 percent of the news on the *USA Today* site during the studied period was sports, 17.9 percent was arts and entertainment, and so on. Undoubtedly, there is more to the story than that, but we do not have data bearing on the content of the sites during the study period. Unfortunately, we are left to speculate to fill in the details. One plausible explanation for the data is that the news readers in this sample chose sites on the basis of the news they expected to find. For example, people seeking sports information believed that they should visit the *USA Today* site rather than the ABC news site. A similar story could be told for people seeking business and personal-finance news on CNN online rather than the other sites.

If the audience studied here was, indeed, looking for a specific set of stories at each site, one would expect to see differences in the characteristics

Table 4.1. DISTRIBUTION OF PAGE VIEWS AT SELECTED NATIONAL NEWS SITES

Site element	CNN	USA Today	New York Times	ABC News
Sports	29.6	41.9	7.9	4.1
Arts and entertainment	4.8	17.9	14.7	7.7
U.S. national	13.9	9.7	9.0	29.8
Features	10.2	3.9	13.5	13.5
Business and money	16.1	7.4	9.2	7.4
Technology and science	7.0	2.0	11.4	13.3
World	6.1	1.2	8.6	9.3
Politics	5.1	2.7	11.4	7.6
Weather	4.8	6.7	0.2	0.8
Other news	0.2	4.5	0	1.1
Health	2.2	1.6	2.2	5.4
Opinion and editorial	0.0	0.6	8.0	0.0
State and local	0.0	0.0	2.8	0.0
Obituary	0.0	0.0	0.3	0.0

Note: Cell entries are percentages of all news topic views. The "other news" category captured URLs that could be identified only to the point of having news content. Topic-selection percentages may not add up to 100 because of rounding.
Source: Tewksbury 2005.

of readers at each. For many years, researchers have noted that interest in different news categories varies by age, sex, education, and other demographic features of audiences (e.g., Bogart 1989; Schramm and White 1949). There is no reason to expect that news readers selecting news sites somewhat randomly—that is, for reasons other than expectations about the sorts of news they will find on sites—should distribute themselves across news sites on the basis of demographic differences. But, of course, differences among sites do appear to exist. An analysis (Tewksbury 2005) of the profiles of specific sites' users shows substantial variation across sites.

Table 4.2 shows user demographic data for the national news outlets discussed previously. The data suggest that the demographic profile of visitors across sites differs markedly. In the time frame studied here, CNN online readers were better educated and less often female than were readers of ABC News online. *USA Today* readers were also typically male and were particularly likely to be African-American. *New York Times* online visitors were uniquely well educated and were often female. In sum, the data in tables 4.1 and 4.2 show that news readers are not randomly distributed across major online news sites and seem to cluster in ways that suggest some correspondence between audience characteristics and the

Table 4.2. DEMOGRAPHIC CHARACTERISTICS OF VISITORS TO SELECTED NATIONAL NEWS SITES

	CNN	USA Today	New York Times	ABC News
Age	40.4 (13.5)	43.3 (12.4)	47.1 (14.8)	41.9 (13.0)
Income over $49,999	68.9	67.0	68.0	70.2
Bachelor's degree or higher	61.1	58.0	77.2	45.8
Female	25.4	27.9	37.0	38.5
Hispanic ethnicity	6.7	3.7	3.9	5.3
Race				
White	88.6	84.6	92.2	92.0
African-American	6.5	11.7	3.3	3.5
Asian-American	3.6	3.2	2.8	3.6
Other race	1.4	0.6	1.7	0.9
Region				
Midwest	30.5	21.4	14.0	21.4
Northeast	19.2	13.1	39.7	16.4
South	28.9	42.8	26.6	37.8
West	21.5	22.8	19.7	24.5

Note: Cell entries for age are mean and standard deviation (in parentheses). Entries for all other demographic items are the percentages of nonmissing data. Entries are weighted by demographic weights and by number of site views.
Source: Tewksbury 2005.

kinds of news that sites feature. Taken together, this is tentative evidence of site segmentation: the division of sites along content lines and audience characteristics.

More recent data concerning self-reported site use reveal complementary patterns. In their 2008 media use national survey, the Pew Research Center for the People and the Press asked internet news readers which sites they tended to visit most often. The respondents volunteered the names of as many as three sites. Later in the survey, these people were asked to report how closely they tended to follow specific categories of news in "newspaper, on television, radio or the internet" (Pew Research Center 2008b). The overlap in responses to these two sets of questions might illustrate how specific news topics can be connected with specific sites in the minds of audiences. If people who follow one type of news tend to say that they visit a certain site most often, it could be that they tend to look at that site for the information they typically follow. If there is no connection between the kinds of sites they use and the news they tend to follow, there would be little observable relationship between where they say they go and what news they say they follow.

A comparison of news interests with news-site use is presented in table 4.3. The top row of the table displays the percentage of online news readers (overall N = 949) whose initial report of the site they visit most often was one of those displayed here. For example, the initial response of almost 11 percent of online news readers was that they visited CNN's site for news. Initial site responses were used here because they should represent what was most accessible to the respondents, and information accessibility is typically related to how often and how recently some concept is used (e.g., Higgins 1996). The next seven rows of data in the table represent the percentage of each site's users who reported following a topic very closely or somewhat closely (as opposed to not very closely or not at all closely).

A number of rather strong relationships are visible in the data in table 4.3. Looking across the rows, one can see that sites vary in the degree to which their users report following specific topics. For example, following business and finance is not uniform across the sites. For most sites, about

Table 4.3. NEWS PREFERENCES OF VISITORS TO POPULAR ONLINE NEWS SITES

	Yahoo! News	Google News	CNN	MSNBC	Fox News	New York Times	Drudge Report
Sample naming site	20.8%	6.2%	10.7%	5.1%	4.5%	2.7%	1.5%
News topics							
Political figures and events	68	64	79	94	87	93	100
Business and finance	63	62	57	54	52	92	63
International affairs	57	70	69	69	74	100	96
Science and technology	59	69	74	53	45	100	100
Crime	75	56	78	73	74	30	57
Culture and the arts	39	24	56	68	20	66	20
Health	62	60	42	63	41	71	91

Note: The number in each news-topic cell is the percentage of visitors to each site who reported following the topic very closely or somewhat closely. Because of the Pew Research Center's use of randomly applied form splits in the survey, twice as many people were asked about political figures and events, business and finance, and international affairs as were asked about the other topics.
Source: Pew Research Center 2008b.

60 percent of their visitors follow the topic. *New York Times* readers stand out for their far more frequent report of doing so (92 percent report following the topic). This sort of variance is found for all of the topics. Thus, news interests are not uniformly distributed.

Looking down the columns, one can discern glimpses of site segmentation. Large percentages of Yahoo! News users tend to follow crime and politics, but relatively few of them report following culture news. Google News visitors are rather high on international affairs and science and technology but rather low on crime and culture and arts. CNN online visitors report following politics, international affairs, science and technology, and crime but not health news. MSNBC visitors are rather similar, although they less often report following science technology and more often follow health. Some large differences emerge for the smaller sites, perhaps as a partial function of smaller numbers of respondents there. Fox News visitors frequently report following politics, international affairs, and crime. They exhibit less interest in science and technology, culture and the arts, and health news. *New York Times* site visitors report very high interest in several topics but a very low frequency of following crime news. Finally, visitors to the Drudge Report closely follow a number of topics, but they report rather infrequently for culture and the arts. Thus, the news sites listed here appear to be drawing rather distinct audiences in search of specific profiles of content areas.

There is also some evidence for topic-based segmentation at the medium level. The Project for Excellence in Journalism tracks the topics of news stories across a number of media. In May 2010, it released a report comparing the news topics in selected segments of the internet with those in the traditional press. It found that across 2009, blogs and Twitter posts focused on different topics from the traditional press. The findings for technology news were most striking. That topic showed up in 43 percent of Twitter news posts and 8 percent of blogs. It showed up in only 1 percent of the news in the traditional press. These findings clearly indicate that content creators in new technologies are deliberately selecting different topics from other news media.

What makes this compelling evidence for segmentation is the fact that the people who rely on the traditional press for news are different from those who rely on the internet. The Pew analysis of its 2008 biennial media-use survey revealed the presence of different clusters of news audiences. The proportion of the American population (46 percent) who rely on the traditional media for news is substantially older, less educated, and lower-income, on average, than the proportion (13 percent) who rely on the internet for news. Furthermore, the survey revealed that people who use traditional media were far less interested

(10 percent) in technology coverage than were the dominant users of online news (24 percent). When we combine the content findings with the survey findings, there is evidence of news organizations employing segmentation strategies by offering tech news online but not offline, of citizens self-selecting a news medium based on content offerings, or both. Regardless of the process that led to the divergence in coverage, the apparent division of news topics across media is a pretty clear sign of segmentation.

Evidence of Style-based Segmentation

News organizations can segment audiences in a unit fashion more subtly than simply by covering one topic or another. An important question for a news outlet to answer is whether to create content for a relatively serious or a casual audience segment. This choice will help determine the content and style of the news that organization produces. When academics talk about "the news," they almost always mean hard news, or coverage of government, politics, and international affairs. This type of information is typically considered the most important for political participation (Berelson 1952) and therefore receives the bulk of scholars' attention. However, this is not the only type of news available—it is not even the most popular type of news available. In a selective media environment, individuals choose both between news and entertainment and among types of news (Rittenberg, Tewksbury, and Casey 2009). Stable preferences for different news are important, because there are substantial differences among the audience segments favoring each type of content (Tewksbury 2003). The two main types of news formats are hard and soft, the latter of which is sometimes associated with infotainment. Although the distinctions between the categories are sometimes fuzzy, we focus on differences in content and effects.

The names suggest the nature of the content for each type of news. Hard news deals with topics that are considered most important—public affairs and international issues—and stories are covered in a serious, direct manner. Network evening news and nationally prestigious newspapers (e.g., the *New York Times*) are classic examples of hard news. Soft news is sometimes defined simply as "not hard news," but our definition of soft news is a news format that—regardless of topic—presents stories with an emphasis on individuals (also called "human interest") and sensationalism over national interests, public policy, or information quality. Television shows such as *Good Morning America* and *20/20* fall into this category, as do magazines such as *Entertainment Weekly*. This definition does not always yield a clear distinction between hard and soft news. A "soft"-format outlet may occasionally break an important story, and a "hard"-format organization may dabble (at least) in trivial subjects. Nonetheless, content comparisons of direct and informational versus individual and sensational provide an effective starting point for dividing news outlets by format.

An outlet's choice of content type and style says a lot about the audience it intends to attract. Hard-news styles tend to appeal to a cross-demographic group that maintains strong interest in politics (Prior 2007), whereas soft news and infotainment are typically assumed to appeal to less attentive audiences. This is not necessarily a definitive typology, of course, as particular types of infotainment can quite successfully appeal to knowledgeable audience segments. For example, whereas readers of the *National Enquirer* and viewers of the CBS evening newscast rate quite poorly on measures of political knowledge, viewers of the *Colbert Report* perform quite well (Pew Research Center 2007). In addition, viewers of soft-news programs that include comedy are likely to be more cynical of and less trusting in government (e.g., Baumgartner and Morris 2006). Research in this area is still relatively limited, however, as scholars are only beginning to tease out the practical differences between hard and soft news.

The distinctions between types of news can be particularly difficult to discern online. We might assume that mainstream news sites target an audience similar to that of their offline counterparts. However, blogs—whether independent or on mainstream sites—have typically focused on partisan and/or sensationalistic topics. Indeed, many of the great success stories of early online news include the breaking of stories focused on individuals (e.g., Senator Trent Lott praising Strom Thurmond's presidential campaign, Dan Rather broadcasting phony George W. Bush military records). These content choices have placed much of the internet's original news more clearly in the soft-news category. However, political-news blogs are a relatively fine slice of all of the possible content available online and are likely to be selected only by highly motivated audiences. Therefore, whereas we could reasonably label many of these blogs as either soft news or infotainment, it is possible that the creators are nevertheless targeting an audience with a level of sophistication typically associated with hard news.

Hard and soft news have traditionally been treated as quite different approaches to selecting and reporting the news. Online outlets are blending these styles to serve a variety of audience interests. A likely reason for this experimentation is that the "long tail" (Anderson 2004) of the internet means that almost any type of content can find some audience.

Regardless of the reason for the evolving news presentation, it is clear that describing news styles is more difficult now than it was 20 years ago. Disentangling the news formats and their likely audiences any further requires a careful consideration of news selection and effects, both of which are discussed in greater detail in the next chapter. For now, the important point is that one way in which internet content providers segment the audience is by providing some mix of the traditional hard and soft news styles.

Evidence of Geography-based Segmentation

Additional evidence of unit site specialization comes in the form of local-news site development. The downsizing of large news organizations in 2009 and 2010 resulted in a modest growth in sites that cater to a geographically distinct audience. Some media observers argue that newsroom cuts at large city daily newspapers have left many cities underserved and a number of seasoned journalists looking for work (McChesney and Nichols 2010). Some internet start-ups have sought to take advantage of the content gap by providing focused coverage of local news. They hope that local audiences will either pay for that content or attract enough advertising to finance sites. In fact, AOL appears to be developing plans to introduce a number of local news sites of this kind (Carlson 2010).

A proliferation of local news sites might play a role in site segmentation. A Project for Excellence in Journalism study in Baltimore found that newspapers (print and online components) were the outlets most likely to break local news (2010a). The study found that online news sites tended to focus on local events to a much greater degree than other media did. This study looked at news about Baltimore produced by news outlets in Baltimore (e.g., newspapers, television stations, radio stations, online-only outlets) for one week in July 2009. Larger news organizations, such as newspapers and television stations, produced quite a bit of local content, of course. But this content still competed with news about national and international events, sports, and so on. For example, about 53 percent of stories in the *Baltimore Sun* newspaper (print and online) were locally focused. Local online sites were much more likely to be geographically focused. The study found that 85 percent of the news on the locally produced Web-only sites was local in nature. It appears that smaller news sites could eschew a model of broad news presentation and focus instead on serving a distinct audience looking for geographically focused news.

In sum, there is evidence that news sites are developing profiles of specific news-topic selection. News sites are associated with specific audience demographic profiles and with distinct patterns of news-topic interest and selection. This may be a sign that audiences are seeing distinct differences among sites and are choosing where to go on the basis of expectations about what they will find there. Of course, this is but one interpretation of the observed data. It might be that there is some third factor that explains why certain people end up at certain sites. It could have more to do with some other features of a site than the news topics it offers, or it could be something about the people other than their news interests that brings them to specific sites. Site segmentation provides one explanation, but others are also possible. Communication researchers will be studying this issue and might have more definitive answers soon.

LIMITS OF SITE SPECIALIZATION

The segmentation of news sites into distinct categories might appear inevitable from a historical perspective, but there are a number of reasons researchers remain cautious about the idea. When satellite-distributed cable television channels appeared in the 1980s, a number of researchers started asking whether the mass medium of television would become a specialized medium (e.g., Becker and Schoenbach 1989). In his 1991 analysis, *The Future of the Mass Audience*, Neuman considered whether proliferation of cable-television channels would increase the diversity of content on television. He reasoned that diversification of content on cable would come as a result of audience demand. Therefore, he examined the evidence of audience diversity. He concluded that in spite of the many ways one can define and observe diversity in American society, media-content preferences are rather homogeneous. He noted the presence of technological and economic factors that facilitate and drive content specialization, but he questioned audience demand for that specialization. In sum, he wrote, "The future of specialized media and the possible fragmentation of the mass audience remain unsettled questions" (Neuman 1991, p. 128).

One of the factors that might inhibit audience demand for diversification of content—through the provision of specialized content channels—is audience perceptions of news accessibility. Neuman argued that "people are passive and only partially attentive to what they see and hear from the media. For most of the people for most of the time, the psychological costs and inconvenience of finding special-interest information and entertainment outweigh their desire to find it" (1991, p. 146). If this is true, the convenience of finding and selecting generalized content could be a large factor inhibiting or facilitating website specialization.

A simple review of internet traffic supports the notion that many users will cluster around a few general-interest news sites. In its 2009 ranking of internet news sites, Nielsen Online reported that Yahoo! News, MSNBC, AOL News, and CNN and were the four most popular news sites for Americans (Project for Excellence in Journalism 2010c). These sites are all, arguably, relatively general sites providing a broad array of news topics. What is more, news aggregators such as Yahoo! News and Google News sample from a cross-section of news sites. Thus, they are perhaps the most general of all news sites, and they are a steadily popular type of news platform. Audiences may select particular content from these home pages, as discussed in the next chapter. However, as predicted by Neuman (1991), the large-scale clustering around general sites may be sufficient to provide some pool of common content and limit widespread specialization.

CONCLUSIONS

As a medium with an almost limitless capacity for content diversity and quantity, the internet may appear to be the ideal environment for slicing content and audiences into very small segments. Most observers of the news industry have expected that this is likely to happen as news moves online. Existing models of media evolution predict that media run through a relatively predictable pattern of development, something that has been dubbed the EPS cycle. The internet is an important exception to the EPS cycle, because it is not clear how to assess its audience and content, as a whole. In some ways, the internet shows signs of a mature, specialized medium, but in others, it has just made the transition away from the elite stage.

These considerations put the focus of the study of online news development on whether sites are specializing their content and audiences. There are a number of ways in which specialization can operate in advanced media, with the most common and powerful being unit specialization. Audience segmentation that could result from that sort of specialization can be facilitated by the increasing popularity of soft news online and the current trend toward a focus on local news for many online outlets. Of course, not everyone in the potential audience will always opt for sites that employ unit specialization. The desire for general content and a certain amount of inertia may place an outer limit on the extent to which sites can create segmented audiences.

Fortunately, there are some data that bear on the question of whether sites are specializing for specific audiences. An analysis of one sample of news sites shows that the demographic profile of visitors to each site is distinct from the profile of visitors to other sites. Similarly, the news that audiences select at each site differs from the news that visitors select from the other sites. Additional data show that the kinds of news topics that people like to follow vary in tandem with what they claim are the news sites that they prefer to visit. In sum, these data show that news site specialization appears to be leading to patterns of audience segmentation. Whether that sort of segmentation has implications for citizen learning about public affairs and for aggregate-level concerns about the quality of public engagement in advanced democracies is discussed later in this book.

CHAPTER 5
Selecting News Online

From the way most of us talk about media audiences, one might decide that people are active selectors of news. They carefully survey the news environment, going online and scanning the available choices as they home in on the sites and news topics that provide the best fit with what they want. In this picture that we often paint of the news audience, people appear quite deliberate but not very human. The true picture is more complex. People resort to a mixture of habit and reasoned selectivity as they choose the news.

In this chapter, we focus on the concept of selectivity. We look at what researchers have learned about how people select the news. We first consider selectivity as a general concept, describing how people choose media and messages. We then focus the discussion on the internet. The Web carries much more than news, so a primary choice that people make is among types of content online. We describe how people select online news sites and stories. Finally, we consider the extent to which people carry selectivity practices online to the point of content specialization. We report the evidence we have for the often-heard claim that the internet will inspire and allow people to focus exclusively on the few news topics that interest them.

Out of this discussion of audience selectivity emerges a picture of both audience specialization and broad news browsing. The research results suggest that news audiences are not acting in concert. Some people engage in very intentional selection of news sites and topics, others seek specific topics but seem to care little about the sites from which they choose, still others carefully choose sites but then browse widely within those sites, and still others choose to ignore news entirely. There is no simple answer to questions about the future of news audiences, but we see some signs of what could be.

Nearly everything online is situated within an interactive environment. That seems obvious, but it is worth pausing for a moment to consider the concept of interactivity. There are many ways to define it (see Kiousis 2002 for a discussion). Many people talk about interactivity as an attribute of a site (Bucy and Tao 2007). That is, a news site that contains options for contacting journalists might be labeled an interactive site. Interactivity could be thought of as a process of reciprocal communication between parties (such as between a site visitor and a site or another visitor), or it could be a perception on the part of a site visitor (Bucy and Tao 2007). The key point is that newer media such as the internet seem to feature more interactivity, no matter how it is defined.

The focus of this chapter is how people interact with sites as they consume the news. The most basic interaction is simply the selection of stories through the click of a mouse or other pointer. Interaction can be more developed as news audiences respond to stories or post items of their own. They can even interact with other users inadvertently, as when their selections or emailed story recommendations are aggregated to indicate story popularity for other readers. Story selection as the most basic unit of interaction has attracted the most research attention, so it is the primary topic here. For this discussion, we draw on the audience-activity concept reviewed in chapter 2. We take a more focused look at activity in news selection in this section. We see that researchers have studied activity and audience selection of news in a variety of ways, and we examine how these approaches apply to the online news environment. We attempt to provide a general picture of how people tend to use the internet. In chapter 7, we apply the general concepts and patterns described here to an analysis of the potential for online news consumption to fragment audiences and ultimately polarize societies.

Selecting News to Satisfy Needs and Desires

In the context of online news, the concept of audience activity points to the potential for people to apply a number of considerations to the choice of how to spend their time. For most people, media content is merely one of the many things in their environment that they can use (e.g., the news competes with other media content, work, friends, sleep, food, exercise, or any number of other options). Considerations about what friends and family are doing or want from an audience member may contribute to a decision to choose a particular media product (e.g., Levy and Windahl 1984). For example, people might choose an online news story because they want to do something online, because they want timely news to share with friends, or because they check online news at a particular point every day. A similar range of considerations will act on how people select news outlets, how they consume and interpret the news they choose, and how they form conclusions about a medium.

There are two important factors in the active selection process. The first is the role of habit. Just because we think of the audience as active does not mean that we need to believe that people start each news-selection and -consumption process from scratch (Diddi and LaRose 2006). Rather, news consumption is clearly like many other parts of life. People have well-worn paths (or "scripts," in the language of cognitive social psychologists; Abelson 1981) that guide how they approach the process. There are specific goals, thoughts, feelings, and behaviors they habitually apply to news selection and processing. People are not automatons, merely repeating the past in an endless loop, but neither are they perfectly intentional all of the time (Rubin 1984).

As people use and explore media, they tend to develop dependency relations with particular media, outlets, and content (DeFleur and Ball-Rokeach 1989). The goals that people have with respect to media (such as learning about other people and places) are relatively stable (McDonald and Glynn 1984). Likewise, what the media offer is often relatively predictable. In fact, the notion of media system dependency introduces a level of stability to news selection that coincides nicely with what media producers likely want to see. An outlet's ability to sell display advertising space on a Web page is likely enhanced when it can predict the audience for the site with some confidence. If the audience is stable and exhibits relatively predictable visit and selection patterns, it should make the job of selling space to advertisers all the easier. Thus, one element of news sites' audience segmentation strategy is the creation of content that fits the goals of a desirable (from the perspective of potential advertisers) audience.

The second factor affecting news selection is the directive action of environmental constraints and options. For most people, the news is not a vital commodity. There is considerable variance in most populations when it comes to the centrality of news to people's lives, but few people need it to live or achieve their most important life goals. Rather, news consumption is one of the many things that they do over the course of a day. People will spend only so much of their available resources (e.g., time and money) to obtain the news. Likewise, people are constrained by how the news is presented in the media they have available. People are not perfectly autonomous in their selection of the news but will choose among the options their environment offers (Prior 2007).

Selective Exposure

A somewhat less predictable element of news selection is introduced by the concept of selective exposure (Klapper 1960). The idea is relatively simple. Based on Festinger's (1957) theory of cognitive dissonance, people consider the potential implications of news and other content for their preexisting beliefs and opinions (Frey 1986). As a general rule of thumb, people want their beliefs and opinions to be consistent with one another. This desire for consistency can motivate people to seek information that is supportive of their predispositions, and it can motivate them to avoid challenging information. These approach-and-avoid tendencies have formed the bases for much of the work on selective exposure.

Despite its simplicity and the commonsense ring to it, audience selective exposure received only limited support in tests in the 1950s and 1960s. Sears and Freedman (1967), in a well-known review of the research record at the time, concluded that there was little evidence that people selected information on the basis of their attitudinal predispositions. Research on cognitive dissonance and information selection continued in social psychology but waned in communication research (Frey 1986). More recent studies (e.g., Knobloch, Carpentier, and Zillmann 2003) and reviews (e.g., D'Alessio and Allen 2007) have renewed interest in selective exposure.

Under the more general banner of audience selectivity—the tendency for people to be purposive in their media choices—researchers are finding that some online news audiences will make exposure decisions that reflect their predispositions and personal characteristics (e.g., Appiah 2004; Knobloch et al. 2003; Lee 2008). For example, Knobloch-Westerwick and Meng (2009) found that some news readers prefer attitude-consistent news. Specifically, readers who were confronted with opposing viewpoints on four different issues spent one-third more time reading supportive articles. This tendency is far from universal, of course. Some members of news audiences are willing and able to use a variety of cues as they decide how to navigate the wealth of information on most news sites. Researchers are turning now to the question of how selective exposure may be facilitated in online environments that both foreground topic and opinion distinctiveness and permit high levels of customization. In chapter 7, we examine evidence bearing on whether that is the case and whether it might result in social polarization.

Before the news can have any direct influence on an individual, that person must first choose to experience it. This may seem painfully obvious, but the process by which people choose between news and other content in the media has received relatively little academic attention over the years. The rise of high-choice media—first cable television and then the internet—has increased the importance of initial media selection (Prior 2007). As all types of content become more plentiful, the news accounts for a decreasing portion of all available content, which means that people need to use an increasingly deliberate process to access news content. This, in turn, makes it more likely that news viewers will develop meaningful differences from people who do not choose news content. This possibility has led a growing number of scholars to take note of media selection processes not only within the news genre but also between news and other genres (e.g., Prior 2007).

News Versus Nonnews Choice

The audience profile of news viewers versus nonviewers is a logical starting point for considering the potential significance of this content choice. If news audiences are demographically different from other audiences, then only certain parts of society are selecting and receiving news. This would suggest a problem in terms of social-economic status: a rich-get-richer type of scenario (see chapter 6 for a discussion of the knowledge gap). If news audiences are demographically similar to other audiences, then news consumption would be better dispersed through society. This finding would then be attributable to a factor that is less obvious than demographics, such as personal preferences. Identifying the nature of news and entertainment audiences is therefore a necessary step toward understanding the nature of the content-selection process.

There are several ways to characterize media audiences. One approach is to identify the demographic profiles of news and nonnews audiences. An analysis of the Pew Research Center for the People and the Press April 2008 Media Use Survey revealed that 14 percent of Americans are completely uninterested in any kind of news, and the profile of this audience is generally low income, low education, female, and apolitical (roughly one-quarter refused to name a political party or ideology). However, this profile—with the exception of political preference—largely reflects Pew's overall respondent profile, suggesting that demographics may not be strongly driving the placement in this category. The same survey report found that 19 percent of the respondents overall—and 34 percent of people older than 24—reported zero news use the day before the survey (Pew Research Center 2008b). Prior (2007) similarly finds that the relatively old, educated, wealthy, and male are more likely to prefer news, but Prior finds that all demographic indicators taken together are only weak predictors of a preference for entertainment over news (accounting for only 13 percent of the patterns of content selection). The evidence from these sources suggests that there are certainly demographic cleavages to news viewing, but these characteristics alone are fairly poor indicators of individuals' selection of news content. We should therefore consider the role of personal preference in media choice.

Preference can exert an influence on news selection in a number of ways. The most direct would be to say that some people prefer news content and some people prefer other content. This direct-preference perspective is often assumed in studies that use some type of news preference measure as a predictor of other factors (see Price and Zaller 1993). A more complex approach is suggested by uses and gratifications. Applying this framework to news selection would consider the more basic preferences of individuals, such as surveillance versus parasocial interaction, as reasons for consuming news (Kaye and Johnson 2002) and then determine whether news content met the needs behind those underlying preferences. For example, a person who wanted to know about the world around him or her would achieve gratification through news consumption, whereas a person who wanted to spend time with others would be better served by watching sports or a popular drama. These are two methods for defining how personal preference could lead to news selection.

Prior (2007) suggests a subtler way to think about the connection between personal preference and content selection. His argument is that people have innate preferences for some types of content over others (applying the more direct definition), but these preferences are moot unless the media environment offers adequate choices. In other words, a person might want to watch a comedy program but will nevertheless watch news if every station broadcasts the news. That preference for a comedy is meaningless until one station decides to air a comedy while the other stations air their news programs. Only at this point can the individual make a choice that exhibits the preference for comedy. Prior labels this the "Conditional Political Learning" model, which essentially states that content preferences exist, but they are not observable in behavior unless individuals are operating in a high-choice media environment.

Survey research generally supports the premise of the Conditional Political Learning model. Prior finds overall support for the idea that people who prefer entertainment content are less likely to watch the news but that this is particularly true for people who have cable television. Prior does not find support for an interaction between preference and internet access (perhaps because his surveys were run before the expansion of broadband services in the United States). This remains a new and under-investigated area of research, but the results thus far do suggest that personal preference, tempered by the availability of media options, plays a significant role in the selection of news over competing content.

Incidental Exposure

Preferences for nonnews content appear prevalent, but this does not mean that people always perfectly select their preferred content. Everyone has experienced incidental—or at least unplanned—exposure to media content. Surfing between E! and Bravo on American television may take a viewer past CNN, and perhaps an interesting graphic will encourage him or her to pause. Similarly, an individual who uses Yahoo! to find sports scores may also view an interesting news headline, or a Facebook user may follow a news link posted to a friend's wall. In each of these examples, people with entertainment preferences could be incidentally exposed to news content. The scenarios certainly seem plausible, and so the question is whether this type of exposure occurs with any meaningful frequency.

Research suggests that the answer is both yes and no. One study found that participants certainly did click on news links even when they were not deliberately seeking that type of content (Tewksbury, Weaver, and Maddex 2001). However, these "accidental" exposures were more likely to occur with people who otherwise preferred news content—not with the people who normally avoid it. Pew surveys tell a similar story (see Pew Research Center, 2008b). The item of interest in this case asks respondents whether they ever come across news when they were online for a different purpose. The frequency was only slightly above 50 percent in the late 1990s, but more than 70 percent of respondents in each survey since 2004 have reported experiencing this incidental exposure. Although a 70 percent rate of incidental exposure may help alleviate fragmentation concerns in some ways (see chapter 7), the research to date primarily suggests that such exposure serves to expand the discrepancy in news exposure between people who prefer news content and those who do not.

Taken as a whole, the current media environment offers an abundance of news content, but it is critical to consider directly the implications of choosing news versus any of the other plentiful types of content. Audience demographics, personal preferences, and available choices are all important factors in the selection of news content—whether deliberate or not. The story does not stop here, however. News content is not all equal, and not everyone arrives at content in the same way. It is essential to consider the people who do choose news media and determine how they arrive at different types of news.

CHOOSING AMONG ONLINE NEWS OPTIONS

The internet makes the news-selection story far more complicated than just the decision about whether to watch the news or to watch entertainment. When a user opens a Web browser, he or she can point it to any desired (non-)news site. On the one hand, choosing among literally thousands of options is a daunting task. On the other hand, the abundant availability of sources means that choosing to view a particular type of news is easier with a medium that provides more choices and a high degree of user control. Chapter 4 discussed the existence of different types of audience-segmented news that people can consume (e.g., specialized by topic or style). This section more explicitly addresses the choices that online news audiences must make: which site to visit and which story to read. Even at these seemingly fine levels of media selection, there is a great deal of potential variability in the content that different people will experience.

Choosing a News Format

One of the important—and broad—distinctions within news content is hard versus soft news. Recall from chapter 4 that hard news covers public affairs and international issues in a serious and direct manner, while soft news covers lighter topics and/or addresses issues in a lighter, even sensationalistic, manner. Media organizations deliberately select some mix of these news formats in order to attract a specific audience. The question here is whether there are differences between people who prefer hard news and those who prefer soft news. Demographic characteristics or personal preference could again play a role in this distinction.

In a direct parallel to the news-versus-entertainment discussion, people who prefer soft news can differ from people who prefer hard news. An analysis of the Pew Biennial Media Consumption 2006 survey[1] reveals that people who are younger, are female, are less educated, and have lower incomes have stronger relative interests in community, crime, and health news—topics that are not typically considered "hard" (Rittenberg, Tewksbury, and Casey 2009). As with the preference for entertainment content, however, these factors (along with employment and location) offer only a very limited accounting of individuals' preference for soft news (together they explain only about 10 percent of the variance in that preference). Demographic background, therefore, appears to be a relatively minor contributor to news preferences, and the evidence further points to the role of personal preference in leading people to different types of media content.

The presence of cleavages between people who prefer entertainment and those who prefer news only describes a very rough split in the total audience. The further division of the news audience into people who would rather consume serious news and those who like softer formats begins to demonstrate the complexity of the specialization available to audiences. Even this level of distinction within the news audience, though, will seem rough once we consider the processes that lead people to select one news outlet over another.

Choosing a Website

The task of selecting a single source out of the collection of news online would be almost impossible without assistance; there are literally thousands of online news sources. Deciding whether to use a specific website for access to the news is the product of two primary factors. The first is learned. This factor comes into play when a person chooses a site on the basis of past experiences with media. The second factor is reputation, which plays a role when the user makes an evaluation on the basis of the popularity or perceived credibility of a site. Considering experience and reputation can help individuals successfully select a satisfying news source.

Learned media use occurs when a person relies on past experience to guide current media choices. For example, a person who has previously preferred the news analysis of a magazine such as *Time* may select slate. com (an online newsmagazine) rather than Google News. Lessons learned from past use commonly play a role in theories of media selection. Selective exposure (Klapper 1960) predicts that people will learn to choose media sources that express agreeable viewpoints. The uses and gratifications perspective argues that individuals learn from experience about which media can best serve specific needs and that people are likely to return to media that have proven satisfying (McLeod, Bybee, and Durall 1982). As with many things in life, when people are happy with the consequences of their current actions, they are not likely to make significant changes to their future behaviors.

Of course, experience and habits cannot entirely explain media selection, as many people will eventually adopt new interests, goals, and sources. Multiple factors can influence whether a person decides to try a new outlet. An individual may find that his or her news outlet of choice poorly covers a topic of interest or does not provide content in a new format. Regardless of the circumstances, reputation is a core component of which outlet will be adopted next. When we talk about the reputation of a news outlet, we are referring to its popularity and/or credibility. Ideally, these would be equivalent; that is, the most reliable content would be read by the most people. In practice, of course, this is not necessarily the case.

Popularity can be—and often is—the result of factors such as brand recognition, advertising placement, and reporting style more than the quality or reliability of the content. Perhaps more than in other media, the line between popularity and credibility is often blurred online. The Drudge Report provides a clear example of this problem, as it is one of the most popular online news websites (Pew Research Center 2008b) but is also notoriously unreliable. Broad news sites attached to major offline brands present a similar challenge. These types of sites are often among the most read on the internet, but it is difficult to determine whether CNN and *USA Today* are read online because of their names or because their informational quality is high. In fact, focused news blogs with sophisticated writers (e.g., fivethirtyeight.com) may be some of the best sources of information about very specific topics, but these sites may never be able to garner much attention. Even more vexing is the role of repurposed content online, which is particularly responsible for blurring the line between popularity and credibility online. For example, three of the most popular news outlets—Google News, Yahoo! News, and Facebook—generally do not do their own reporting. When Americans had the option to choose among only one or two major newspapers and three television networks, it was likely that any choice would be at least relatively popular. However, the dominance of a few news outlets on a medium that features thousands of them certainly raises questions about the degree to which source popularity matters over substance.

Despite the apparent importance of source popularity, people probably do not completely ignore information credibility when they choose outlets. Credibility is a highly variable concept for many different online news outlets, because the internet audience is particularly segmented. Some news outlets might be deemed credible go-to information source by liberals, whereas other sites are recognized as such by conservatives (Pew Research Center 2010). Similarly, some sites will be seen as the credible voice for foreign affairs reporting, some for tech reporting, and some for reporting topics of interest to East European immigrants currently residing in America (see chapter 4 for a discussion of site specialization). A relatively few sites may be able to achieve credibility for "the news" in general, but even these may be seen as particularly credible in some areas versus others. For example, the *New York Times* is a credible overall news source, but it is seen as particularly credible for world affairs. In many cases, it is likely that online readers use their experience to decide which sources are credible and/or worth selecting.

Selecting News within Sites

The demands that the internet places on potential news readers do not end with a source selection. Whereas a television news viewer can choose a channel and then sit back and absorb what comes, the internet user has more work to do before receiving the news. This is because most news sites (smaller blogs being the prime exception) offer a home page with little more than a headline and a blurb for each story. In order to find a news article, the user must decide which of these articles to select. Once again, this choice is informed by many factors, although these are generally divided into two broad modes of story discovery: deliberate and serendipitous.

Deliberate story selection refers to times when the reader enters a site with a somewhat specific interest in mind. This does not have to be as specific as "I am going to find story X" but can instead be more along the lines of "I feel like reading about topic X." When a user enters a site with this mind-set, his or her story-selection process is likely to be far more direct than that of other users. This is demonstrated in studies of browsing behavior that find that users who are either strongly interested in a topic or are given directions on what news to find browse news sites in a relatively linear fashion (Rittenberg and Tewksbury 2007). This means that the users go directly to their topic of interest rather than clicking around through more popular or prominent articles. This type of purposeful behavior suggests that users with this approach will give a greater level of attention to and consideration of the news content they select than other users will.

Serendipitous story selection comes into play when an individual is more interested in reading simply any news than in reading a particular type of news. The uses and gratifications approach to media exposure might suggest that such individuals are using the news for personal entertainment or environmental surveillance (Levy and Windahl 1984), rather than to learn about a given subject. Browsing studies find that users without a goal are more likely to click back and forth through a site, visiting stories but constantly backtracking to earlier menus (Catledge and Pitkow 1995). This method means that such users can be, at least theoretically, exposed to a wider variety of stories than deliberate browsers. The major question with the serendipitous approach is how the users determine which stories are worthy of selection. Broadly speaking, article worthiness most likely comes down to either the interests of the individual (e.g., "Is this a topic I care about?") or the estimations of others (e.g., "Is this article popular?") (Knobloch-Westerwick et al. 2005). When personal interest dominates the selection mechanism, the individual will browse until he or she sees an interesting story, checks on that article, and then returns to the menu to find another potentially interesting article. Graber (1988) observed this pattern with print-newspaper reading.

When the user is focused on external evaluations, the process is more complicated. The news editor is the traditional evaluator of worthy topics, and editors have long held a great deal of sway in helping people decide what stories to read (Graber 1988). Of course, the editor still decides which stories are published and where they are placed (more on this below)—both of which are important factors in determining article selection. However, one of the things the internet changes about news consumption is that editors no longer necessarily dominate (although they are still obviously important) the article-evaluation process for the public.

Many, if not most, major news sites provide some sort of peer recommendation system that reveals which articles are the most read or most shared on the entire news site. Facebook, for example, provides many news sites with a plug-in that allows the outlet to reveal not only how many Facebook users have shared which articles but also which articles have been shared by people in a member's networks. Research by Knobloch-Westerwick and colleagues (2005) suggests that the presence of popularity indicators at a site can increase the number of stories that people select and how long they spend reading them.

Of course, news search algorithms can influence how news is presented and, therefore, what people read. As we noted, sites such as Google News use proprietary formulas for selecting and prioritizing news from a large number of sites. The selection and placement of news on a page will likely influence news selection. One of the most reliable findings in news-reception research is that people will start reading at the top of a page and work their way down (e.g., Adam, Quinn, and Edmunds 2007). Thus, the seemingly simple process of prioritizing stories in a search result can have substantial consequences.

Even subtler cues can influence what people read. Research in selective exposure has found that the framing of story topics affects whether people will select articles online. In one study (Zillmann et al. 2004), comparable groups chose from identical story texts and headlines, but they saw different lead paragraphs. People spent more time reading stories with leads that stressed group conflict and personal suffering. Similarly, the presence of visual imagery has been found to influence story selection (Knobloch et al. 2003), with stories that featured threatening images typically garnering more selection and reading time than stories with more innocuous images. With personal interests, editors' placements, peer recommendations, and story cues all informing readers, it is easy to see that even serendipitous news selection is not a random process.

Web-page Layout and News Selection

News selection is not exclusively a set of deliberate, physical actions, such as navigating to a website or clicking on a hyperlink. An even deeper level of selection is always simultaneously in play. People also "choose" content—sometimes consciously and sometimes not—simply by looking at different portions of their selected Web page. Where a person looks can determine many crucial aspects of exposure, including what news, links, ads, or other information even has the opportunity to affect the individual. The research methodology that focuses on news readers' gaze is called eye tracking, and a number of findings from these studies offer additional insight for our discussion of content selection.

One set of results from eye-tracking studies speaks directly to where people look on a news website. Several studies indicate that readers will generally begin looking at a Web page near the top left of the screen, proceed across the screen horizontally, and then return to the left and scan vertically down the page. Some readers expand on this by viewing horizontally across one (or sometimes two) more times, but such a pattern is referred to as either an F pattern or a Golden Triangle (Enquiro 2005; Nielsen and Pernice 2010).

One factor that can disrupt this common reading path is the presence of graphics. Poynter studies have found that photos, particularly ones featuring faces, draw some attention, and charts or tables can be somewhat effective in attracting a reader's gaze (Adam, Quinn, and Edmunds 2007). The dominant attention grabber is weather graphics. One study found that 88 percent of the time users spent looking at a graphic was spent with a weather graphic (Adam, Quinn, and Edmunds 2007).

These findings are informative, because they reveal that news in certain positions is more likely to be viewed than other content on the

same page. The eye-tracking findings are confirmed by other experiments on online story selection (e.g., Knobloch-Westerwick et al. 2005).
For example, Eveland and Dunwoody (1998) found that people select
more topics from the top left corner of a science news page than from
other parts of the page. Thus, editorial decisions about what makes it to
which portion of a Web page affect the likelihood that a story is selected.

These studies offer an interesting perspective on broader news effects.
The information about article placement may not be surprising, but it is
helpful to have verification that placement affects article attention, as does
the inclusion of graphics. This knowledge can improve our ability to
understand news effects, because when we look at a website, we can predict likely news exposure partly based on placement, rather than simply
on what is available anywhere on that page.

What these findings tell us about readers, however, may be both more
interesting and disturbing. People appreciate graphics, but mostly when
they are about weather, and people are very willing to read news articles
that they select, but probably only the summary information. The good
news is that online news readers are attracted to a fair amount of content,
and they may even be more likely than print readers to read the content
they select thoroughly (Adam, Quinn, and Edmunds 2007). The bad
news is that many seem hesitant to pay attention to the most useful content. The eye-tracking research, therefore, serves to supplement a meme
that is present throughout this book: the internet can provide excellent
news content, but the challenge is in getting the general public to use (or
see) that information.

SITE SPECIALIZATION AS A SELECTION STRATEGY AND OUTCOME

The hopes and fears of a good many academic observers and news site operators rest on the extent to which people specialize their news selection
online. Site operators hope that people will choose their sites exclusively,
spend a lot of time there, and select consistent (and advertiser-friendly)
patterns of news content. Communication researchers often fear that
people will limit their news exposure to a few content domains that limit
the range of what they learn and feel about public affairs. Thus, the extent of
news specialization online is the source of some trepidation and a central
topic for study. Fortunately, we have some data we can use to examine
whether site selection specialization is developing online. There are two dimensions to news site selection. Along the first, we can assess the number
of sites that people tend to use for news gathering. The second dimension is
the diversity of sites they select. We will start with the former.

Number of News Sources Online

An analysis of site segmentation in chapter 4 used an April 2008 Pew survey question that asked people to name "a few of the websites" they visited most often. Of the people who were willing to volunteer the name of any news site, 53 percent named a second, and 17 percent named a third. Thus, more than half of the respondents named multiple online news sites. This is a sign of at least some willingness to consult multiple sources.

The survey also asked people whether they tended to rely on "just a few publications, programs and websites" for news or if they obtained it "from many different sources." Overall, 51 percent of people who were asked that question said that they consulted only a few sources. That left 46 percent of people (with others not giving a valid answer) saying that they received news from a number of different sources. If people tend to use several different sources, the issue is whether use of the internet is a positive contributor to that tendency. The most basic version of the news-specialization hypothesis suggests that people who rely on the internet for news may find one or a few highly specialized news sources. If that is what they want, then heavy use of the internet for news would be associated with exposure to only a few sources (if use of other news media were held constant).

Data for testing that suggestion are available from the April 2008 survey.[2] If people are using the internet to narrow their exposure to news sources, then use of the medium should be negatively associated with the use of many sources. The results of the analysis strongly contradict the expectations of internet news-source exclusivity. With a number of controls and the two predictor variables in the analysis, self-reported reliance on the internet for news bore no relationship to the use of many sources of news. Most strikingly, the frequency with which people used the internet for news was *positively* associated with the tendency to use multiple sources of news (the opposite of what was expected). In sum, there is not much evidence of internet news users taking advantage of the medium's capabilities to limit their news exposure to a small number of news sources. Indeed, the opposite seems to be the case; frequent online news consumers prefer a number of outlets.

Diversity of News Sources Online

People might not be limiting the number of news sources they use online, but they might still be using the medium to focus on specific topics and ideological positions in the news. Again, there are some survey data that may speak to this potential orientation to the news. The 2008 Pew survey asked people to report whether they thought that the news media were all about the same as one another or if they tended to trust some news sources more than others. A slight majority of people (53 percent) agreed with the statement "There are a few news sources I trust more than others." Thus, on the most basic level, at least half of Americans appear to have preferences among the sources they use. That is interesting, but it hardly suggests that many people have strong feelings about the superiority of some news outlets over others.

One way in which people might specialize their news exposure online is through the selection of news outlets along ideological lines. This has been the concern of political communication researchers, certainly. If people are consciously concerned about ideology in the news, we can expect them to say that they seek out ideologically consonant news. Fortunately, the 2008 Pew survey asked a question about this issue. About a quarter of the respondents (23 percent) reported that they preferred to receive news from sources that shared their political points of view, as opposed to the two-thirds (66 percent) who said that they preferred news from sources that did not have a political angle (the remaining people did not give an answer). Thus, a general tendency to seek out like-minded news could be limited. One caveat, though: the respondents to this survey might have been motivated by social desirability concerns to avoid reporting ideological news biases. It is hard to know how much confidence to place in responses to this question, but we will assume that a majority of Americans believe that they prefer nonbiased news.

The majority of Americans might prefer ideologically neutral news, but perhaps there are differences among the media that people use. It might be that people who use the internet are those most likely to seek specialized news. Earlier, we noted that the 2008 Pew survey asked people to report the medium they tended to use most often for news. Among those who reported using television news and newspapers most often, 24 percent said that they preferred news that shared their points of view. Among those who used the internet most often, only 19 percent reported that. Thus, inasmuch as this question is tapping actual preferences and behavior—an open question, to be sure—it appears that internet news users are no more likely to prefer ideologically consonant news. They may even be slightly less inclined to choose news outlets that way.

Another way to approach the question is to compare how people seek ideologically slanted news in the traditional media with how they seek it online. Whereas the Pew survey data suggest that relatively few people see themselves specializing along ideological lines, there could still be some tendency for online news to facilitate this type of specialization. Fortunately, this possibility was the partial focus of a recent study of cable television and online news exposure (Nie et al. 2010). Researchers posited that the greater availability of ideologically slanted news on the internet than on television should lead people who rely on the internet for news to be more ideologically extreme. In their study, the researchers looked at people who obtained news from both cable television and the internet. If people engage in more partisan selectivity online, one should see more ideological extremism among people who use online news than among those who use only television news. Analyses of survey data about news-exposure behavior show that this is the case. Viewers of CNN who searched for online news were more liberal than those who did not go online for news, and viewers of Fox News who also searched for online news were more conservative than other Fox News viewers.

In sum, there is a complicated picture in the available data regarding site selectivity. It appears that for some people, choosing among news sites is partially a matter of matching ideological slant in the news with personal ideological preferences. This tendency is not widespread, though. There seems to be a majority of people, particularly among internet news users, who see themselves choosing news sites that are ideologically balanced (or, at least, not overtly partisan). The data described here are still rather limited. More work is needed, particularly as the political and media environments evolve. People might increasingly rely on partisanship, if more overtly partisan content emerges in the marketplace and if audiences shift their normative perceptions of what news should be.

CONTENT SPECIALIZATION AS A SELECTION STRATEGY AND OUTCOME

Once people reach a news site, they still must choose the news stories and topics they will consume. Do they tend to focus on specific topics over time, or do they sample from the range of stories that sites carry? We will examine this question in two parts. First, we can look at what people say about their attention to different topics (as opposed to sites or sources) in the news. Then we can examine some data from observations of what people read when they visit news sites. Overall, the data will show that content specialization is far from the rule. There are plenty of people who seem to follow one or two topics exclusively. Yet there are ample signs that many people are broad readers of news topics.

We noted in chapter 4 that the April 2008 Pew survey asked people to say how closely they followed different topics in the news, "either in the newspaper, on television, radio, or the internet." Not everyone was asked about every topic, but the responses to these questions provide a relatively clear picture of how people think about their interest in different types of news. Within the topics that cover public affairs (i.e., international affairs and domestic American national and local politics), the people who followed one area tended to follow others to a moderate degree. For example, the correlation between national political news and international affairs was .51. With a possible absolute range of 0 to 1 (a perfect correlation would be 1.0), that is a pretty strong relationship. Between local and national politics, it is .47, another relatively strong relationship.

People who followed public affairs did not always follow other topics, however. For example, the data reveal weak relationships between following national politics and following sports, entertainment, and celebrity news (correlations all less than .15). What is more, among topics outside of public affairs, the relationships are relatively weak. For example, among entertainment, consumer, travel, and environmental news (one subgroup of the sample was asked about these topics), none of the correlations is larger than .33. Still, there are positive relationships, even if sometimes small, between all of the news topics in the survey.

The data from this survey suggest that people who follow news generally tend to follow multiple topics (at least in terms of what they report to survey interviewers). A fully specialized audience, in which each person follows one topic only, would reveal systematic patterns of negative relationships among the variables in this analysis. People following one topic would tend to avoid other topics. The universally positive relationships, even if most are small to moderate in size, indicate that a good portion of the people tended to report following multiple topics. Indeed, the mean number of topics that people reported following at least somewhat closely is 3.5 out of the eight questions on the survey (SD = 2.06). Thus, these survey data suggest that for news across a range of media, audiences are not as specialized as one might think.

A more focused analysis of whether people specialize their online news exposure can be conducted with records of online behavior. Such an analysis could determine how extensively people focus their news selection on specific topics. If there are a good many highly specialized readers, they would read only a few topics very extensively. One would not see them selecting news across a variety of areas. The presence of very broad readers, on the other hand, would be visible in people selecting a relatively large number of news topics.

The news-site visitation data introduced in chapter 4 can be used for a search for specialized online news audiences. The Nielsen//NetRatings data from March and May 2000 provided the Web addresses for news articles viewed by a sample of 2,100 American news readers when they visited one of 13 selected national and local news sites.[3] These addresses were categorized by their overall news topics (e.g., national news, politics, arts and entertainment, or sports).[4] A cluster analysis of the page-view topics revealed the presence of 13 different reader types. These types are listed in table 5.1.

The first column of the table supplies a general label for each group based on the news topic that group members read most frequently. The table also lists other topics that accounted for at least 5 percent of the views by people in the group. The final column on the right reports the mean number of views of news menus or stories that was observed for each group (this does not include home-page menu views) in the two-month observation period.

The data show that the cluster analysis produced only two groups (together accounting for about 35 percent of the panelists) whose members read widely. Specifically, a relatively small group of menu browsers focused exclusively on site home pages and general menus, never going beyond that level to select topic menus or specific stories. In addition, there emerged a substantial group of broad readers, panelists who selected a wide variety of topics. On the other end of the spectrum, the data in Table 5.1 show three groups with rather focused behavior. These groups—the largest is the sports specialists and the smallest is the U.S. news specialists—all averaged at least 75 percent of their viewing focused on one topic, and none viewed a second topic more than 5 percent of the time. These groups together accounted for more than a third (40 percent) of the sample.

In general, about equal thirds of the people in this sample were general and specialized readers. The remaining third (or so) of the sample consisted of mixed audiences who tended to focus a bit on a particular topic but chose other topics on a regular basis. These results suggest that American internet audiences at the time of the study were not overwhelmingly inclined to specialize in their online news selection. Of course, the data covered 13 relatively general news sites, so it might be that people were much more selective when they visited more strongly segmented news venues online. Ultimately, the evidence gathered here suggests the presence of some audience news specialization, but broad exposure is the norm.

Table 5.1. VIEWING CHARACTERISTICS OF ONLINE READER GROUPS AMONG PANELISTS WITH PAGE VIEWS ON MORE THAN THREE DAYS

Reader Group	% of Sample	Lead Topic	Other Common Topics[a]	Mean News Views (SD)
Menu browsers	5.0	Home page/menu[b]	National, technology, business, entertainment	7.9 (11.7)
Broad readers	30.4	U.S. national	Technology, world, politics, entertainment, business	66.9 (112.0)
Entertainment readers	7.9	Entertainment[b]	National	58.1 (116.4)
Weather readers	3.4	Weather[b]	National	24.1 (37.6)
Features readers	3.0	Features	Sports, entertainment	31.2 (37.0)
Politics readers	2.3	Politics[b]	Business, national, world	25.8 (34.7)
Health readers	1.6	Health	National, technology, entertainment, features	19.3 (26.2)
Style readers	1.6	Style/home	Sports	58.3 (106.2)
Public affairs readers	1.3	Opinion/editorial	Politics, national	63.1 (98.4)
Local readers	1.0	Local/state	National, technology, features, business	28.3 (30.2)
Sports specialists	27.5	Sports[b]	Sports	54.1 (76.2)
Business specialists	11.1	Business[b]	Politics, national	35.6 (43.5)
U.S. news specialists	1.3	U.S. national[b]		9.4 (10.3)

Note: A total of 2,100 readers had page views on more than three days and fell into a cluster that contained at least 1 percent of the sample.
[a] On average, these topics represented at least 5 percent of page views for readers in this group; shown in descending rank by percentage.
[b] On average, this topic represented at least 55 percent of page views for readers in this group.

Thus far, the evidence suggests that the online news audience is made up of different sorts of news consumers. Some are inclined to limit their news exposure to specialized areas, but a good many people are willing to select a broad range of news. Thus, there are a substantial number of news generalists online, and the data suggest that exposure to national current events topics forms the backbone of their news consumption. For the majority of people, the selection of national news is linked with the selection of a range of other topics.

The presence of news generalists online fits nicely with survey data that show that a substantial majority of Americans believe that they have a civic obligation to consume public affairs news. People who say that they believe they have such an obligation are more likely to consume news, both offline and online (Poindexter and McCombs 2001). There are additional reasons for the presence of relatively large numbers of online news generalists. Internet technologies certainly make it easier to specialize news exposure than was the case with television news, but browsing the news at a major news site such as CNN or Yahoo! News is relatively effortless. A recent study of news audiences also found that people who browse through a number of news topics do so, in part, because they are socially efficacious (Tewksbury, Hals, and Bibart 2008). They read widely because it facilitates their social relationships. Specialization may be functional for some goals, but generalized news exposure is more useful for others.

CONCLUSIONS

This review of the online news selection process suggests that the internet provides audiences with a daunting number of choice points and options. People apply their preexisting needs, desires, and interests to the selection of media, news outlets, and story topics. Of course, not all of the news-consumption process is deliberate and conscious. People often follow habits that they have developed over time (Diddi and LaRose 2006). These habits lead them toward and away from the news and particular topics. One habit that many people appear to have adopted is a pattern of reading news headlines in a predictable order, starting and finishing from particular points on a Web page. What is more, some news exposure is accidental, largely a function of the variety of sites that carry news today. The picture that emerges from this consideration of how people choose the news is that selectivity occurs through a mixture of purposeful evaluation of sites and topics and healthy doses of habit and chance.

With these observations as background, we turned to an evaluation of the prediction that Web audiences tend to focus their news selection on a limited number of sites and topics. The accumulated evidence suggests very mixed support for this prediction. By a number of different measures, it appears that a sizable minority (large but still not a majority) of internet news users tend to focus on a limited set of news sites and topics. In many cases, equal numbers of people cast a rather broad net when they look for news online. Indeed, research suggests that a good many people see broad exposure to the news as a socially valuable good.

Looking to the future, the question for news-site producers and outside observers is whether the news selection patterns that have developed over the first 15 years of online news will remain static over the next 15 years. It may be that the habits people have developed reflect long-term orientations toward the news and the technology. If so, the mix of selective and broad readers could persist as the internet continues to evolve and technologies for content specialization develop. At the same time, the current population of internet users includes a substantial majority who developed news consumption habits before the internet's popular adoption. The influence of this legacy of the traditional media may lessen over time as more of the audience initiates news consumption with the internet in the mix. These people may develop higher levels of selectivity if they are exposed to more options from the beginning. These are speculations, of course. The research evidence does not yet reflect this possibility.

CHAPTER 6

Learning from Online News

W e know that people will choose and consume news online. The next issue for discussion is what people learn from it. The literature on medium differences suggests that people will process news content differently through one medium from how they process it through another. The evidence thus far points to some differences in how much people learn about public affairs from exposure to different formats of online news.

Learning from the media is an important topic for several reasons. The most basic is that what people know about politics helps them understand new information (see chapter 1 above for a discussion of information and citizenship). Existing knowledge provides a context for interpreting novel information and opinion. Thus, knowledgeable people are generally able to do more with the news. Knowledge is also related to participation in politics. Knowledgeable people are more likely to vote in an election, donate their time and money to campaigns, and so on (Delli Carpini and Keeter 1996).

This chapter addresses several key components of the relationship between learning and online news. We discuss the learning process and how the internet facilitates (or disrupts) this process. This background sets the stage for a review of online learning, in which we define differential learning and its implications for society. Some of the available research suggests that what people learn online is a function of how news sites present stories. Audiences respond to how the news is presented in a very sensible fashion; they use search functions, follow hyperlinks, and utilize topical menus. What might be surprising is that reading a news story online seems to be much the same as reading it on paper. The format of news presentation, though, seems to allow audiences to build relatively sophisticated mental models of concepts and their interrelationships. Before turning to this evidence, however, we first clarify how each medium offers different opportunities for learning.

LEARNING FROM DIFFERENT MEDIA

When it comes to potential knowledge gain, all news is not created equal. Differences among stories can arise from many factors. One of the foremost is the medium used to deliver the news. Audiences do not have the same experiences with—and, therefore, not the same effects from—print, television, and the Web. A second factor is the type of news that a user selects. Whether an individual selects hard news, soft news, or just poor-quality news has a significant influence on the learning potential from that content. Understanding these factors is a critical component of understanding how the news can inform people about public affairs.

Comparing News Through Audio, Video, Print, and their Combinations

The question of whether the medium of news presentation matters for what people encounter and learn has been a central interest of social scientists studying political communication (e.g., Chaffee and Kanihan 1997). There are two core emphases in this research. The first centers on the question of whether the character of news differs across media. Some observers have noted that news content in the various media is typically more similar than it is different, often largely a result of the corporate structures that underlie them (e.g., Parenti 1993). Nonetheless, most social-scientific studies have pointed to substantial variance in the amount and type of news one finds in different media (e.g., Neuman, Just, and Crigler 1992).

The second focus of research on audience learning from media exposure is whether the mode of presentation has a substantial impact on audience experiences. Initial studies of learning from television news suggested that audiences gained little from that medium (e.g., Neuman 1976). That finding did not stand the test of time, though. Subsequent research using better conceptualizations and measures of television content, use, and learning demonstrated that television audiences can learn quite a bit (e.g., Graber 2001). Nonetheless, most studies comparing the traditional media continue to observe more learning from newspaper reading than from television viewing (e.g., Bartels 1993; see also Drew and Weaver 1998). Studies have also suggested that how researchers assess knowledge gain has a substantial effect on what they find (e.g., Eveland, Marton, and Seo 2004). Graber (2001), for example, has argued that tests of facts about politics (e.g., which party has the majority in the U.S. Senate) fail to tap how people acquire and use information in the news. Graber advocates a conceptualization of learning from the media that focuses on how people incorporate new information into what they already know and feel about issues, people, and institutions.

Research comparing media took up the impact of computer-based news in the 1980s. Comparisons of existing media with what were termed "new media" ventures examined whether the interactive elements of emerging technologies substantially changed the news-exposure experience for audiences (e.g., Edwardson, Kent, and McConnell 1985). Fico et al. (1987), for example, observed that computer-based news media—such as videotex, an early interactive information-retrieval system—could substantially change the way people select news stories. News options built on a menu structure were thought to encourage users to select news by general category rather than on the basis of headline content or physical features of the story (e.g., headline font size). This early research found that layout differences resulted in some differences in what news people selected (Fico et al. 1987) but few differences in their issue agendas (Heeter et al. 1989). Videotex systems were never widely adopted except in a few cases, so this line of research lay dormant for some years.

More recently, Eveland (2003) has argued that comparisons of media should incorporate clear explication of the attributes of various media. Such an explication should allow researchers to develop specific expectations that are tied to the elements that make one medium superior or inferior for specific kinds of information acquisition. Eveland suggests that one could classify media technologies in terms of the interactivity they promote or allow, the structure of content they carry (e.g., narrative or use of hyperlinks in text), the control they provide users, the information channels they provide in the content (e.g., visual, audio) and their emphases, the level of textual sophistication they incorporate, and the content of messages (Eveland 2003). Such a framework specifies ways in which researchers can conceptualize differences and similarities among media.

Selecting and Learning

The research suggests that people can learn about public affairs in varying degrees. Information gain can range from mere familiarity with a topic (e.g., knowing that government budget deficits are a political issue) to in-depth knowledge (e.g., understanding the relationships among government debt rates, trade balances, and budget deficits). For the barest knowledge about an issue, people probably need go no further into a news website than the home page. Headlines and subheadlines may provide enough information to create some awareness that an issue, person, or event exists. In that case, learning can occur in the absence of the selection and careful consumption of a news story. Studies that show the effects of incidental exposure to the news may be tapping just such a level of exposure (e.g., Tewksbury, Weaver, and Maddex 2001).

Researchers and other observers often think about news exposure merely in terms of time spent with a medium or outlet. Such a level of consideration distinguishes well between surface and in-depth news consumption, but it does not allow for the comparison of effects of exposure to different news topics. Looking at news exposure in terms of the topics that people select reveals the interests they have, and—more important— it allows for some predictability in what they learn. People who read solely sports news can learn only so much about politics, and vice versa. For this reason, we spent time in chapter 5 reviewing what research has shown about online news-selection processes. Contemporary research on how people learn from the news increasingly looks at what people want and expect from the press.

THE PSYCHOLOGY OF LEARNING FROM ONLINE NEWS

Research on learning from the news tends to focus on attributes of audience members, the structure of the news, and the interaction of these two factors. Elements of the audience members that seem to matter most are characteristics that affect the motivations and skills that people bring to news exposure. As we noted above, there are several ways to conceptualize the attributes of a news medium. For online news, most of the research attention has been focused on the effects of the hypertext environment on how people navigate and consume news stories.

Motivations and the News

Research on learning from the media has pointed to the importance of motivations that people have for news consumption and the amount of effort they put into thinking about the news they receive. In previous chapters, we described the uses and gratifications approach to media research (Katz, Blumler, and Gurevitch 1974). A basic tenet of that approach is the suggestion that what and how much people acquire from the media is a partial function of their reasons for exposure. Researchers have focused on the kinds of things people tend to seek from the news. Commonly identified reasons include consuming news to obtain entertainment, information about the social environment (often called surveillance), and things to use in conversations with friends and relatives (Kaye and Johnson 2002). Over the years, a range of reasons for news exposure has been identified.

A few studies have looked at the relationships between the reasons for audience news exposure and patterns of news consumption and effects. Survey studies have repeatedly shown that people with a surveillance goal in their news consumption know more about public affairs (e.g., Eveland 2002). One study of television news exposure demonstrated that when people have a surveillance goal, they pay more attention to the details of a news report and may emerge from the story with rather different beliefs and attitudes about the topic from what they would have if they were merely passing time with the news (Tewksbury 1999). A more broadly defined study of motivations found that college students effectively tended to pair what they said they wanted from the media and the types of sites they said they visited (Tewksbury and Althaus 2000a).

Most models suggest that audience members' motivation to learn from the news increases the amount of attention they pay to stories. Researchers often focus on elaboration of the news as the mechanism that translates attention to news stories into ideas and feelings that people can store in long-term memory (e.g., Eveland 2002). Elaboration is the amount of thought that people devote to a topic. The more people elaborate on the subject of some news story, the more they consider what the story contains, think about related concepts that they have in their memory, and possibly form attitudes toward the topic of the news (Eveland 2002). On the Web, the presence of site-navigation aids, video and other multimedia features, and page layout can all affect the level of elaboration in which audiences engage.

News-consumption Skills

Research on learning from the news examines the skills that people bring to news exposure. Skill is an umbrella term to represent basic attributes of an audience member. Under this heading, researchers consider how much people know about a medium and a news topic. The more audience members know about how a medium works, the better prepared they are to understand and decode messages in it. For example, television news stories often have a rather predictable set of elements. They typically start with an introduction from a news anchor, proceed to a voice-over and video images that bear on the central topic of the story, and finish with some summative remarks about the future of the topic. Television watchers are better able to understand the content of the story if they know to expect these elements of the television format. Similarly, online news audiences are most likely to process and retain news information when they are familiar with the presentation of news online. The more they know about how news sites are formatted and how hyperlinks work, the more resources they can devote to the stories themselves (Eveland and Dunwoody 2001a).

Researchers have also suggested that expertise in the domain of specific news topics can affect how much audiences learn. Not surprisingly, the more people know about a topic, the more they are able to acquire from exposure to a story (e.g., Graber 1988). Of course, there is an upper limit to this effect. Particularly high levels of expertise might mean that an audience member knows all of the information in a story before exposure. These two elements of prior knowledge—format and content expertise—play a role in the knowledge gap, described below.

Hypertext and the Structure of the News

As we observed in chapter 3, the structure of much of online news mirrors the structure of offline news stories. For example, most major news sites that carry video news stories use repurposed video from offline sources. Likewise, a print story online can contain much the same text as can be found in a newspaper. As a result, we can expect there to be some basic similarities in how people consume news online and offline.

That is not the entire story, of course. Researchers have focused on the unique elements of online news and have suggested how these features might affect learning from the news. The primary unique attribute of online news is the use of hypertext to structure news sites and stories (Eveland and Dunwoody 2001a). Hyperlinks are the mechanisms that sites use to lead visitors from news page to news page, from headlines to stories, and from stories to related content (see chapter 3 for more on the use of links and other design elements). Hyperlinks also are navigation devices within stories, moving readers between sections of a story or guiding news readers to information that is supplementary to a story. For example, a story about a volcanic eruption might include links to previous stories about volcanoes, to maps of the affected region, or to information about emergency-relief organizations.

Some researchers have suggested that hyperlinks can affect the ease with which audience members browse sites and consume stories. In theory, hyperlinks simplify the presentation and consumption of information. But this is not always the case. Some researchers suggest that overly complex site design can strain a reader's resources (Eveland and Dunwoody 2001b). People generally limit the amount of effort they are willing to devote to news consumption (Lang 2000). The effort it takes to navigate a site can reduce an audience member's attention to the news content. Researchers have looked at site-design features that affect the cognitive load that a site or a story creates for audience members.

Cognitive load or information complexity is an important moderating variable in models of news consumption (Lang 2000). All else being equal, people learn more from the news when the load is relatively light. Of course, a story's cognitive-load effect is a partial function of the content and structure of the story. These factors also directly exert an influence on what people learn from media exposure. Thus, cognitive load is a complex concept that is hard to separate from other features of online news consumption.

Researchers have speculated that the hyperlinked structure of online news may facilitate learning in a subtle way. Some researchers (e.g., Eveland and Dunwoody 2001b) suggest that the links between concepts in a hyperlinked information structure might resemble the neural networks of human memory. Similarly, Manovich (2001) argues that links allow readers to re-create an author's thought process. Network models of memory posit that people retain links among concepts such that when one concept (e.g., the U.S. president) is activated to consciousness, related concepts (e.g., political-party affiliation or affect toward the president) are also activated. Hyperlinks at a news site or other website can function in a similar fashion. Audience members reading a news site that describes a political policy might find links to related concepts, images, and opinions. If they explore those links, they will develop a network of linkages among concepts. Such a network may improve audience members' memory for people, policies, and other political information.

WHAT PEOPLE LEARN WHEN READING NEWS ONLINE

Here we get to one of the central functions of the press in a democracy. What do people learn from the news media? Once people have selected news stories online, what do they learn there? In general, empirical research on audience learning online can be divided into two types. Survey studies ask a sample of people—usually representative of some population—to report their internet and other news use and to answer questions about politics and current events. Experiment-based studies, on the other hand, typically direct participants to news websites and measure what they learn there. Often these studies will assign groups of participants to conditions that compare news sites with other media or compare different versions of sites or online news formats.

The overall results of these studies are interestingly complex. The survey results tend to support the notion that people acquire information when they go online for news. The experiment-based studies are more mixed. What people choose from news sites affects what they learn from the news, and site design affects how people browse sites and select stories. The consumption of the news is likewise influenced by how sites are constructed.

Survey-based Studies

On the whole, survey-based studies show that the frequency with which people visit online news sites is positively related to how much they know about public affairs. For example, using data from a large U.S. national survey administered during the 2004 presidential election, Kenski and Stroud (2006) found that people who reported being exposed to campaign information online knew more about candidates and their positions. Kwak, Poor, and Skoric (2006) similarly found that people in a local sample in Michigan who reported attention to domestic and international news knew more about those topics. At a very basic level, these studies show that people can learn from online news much as they do from exposure to other news media.

Researchers have examined whether this positive relationship applies to everyone receiving news online. There is some evidence that how much people learn from online news sites depends on other things. For example, one study of South Korean adolescents (Kim and Kim 2007) showed that using online news for general information or for things to use in conversation with others was associated with learning about politics. Going to online news for entertainment purposes was not associated with political learning. So, what people want from the news appears to direct attention and exposure in a way that can influence how much they learn about public affairs.

Experiment-based Studies

The basic question underlying experiments on internet-based learning is whether the format of news presentation online is conducive to learning about public affairs. Studies in this area can take one of two general forms.

In one, a study compares the effects of exposure to the natural mixture of news in one medium with the effects of exposure to the natural mixture in another. In the second form, a study looks at how different formats (online versus offline and different online formats) affect the processing and retention of the news when the content is the same.

Naturally Occurring News

As we have noted, learning from the news begins with selecting sites and stories. Studies that examine the effects of medium differences include some that test whether people going online choose different news topics from those chosen by offline audiences. Tewksbury and Althaus (2000a) conducted an early study of this sort. In it, undergraduate students in 1998 read either print or online versions of the *New York Times* for five days. Online readers were less likely to select public-affairs topics and could recall less information from the news that week. A comparison of learning from television news, print newspapers, and online news sites during the 2000 U.S. presidential election (Eveland, Seo, and Marton 2002) revealed that audiences of online news recalled less political campaign information than did audiences of the other media.

D'Haenens, Jankowski, and Heuvelman (2004) replicated the Tewksbury and Althaus study in 2000 in the Netherlands with two Dutch newspapers. They found some differences in what readers of the online and print versions of the papers read. Online readers spent less time with international-news stories. This was not surprising, given that the online version of one paper supplied a particularly large amount of national news on its site (relative to what was in the print version). It might be that the presence of so much national news diverted attention away from international stories. Indeed, analyses of differences in the content of the online and print versions of the papers suggest that news audiences encountered different sets of stories there. Overall, this experiment revealed fewer medium differences than did the Tewksbury and Althaus study.

The contradictory findings described thus far bring up an important caveat with studies of this sort: the design and content of news sites can affect how people learn from them. Some sites present the news in essentially the same format as newspapers, but differences in layout and site content can affect how much people learn. Given that the mixture of stories and formats at news outlets can affect what people learn from the news, researchers have devoted more attention to how specific attributes of the medium affect the consumption and recall of essentially the same set of information.

Some studies in this vein compare how the attributes of online news can exert different effects than the attributes of television news and print newspapers. The internet offers more space and interactivity—among other features—but it is not obvious how these might affect user learning. The question in this research is whether hyperlinks and other special features of online news help audiences or—counterintuitively—create impediments to learning. Research in this area tends to focus on the volume of content, the interactivity of the site, or the inclusion of links.

The number of story options at a site can affect how people process the news. The large number of stories available at news sites (relative to what can be found at offline news outlets) is often identified as a positive feature of online news. Aren't more options always better? One experiment put this suggestion to the test (Wise, Bolls, and Schaefer 2008). The study participants were asked to choose and read unpleasant stories (e.g., stories about bug infestations, child molestation, or addiction) from a set of options hyperlinked on a Web page. Half of the people chose from a page with five stories presented; the others chose from 15 stories. People who had more options retained more information from the stories they read. The study results suggest that the larger number of options increased readers' emotional arousal and elaboration during the reading task.

Bucy (2004) suggested that the level and type of interactivity at a news site also might have a primary influence on audiences' emotional reactions to the site. The results of an experiment that manipulated the interactivity of a news site show that people like highly interactive sites and activities (e.g., voting in a daily poll on the site), but they often find these activities more confusing and frustrating than simply reading the news on a site (Bucy 2004). This means that the cognitive load imposed by some types of interactivity could work against acquiring information from the news. Indeed, this has been the conclusion of several studies of audience use of multimedia and interactive elements at news sites (e.g., Sundar 2000; Sundar, Kalyanaraman, and Brown 2003).

At the same time, some studies have found that interactive features can have positive effects that go beyond the amount of information people acquire. Earlier, we noted that an important part of memory for information is how concepts are mentally linked to one another. People are better able to understand and interpret new information when they have well-developed networks of knowledge. Dense structures have a good number of redundant links among concepts, and these links help people integrate new information with what they already know. Dense structures also help them evaluate people and institutions.

Studies by Eveland and his colleagues (Eveland et al. 2004; Eveland, Marton, and Seo 2004) have examined the effects of hyperlink design on audience-knowledge structures. One study found that in-story hyperlinks that connect articles to related stories increase the disorientation that users feel (relative to what is experienced by users of unlinked stories). As a result, readers of linked stories recall fewer facts from the news. More important, though, is that these readers have denser knowledge structures. They report more connections among concepts than do the readers of unlinked stories. Thus, hyperlinks can have cross-cutting effects. Some appear to inhibit the retention of information, but others seem to encourage a kind of memory that can be useful for audiences. This research is still young, however, and more needs to be done to explore these patterns and their implications.

KNOWLEDGE GAP AND ONLINE NEWS

We must highlight the fact that saying that audiences "learn" from the news describes an overall effect, but in reality, some people learn more than others. The knowledge gap refers to the hypothesis that there is a large difference between people who know about politics and those who do not. This idea is important, because it runs against the societal-level patterns of many other phenomena. The standard expectation for any given variable (e.g., height, SAT scores, media use) is that it will be normally distributed in society, which means that some people will be at one of two extremes (high or low), but most people will be clustered around a central value. The normal distribution offers a nice approximation for many variables. Observers have long been concerned that political knowledge is not a concept that fits a normal distribution. Instead, the fear is that some people know quite a lot about politics, while many others know almost nothing, with a smaller than anticipated group occupying the middle space. The space between the peaks representing those with knowledge and those without is the knowledge gap.

Two additional factors make the knowledge gap such a cause for concern. The first is that (a lack of) knowledge is not randomly distributed across society, but it is instead concentrated in particular pockets of society. More specifically, people with higher incomes and more education are more likely to know a lot about politics (McLeod, Kosicki, and McLeod 2008). This, in turn, suggests that the disadvantaged groups might have a more difficult time voicing political opinions or selecting adequate governmental representation. The second factor is that new knowledge tends to spread faster among individuals who are already knowledgeable than it does among other people. This means that most informational messages simply widen the extant knowledge gap (Perloff 2007). These factors suggest that the knowledge gap is not only a concern but also one that is difficult to address.

Knowledge and Medium Differences

The problem posed by the knowledge gap for news scholars is that mass media should be particularly ill suited to correcting the informational disparity. Research demonstrates that this is indeed the case. Newspaper use has been associated with knowledge increases only—or at least primarily (Kim 2008)—for relative elites (the worst-case scenario), while television has been found to add knowledge for both elites and nonelites, which maintains the gap (Jerit, Barabas, and Bolsen 2006). Such findings have led to speculation that targeted campaigns are necessary for decreasing the difference in knowledge levels (Perloff 2007), but mass media are intended for broad audiences and are necessarily clumsy tools for delivering specialized messages.

The internet is much better suited for targeted campaigns than either print or broadcast television. After all, the internet is not only effective at matching specific messages to specific audiences, but it is also a relatively inexpensive and accessible medium. Surprisingly, the research conducted to date does not offer much hope. At times, people with low initial knowledge can learn from internet messages (e.g., Kim 2008; Valentino, Hutchings, and Williams 2004), but a common result is that more knowledgeable individuals are more likely to find online news (Prior 2007; Tewksbury, Weaver, and Maddex 2001) and more likely to search for additional information after that initial exposure (Valentino, Hutchings, and Williams 2004). These findings strongly suggest that the mere existence of online news is not going to help address the knowledge gap.

Structural components of the medium also appear to undermine the ability of less knowledgeable citizens to use the internet for political knowledge gain. The internet is a relatively accessible medium, but even browsing the Web requires more skill and experience than people typically recognize (Hargittai 2002). Even when individuals without prior political knowledge do successfully use the internet, the fact is that easy content selection enables people to have access to different-quality materials. The conditions reaffirm the analysis that deliberate efforts are a necessary precondition for addressing the knowledge gap, even when considering the informative, accessible, and specialized media environment that currently exists.

Research has recently suggested that the principal elements of the knowledge gap also apply to political participation—specifically to voting. Despite the fact that turnout rates have improved in the last few elections (McDonald 2008), social- and economic-status indicators continue to predict voting likelihood reliably (e.g., Cho and McLeod 2007; Leighley and Nagler 2007). Once again, the media seem to play a role in contributing to the disparities in political participation. Individuals who have a preference for news that doesn't focus on public affairs (Rittenberg, Tewksbury, and Casey 2009) are less likely to report voting than people with (hard) news preferences. Similarly, factors such as age, prior engagement (Jennings and Zeitner 2003), and news use (Shah et al. 2005) have all been demonstrated as important conditions for people to use the internet as a means of political participation. The contribution of the internet to the participation gap does seem slightly better than for the knowledge gap. Internet access in general has been associated with improved turnout rates (Tedesco 2007), and young citizens—who are traditionally infrequent participants in politics—seem more likely to engage through new media (Pew Research Center 2010). The internet may therefore be helping to close the participation gap in some ways, even while the selectivity of the medium is exacerbating the problem.

Addressing the Knowledge Gap

The relationship of online news to the knowledge (and participation) gap is not positive, at least on the surface. If information simply exists online— that is to say, if content is posted and no particular efforts are made to target specific users—then the people who already know and care about politics are the ones who will find and share the most sophisticated news content. Under this scenario, the knowledge gap will widen. Whether the medium could instead serve as a tool to diminish the problem is a complex question. The optimistic perspective is that content creators or other interested parties could deliberately use the internet to target low-knowledge audiences with specialized news messages. If used specifically in this sense, then online news could serve as a tool to bring the two segments of society closer together in terms of their political knowledge.

It might be understandably difficult to get users to adopt more informative browsing habits, as people arguably already get the content they want online. Furthermore, it is admittedly somewhat elitist to say that some people should make better content choices. However, if people are making choices that lessen their knowledge of and participation in politics, this does seem to be a problem for the potential equitable operation of government. It might be worthwhile to risk the charges of elitism and develop content (perhaps similar to soft news; see chapter 4) that will appeal to the less politically knowledgeable audiences. Despite these possibilities and hopes, it is likely that online news will serve to widen the knowledge gap in the long run, unless deliberate efforts are made to avoid this outcome.

CONCLUSIONS

In a democratic society, the news media are critical to helping citizens make informed voting decisions. This continues to be true, despite the fact that much original, citizen-generated content is available. The news media act as editor and filter of information, helping citizens decide what content is important to understanding current politics. The centrality of this role does not mean that the connection between media and learning is an easy one.

Many factors condition whether news exposure will lead to any measurable learning. Of the factors that are not internal to the user (such as attention or knowledge), the characteristics of the medium used to deliver the news are particularly important. This chapter applied the design elements discussed in chapter 3 to the likelihood of audience learning. The safest conclusion at this point seems to be that moderate use of online features is helpful, but high use is disorienting. Overinforming audiences is a fairly unique component of online news—at least, it is not a charge that has been often applied to television news—and it illustrates the importance of considering each news medium on its own terms.

Whether the internet facilitates the learning process requires further study. The results obtained thus far are mixed, although it does appear that the internet may succeed if we are willing to define learning as understanding connections and complexity in politics. The safest conclusion at this point, although tepid, is that online news can—at least, given certain favorable conditions—help citizens learn about politics. Further research is certainly required in this area the better to tease out these conditions.

There is one key limit to online news learning that we must bear in mind. Studies demonstrating positive results almost always assume (or require through experimental design) that individuals select content that is informative. We know that such a condition is unfortunately not always realistic. However, the widening knowledge gap is only one possible consequence of a selective news medium and an active audience. The next two chapters will explore other hazards that can arise when citizens use—and potentially overuse—content selection.

CHAPTER 7

Fragmentation and Polarization of the Audience

The processes and effects of audience selection and learning from news help us predict the amount and type of information that people acquire from online news. On a very basic level of understanding the effects of news, that seems pretty useful. Recently, though, scholars and other observers of the news industry have been asking whether current and developing online news consumption processes may have implications for society-wide patterns of what people know and feel about politics. That is, research results suggest that people can learn about events and people in the world when they receive news about them. But what happens when some people receive certain stories and others do not? What are the effects for how social and political groups interact with one another and with the political system?

In this chapter, we discuss how fragmentation and polarization—concepts introduced in chapter 1—might operate, and we review available evidence for their presence in contemporary democracies. Ultimately, definitive evidence to substantiate or dismiss fears of fragmentation and polarization is elusive. Our review of the research literature suggests that some people are being selective in their consumption of categories of information, but there is insufficient evidence to conclude that knowledge and opinion are becoming highly fragmented. Similarly, there are tantalizing signs that some people are basing some of their news exposure—and so grounding some of their knowledge and opinion—on group divisions such as political predispositions. Nonetheless, we cannot yet determine the scope and ultimate effect of information and opinion polarization. Researchers are just beginning their hunt for answers in this area.

A NOTE ON TERMINOLOGY

In this chapter, we review the state of what researchers know about two phenomena: fragmentation and polarization. We both integrate research from a variety of perspectives (e.g., surveys and audience analyses) and define fragmentation and polarization in specific ways. Our reading of the extant literature suggests that observers have used these two terms to cover relatively broad swaths of phenomena. For example, the single term "fragmentation" has been used to refer to audience behavior (e.g., Webster 2005), media content and outlets (Hollander 2008), audience interests (Neuman 1991), public discussion (Dahlberg 2007), and public agendas (Lee 2007). Similarly, "polarization" has been used to refer to audience behavior (e.g., Webster 2005; Webster and Phalen 1997) and group opinion (e.g., Sunstein 2001). Each of these approaches has merit within the context of individual studies, but forming generalizations across them is challenging.

Our desire to evaluate current patterns of fragmentation and polarization and offer some predictions about future development motivates us to be very specific about the phenomena under consideration. If fragmentation can refer to several different potential phenomena, we see the need to evaluate the state of affairs within each of them. This means that we need to draw distinctions—some of which might appear a little blurry—among the different types of fragmentation and polarization. We realize that our need to make distinctions among concepts that are very closely connected (and may have been described with interchangeable terms in the past) will bring us into some conflict with the extant literature. We hope that our framework will prove useful in the current context nonetheless.

For our purposes, fragmentation is the dissolution over time of audience news exposure, public affairs knowledge, and political beliefs into smaller units in a society. Webster, describing the distribution of audiences across television channels, describes fragmentation as "a process by which the mass audience, which was once concentrated on the three or four news options, becomes more widely distributed. As a result, the average channel audience becomes smaller" (2005, p. 367). The online news environment might be allowing, and even encouraging, people to focus on a wide variety of news topics. The wealth of information on these topics, coupled with the user control that the technologies provide, means that people can spread their time and attention across a wide range of topics and sites, both news and entertainment. More important is that they may not be exposed to any depth of information about consequential topics in the public domain. Most topics in the news have an audience—we have talked about how online news systems, in particular, allow news producers to adjust their presentations to track audience demand—but the audience for any one topic need not be large. Thus, observers talk about an overall fragmentation of political knowledge over time into smaller social units.

Polarization can be thought of, in part, as a specific form of fragmentation. A fragmented knowledge environment is one in which relatively few people know about any one thing. This concept does not make any predictions about who will know what. Indeed, in its most basic form, fragmentation suggests that knowledge about public affairs will be somewhat randomly distributed in a population. Of course, that is not a very realistic approach to how people consume news. In chapter 4, we described how news providers and other sites have an incentive to tailor their content to specific segments of an audience. In chapter 5, we discussed how some members of audiences may respond to segmented news content by engaging in active content selection. When people conform to the segmentation strategies of news outlets, they divide themselves into clusters of a sort. Webster refers to them as "small, relatively exclusive communities of interest" (2005, p. 366). In most of the literature in this area, those interests are defined as based on political opinion. But they could just as easily derive from topical or professional interests. Knowledge clusters on any one topic can become increasingly unlike other clusters with which they share few topical inclinations and little news exposure. Most descriptions of polarization suggest that the opinions of polarized groups can develop in opposition to one another (e.g., Sunstein 2001). What polarized groups believe and feel about political events, people, and issues becomes more extreme over time (e.g., Sunstein 2001).

AUDIENCE FRAGMENTATION AND ITS CAUSES

Fragmentation can occur when news outlets specialize. In chapter 4, we described how news providers online can focus their products on specific topics and perspectives, aiming for a specific audience. We suggested, in short, that news outlets and sites have the ability and often the incentive to focus their content on a defined set of topics. The news industry has been following the very general trend characteristic of almost all media to abandon earlier attempts to appeal to large, mass audiences. Recent economic turmoil in the news business has hit general-interest news outlets such as newspapers and network news programs particularly hard, resulting in the reduction of newsroom budgets and the shuttering of some organizations. At the same time, the online environment has seen an increase in the number of news outlets with a limited focus area (Carlson 2010). These outlets encourage news audiences to select sites on the basis of specific news topics. In such an environment—in which the number of broad news outlets is shrinking—general news exposure could become less likely.

The behavior of members of the news audience is another factor that can affect the likelihood of fragmentation. If all members of the potential audience sample widely from a broad array of news topics and stories, they are likely to receive a shared diet of information. If, on the other hand, people focus on specific sites and topics, it is far less likely that they will be exposed to a common set of information about public affairs. The more focused the news exposure of audience members, the more widely scattered will be awareness of problems and policies.

There are a few considerations related to the probability of fragmentation becoming a substantial concern. On first glance, we may assume that the likelihood would be reduced by the presence of general news aggregators online. Aggregators typically sample broadly from a large array of news sources to construct a menu that includes a number of blogs, news outlets, and opinion perspectives. People can use them for one-stop browsing of multiple topic areas. Of course, people can also use search-based news aggregators such as Google News to seek rather narrow news topics. For example, imagine that a user of Google News searches for news about the health care insurance bill signed into law in the United States in 2009. When the results of the search are presented, the user is asked whether he or she wants to add health care reform as a regular news topic of interest. With hundreds of articles on this topic provided by the aggregator, this user can easily focus his or her news exposure solely on health care reform for the foreseeable future and still not exhaust the available content.

A second key point with respect to fragmentation is that an increase in the number of news outlets available for people does not necessarily lead to fragmentation of the audience. If the outlets generally carry the same content areas and give them roughly equal emphasis, different people looking for general news content will come across the same topics as one another. Likewise, if all members of the audience for news have the same interests, they will seek and consume similar sets of information. If either of these conditions—a homogeneous distribution of content or a general news audience—fails to describe the news environment, then fragmentation could result.

In summary, researchers and media observers have described the sort of media environment that seems most conducive to audience fragmentation. News outlets that permit or encourage specialization may facilitate fragmentation, but the active involvement of audiences who specialize their consumption is certainly a requirement. Given these parameters, neither online news selectivity—and so fragmentation—nor broad news browsing seems inevitable today. We will examine the evidence that has accumulated so far to determine what patterns can be discerned.

Types of Fragmentation

We can speak about at least three types of fragmentation. These types are related. Indeed, they can be arranged in a causal sequence of sorts. A simple example of one person's online news use may help illustrate the three types. Imagine that someone—we will call him Dan—enjoys using the internet for entertainment, news, and work-related information. On an average day, he may hear some news headlines on the radio or browse a cable-television news channel for a few minutes. But for the most part, he gets his news online. Typically, he receives a good amount of news from specialized sources and a few topics from the mainstream press. Over time, Dan comes to know quite a bit about events and issues that touch on the topics he follows at the specialized sites, but he sees and hears little about politics and government. As a result, he knows enough about public affairs, perhaps, to hold opinions about some issues in the news, but his knowledge is not very deep. He also has perceptions, as most people do, about which issues the government in his country should be addressing, but those perceptions are based on his rather idiosyncratic browsing of the news.

This example illustrates that fragmentation has three primary levels. The first is the structure of audience members' news consumption. An environment in which few people are attending to news outlets that provide a broad cross section of the news but, instead, attend to a number of specialized news sources represents the *fragmentation of audience news exposure*. This is essentially the type we have been describing in earlier chapters. When audience members consume news about only a few topics that interest them, they may learn quite a bit about some topics but not a lot about a broad range of other topics. This describes the *fragmentation of public-affairs knowledge* (this is in contrast, by the way, with the polarization of knowledge—the development of segments of people with specialized knowledge; we will turn to that outcome below). When people are consuming news and learning about current events, they are building knowledge that they can use to assess the state of issues facing a country. When people are exposed to only a narrow band of the news, they may view the issues they encounter most often to be the issues that require the most government attention. This represents the *fragmentation of the public agenda*. We will review each of these, in turn, to determine whether they are developing today.

Fragmentation of Audience News Exposure

As we have stressed, fragmentation is the result of online audiences focusing their attention on a limited set of topics. We review the evidence here that addresses exposure fragmentation in the traditional (offline) media and on the internet. We are looking for evidence bearing on whether people systematically approach or avoid broad news exposure.

Fragmentation in Traditional Media Exposure

First, we should look at fragmentation in the traditional media to see how high-bandwidth media have affected news use there. At the height of rapid growth in U.S. cable-television adoption, Neuman (1991) examined how Americans adapted their television viewing when faced with substantially more channels than they had seen before. He noted that people do not always respond to increases in content options with more content-choice diversity. Rather, people only marginally increase the diversity of their television viewing. Existing viewing habits are hard to break, and it appears that some people agree that it is possible to have too much of a good thing.

Several years farther into the world of multichannel television, the character of the American media system changed. Looking across both news and entertainment broadcast and cable-television channels, Webster (2005) concluded that television audiences exhibit signs of substantial fragmentation. In one relatively average week in 2003, each of about half of the 65 U.S. cable channels he studied garnered viewing from at least 20 percent of the viewing audience. Thus, viewers were widely spread across a range of channels in that period. This is strong evidence of exposure to multiple sources of news and entertainment, a basic component of exposure fragmentation.

Looking just at Americans' consumption of news content, we can see evidence of shrinking exposure to general news outlets. National surveys by the Pew Research Center for the People and the Press have revealed that Americans' news habits have changed dramatically in the time since popular adoption of the internet began (Pew Research Center 2010). For example, people reporting regular use of a daily newspaper dropped from 66 percent in 1993 to 40 percent in 2010. Similarly, data show that 58 percent of people in 1993 reported regular exposure to a network television (ABC, CBS, or NBC) newscast; in 2010, that number was down to 28 percent. These figures do not suggest that people have given up on the news. Rather, Americans have increasingly turned to more specialized outlets. In the realm of cable television, relatively specialized channels such as ESPN and CNBC appear to have reduced the audience for the general-topic network broadcasts.

Fragmentation in Online News Use

Online, American audiences are using both broad and specialized news sites. News aggregators such as Yahoo! and Google News and general providers such as CNN and the *New York Times* remain among the most popular sites (Pew Research Center 2010). In fact, the types of sites most commonly reported for news consumption are aggregators and mainstream news providers. A 2010 Pew survey reported that 28 percent of self-professed internet news readers received news and information from a Yahoo! site, 16 percent said they received it from cnn.com, 15 percent said Google, and 14 percent said MSN. Thus, a good number of people say that they receive their news and information from general-focus media.

At the same time, though, just a little farther down the top-20 list are the more specialized Drudge Report and *Wall Street Journal* sites (Pew Research Center 2010). Thus, some people also appear to find relatively specialized news outlets attractive. It is not clear that specialized sites and segmented news will entirely replace general-news outlets, but they appear to have made it more difficult for general-news providers to attract and hold audiences online.

There is also some evidence of countervailing use patterns among news audiences. Hindman (2007) presents compelling evidence that there may be more concentration of news reading online than offline. He examines the level of audience concentration for the print and online audiences of America's largest 150 newspapers. He finds more evidence of concentration (a relatively small number of outlets garnering large audiences) online than offline. He notes, for example, "The New York Times' share of online newspaper traffic is 3.5 times its share of the print newspaper market" (p. 343). He finds similar results for the *Washington Post*, the *Boston Globe*, the *San Francisco Chronicle*, and the *Washington Times*. But "at the other end of the scale, 126 of the 150 newspapers attract a smaller portion of online newspaper traffic than they do print circulation" (p. 343). That is, a few newspapers garner larger audiences online, but most draw smaller ones online. This belies some arguments about the proliferation of locally distinct news providers splintering the national news audience along geographic lines.

In total, some, but not all, of the evidence points to exposure fragmentation. Analyses of the online audience continue to find that search engines, news aggregators, and other general-information sources attract very large audiences online. What remains to be seen is whether people use these sites for general news browsing or more focused, specialized news selection.

Fragmentation of Public-affairs Knowledge

If people are selecting websites that focus on entertainment and specific news topics, they might not be exposed to a common body of news. If that is the case, we can expect that different groups of people will know less about a core set of events and issues. That is, public awareness of a range of information will fall over time as the people in a population decrease their reliance on general-news outlets.

It may be hard to visualize that sort of fragmentation, so let's take a hypothetical example. Imagine that news media in some country tend to focus on five major topic areas: the central government, professional sports, the arts industry, the business sector, and medical research. We can assume for this example that over the course of a week, one major event happens in each of these areas. The question for the study of fragmentation is whether people in this country become aware of all or some number of these five hypothetical events. For the sake of argument, we could assume that people regularly consuming the products of general news outlets in this country have the time and motivation to attend consistently to about three topics in an average week (i.e., each topic has a 60 percent probability of selection). Thus, within a random sample of 1,000 people, about 600 will know about each event. This represents a relatively cohesive system of news presentation and consumption.

Compare that with a situation in which the number of news outlets is much greater. Imagine—as is the case in much of the developed world today—that the larger number of news outlets has encouraged news companies to cover a wider range of topics in greater depth. As a result, the residents of our hypothetical nation have 10 topics from which to choose, rather than five. If people still have the time and motivation to attend to three topics, the probability of any one person attending to any one of the topics is only 30 percent. Thus, 300 people know about each event. In this situation, the profusion of news outlets has led to the aggregate population learning about a greater range of things, but together people share less awareness of any one topic. If public-affairs news is one of those topics, the implications for the maintenance of an informed citizenry are clear.

Naturally, there are many potential flaws in this simple analysis. Perhaps the most important is the omission of any role for interpersonal communication about the events. That is, might not people focusing on three topic areas hear about other areas from friends, family, and acquaintances? That is certainly possible, and some research has found that online news exposure may facilitate conversations with others (Shah et al. 2005). Almost as important are the assumptions we made about the various probabilities that people will become aware of any event. Also, the distribution of an equal number of people into each focus area is certainly unrealistic. There would be areas of greater and lesser interest.

The key point, though, is that the fragmentation of audiences among different news topics may lower overall awareness of events. Notably, there is little empirical evidence that this is occurring. A recent analysis of public knowledge about politics and current events found no direct evidence of a reduction in general levels of knowledge from 1989 to 2007 (Pew Research Center 2007). We noted in chapter 5 that there is some evidence that people reading news online might be more selective in the topics they read, but thus far, this has not been observed outside the laboratory. One experiment found that online news readers recalled fewer facts than print readers about events in the news (Tewksbury and Althaus 2000a), but subsequent studies have failed to replicate that finding (Eveland, Seo, and Marton 2002; D'Haenens, Jankowski, and Heuvelman 2004). There is little clear support here.

The lack of evidence that general levels of knowledge are falling does not necessarily rule out that the fragmentation of news exposure is affecting what people know about public affairs and other topics. Returning to the example above, we could change the circumstances slightly, perhaps making them a bit more plausible. Imagine that in this hypothetical population of news consumers, each person takes advantage of the wide range of news topics available and focuses on six topics rather than three. If people double the amount of time and attention they give to the news, it would again give us 600 people who know about any one event. If people skim the news more lightly, however, the probability of any one event being noticed must drop. Knowledge has fragmented, and overall knowledge in the society drops.

Again, there is not a lot of evidence that this situation applies. No surveys or experiments have specifically measured the distribution of public-affairs knowledge within a population over time. One could imagine such a study. It would have to identify groups of people and assess their awareness of a class of issues or events over a specified period. In a highly fragmented environment, knowledge will be unevenly distributed in a population, even when citizens' total time with news media, general interest in news, and other factors are controlled. If knowledge about specific classes of information becomes chronically housed in specific areas of the population, then it may be polarization rather than fragmentation that is taking place. We discuss that further below.

Fragmentation of the Public Agenda

Another visible outcome of the fragmentation of news audiences is the dissolution of the consensus that often exists about the issues facing a nation or other society. During the second half of the 20th century, journalists, political leaders, and researchers came to expect broad public agreement on the issues that a nation must address. The issues would change over time, but the public seemed to keep track of that change easily through news coverage. Not everyone was happy about the power of the news media to set agendas, to be sure (e.g., Bennett 2009), but it was a predictable phenomenon that likely proved helpful to some government leaders and journalists.

The fragmentation of audiences across multichannel television systems and the internet now threatens that easy consensus. At least, that is what some researchers have suggested (Katz 1996; Chaffee and Metzger 2001). Fortunately, this possibility has received some attention in communication research. Even before the development of the World Wide Web, researchers looked for evidence that new electronic news-delivery services may affect the operation of agenda setting (Heeter et al. 1989). Heeter and colleagues examined the effects of reading news through an electronic news service—one that provided readers with substantial control over news selection—for a week. At the end of the week, they detected little to no difference between the agendas of users of an electronic news system and a control group whose members went about their normal news routines in that week.

One experiment conducted in 1998 found some evidence of an agenda-setting effect of online news consumption (Althaus and Tewksbury 2002). Participants in this study read either the print or online version of a national newspaper for five days. On the sixth day, they attempted to recall news events in that week and named the most important problems facing the nation. Readers of the online version of the paper recalled fewer stories about international events—presumably because either the online version displayed them less prominently, or the readers took advantage of opportunities to read other topics—from the previous five days. The online readers were also less likely to mention international issues among the problems facing the nation. Thus, there was some evidence in this study that audiences of different presentation formats could come away from news exposure with different agendas.

These experiment-based findings provide a mixed picture. More recent studies have relied on survey measures of media use and the public agenda. Using data from a survey of a representative sample of the Dutch population, one research team compared the relationship between the number of issues people consider important to the nation and the frequency of their use of print and online newspapers (Schoenbach, de Waal, and Lauf 2005). According to the fragmentation argument, consumption of the print version of the paper should have led to more agenda diversity (through exposure to more issues in the news); consumption of online sources should lead to less diversity (through exposure to a more specialized diet of news). Indeed, print-newspaper exposure was positively related to the number of issue mentions, but there was no overall relationship for online news reading. The one exception to that was for people with a high level of education: reading more news online was associated with the ability to mention more issues. This is not a strong endorsement of the agenda-fragmentation thesis.

Coleman and McCombs (2007) compared the relationship between coverage of issues in the traditional media with what people of different ages considered the most important problems facing the nation. They expected that people between the ages of 18 and 34 would use online news sources more than older people, and so their issue agendas would conform less closely to the agendas of the traditional media. Examining data from two state-level surveys in the United States, they found that survey respondents of all ages reported agendas that closely mirrored the agenda in the offline media. This agenda-setting effect was stronger for older respondents than it was for those between 18 and 34, though. This conformed to the authors' expectations.

The fragmentation thesis would also suggest that younger (internet-reliant) people would exhibit less agenda cohesion. Without exposure to a shared news agenda, individual people would develop relatively idiosyncratic agendas. Some evidence on this point comes from a survey study of American internet and cable-television news audiences. Nie and colleagues (2010) report that people who consume news online show more diversity in the issues they consider important than do people who watch television news but do not use the internet. Together, these survey results suggest that reliance on the internet can fragment the public agenda somewhat.

It is worth highlighting the point here that agenda fragmentation, if it is happening today, is a normatively mixed picture. On the one hand, some observers have argued that effective governance is difficult when members of the public disagree in their basic expectations of the government (e.g., Katz 1996). On the other hand, one can certainly argue that people who come by their issue perceptions through interest-based selection and consumption of news topics might be more committed to their agendas. As a result, the diverse agendas that might emerge from a fragmented society could be more lasting and responsive to actual social phenomena than might agendas that are based on media-generated cues. What is more, if the agendas that people acquire through online news use are influenced by audience-generated content, they may be more responsive to the interests of fellow citizens than those of powerful elites (Chadwick in press).

The reasoning behind concerns about agenda fragmentation posits a relationship between the variety of news outlets to which people are exposed and the diversity of the issues that they consider to be consequential for the nation. Both the scant experiment-based evidence and the survey-based findings point to a modest agenda setting effect of online news consumption (primarily compared with print newspaper reading). This research area has few empirical studies on which to draw, though. It is too early to form concrete conclusions.

Fragmentation is a pretty blunt-edged way to think about the effects of online news consumption. In pure fragmentation, people do not have an enduring loyalty to particular outlets and content (Webster 2005), an unlikely state of affairs. The more loyal audiences and news outlets are to one another, the more likely it is that polarization, rather than fragmentation, will result.

AUDIENCE POLARIZATION AND ITS CAUSES

Fragmentation is the rather simple result of people following their individual interests in the news. If you think about people as individual actors, then that is as far as things may go. In reality, though, people often behave rather similarly to one another. That is, two people who share an enduring interest in a topic are both likely to want to read news on that topic regularly. When many people are so motivated, then some segment of society has developed a specialized news interest. The easier it is for the segment to find news on that topic, the more pronounced the segment will become.

These segments—which may be distinct from one another in terms of age, sex, race, occupation, education, political ideology, or a similar demarcation—may come to develop shared patterns of news consumption. Members of these segments learn things from their news consumption that people outside their group might not. If that happens, the society as a whole might become polarized into factions and groups that do know the same things about events in the world. These factions then might develop different opinions, goals, and behaviors.

Polarization is likely rooted in a set of characteristics of the audience and the media environment. Audiences must be relatively selective in their news consumption. People must not be random grazers of the news but must view news content as related to other parts of their lives. They might see the news as a source of information for their jobs, their hobbies, or their political beliefs. As a result, they choose among available options to pursue their interests in information and entertainment (after all, even news viewing may be entertaining to audiences).

We described earlier how news outlets need to attract loyal audiences. Many sites have responded to audience selectivity by segmenting their coverage along specific topical lines. Websites offer ways for people to receive more news of the type they want. People do not have the time and other resources to consume all of the news available to them, so they may choose to focus on their specific interest areas and not select from a broader set of topics. To the extent that audience specialization follows site segmentation, political awareness and opinion can separate along demographic or other lines in the audience.

By its nature, polarization—like fragmentation—describes a change in how things work. That is, polarization is a type of change in how a society functions. It represents a departure from how news exposure, knowledge, and opinion had been shared in a society. So, for many people, it describes the dissolution of consensus, a breakdown in a system. This is certainly not the only way to think about it. Polarization is also a relatively normal state of being for many people in many situations. We would expect, for example, that people working in a large organization would focus their information gathering on topics that affect their productivity. They, and others like them, would become quite well informed about certain topics and would develop strong attitudes about how their work should be done. That is a quite functional and natural outcome of life in a large organization. For similar reasons, it makes perfect sense for social polarization to occur. How we evaluate the normative implications of the process and outcomes will depend on many factors.

In summary, neither online news producers nor people act randomly. People often pursue specific goals when they seek the news, and news outlets will want to help them. When they do, public knowledge and opinion on specific topics will become divided among different segments of society. We describe below different levels of polarization and review the evidence for whether they are operating today.

Types of Polarization

As with fragmentation, there are different types, or levels, of audience polarization. They are not mutually dependent, but they are likely highly correlated. The conditions that facilitate polarization of one type should function that way for the others, but it is not a certainty. It may be useful to provide a sample of someone who is experiencing polarization from news exposure online. Imagine that Isobel—a fictitious example—is very selective in her news consumption. She works in a textile factory and is a member of a labor union. She is politically liberal and likes to follow politics. Like many of her coworkers, she also is very interested in the clothing industry.

Isobel watches news on television occasionally, but she gets most of her news from the internet at home. Yahoo! is the home page on her Web browser, and she has customized it to put news headlines about politics and the clothing industry at the top of the page. She also has signed up with a news service to receive breaking news about the clothing industry by email. She receives as many as a dozen such messages in an average week. Her union also sends frequent email updates with information about the industry. When she is online, she frequently visits DailyKos, a popular liberal American blog (Baum and Groeling 2008). Isobel talks about politics and her industry with friends and coworkers. She often knows quite a bit about the latest labor and technical issues in the clothing industry, although she does not seem to know much about other industries or their issues. She is politically very active and frequently voices strong support for restrictive international-trade policies.

This example illustrates three potential levels of polarization. The distribution of audiences into internally homogeneous consumers of segmented content represents the *polarization of audience news exposure* (Webster [2005] calls this merely polarization). When they are distributed in this way, audience segments can focus their attention on the topics that most interest them. If clusters of people share specific interests and pursue them in a consistent fashion, this suggests that they are not attending to other topics. In such a situation, one segment of a population becomes more deeply informed about a topic, but the rest of the population becomes less so. In that situation, the population has experienced a *polarization of public-affairs knowledge*. Similarly, people who share an interest and consume news about it may develop opinions and behaviors on the basis of what they receive. People who have a different set of information or even little information at all may develop different opinions and behaviors. As these two types of people develop in different directions, they are experiencing a *polarization of opinion* (Sunstein [2001] calls this merely polarization). We will discuss all three of these levels of polarization in turn.

Polarization of Audience News Exposure

In chapter 5, we reviewed how people choose among news-content options online. People can be quite selective about the sites and kinds of news that they consume. In this section, we look at whether people are engaging in the type of news selection that may result in knowledge or opinion polarization. There are many ways in which people can specialize their news consumption and join other people within topical, social, and ideological segments. We review how this has tended to operate in the offline media and examine the evidence for its occurrence in internet use.

Polarization in Traditional Media Exposure

If people choose news sources in ways that place them in a relatively stable community of news exposure, they experience exposure polarization. In some ways, polarization has occurred in news consumption for some time, perhaps for as long as the press has sought to attract a wide audience to its products. For many years, studies of newspaper reading observed that different people learn different things from the news. For example, Bogart showed that men devoted much more time and attention to sports and business news and women spent more time with features and arts news (Bogart 1989). Similarly, newspaper readers with higher levels of education have been shown to spend more time with news about government and international affairs (Bogart 1989). Even race has been found to be associated with news-reading patterns. One study found that more African-American than white news readers expressed an interest in news about religion, fashion, food, and celebrities (Bogart 1989). A new twist on these well-established patterns comes with newer technologies. As is the case with most effects of the internet, the technology appears to take what people already do and magnifies it.

One way to think about how polarization of use has been observed in the newer media is to count how many channels or outlets people visit. Research on cable television has found that people react to sudden increases in the number of channels from which to choose by adding only a very small number to their existing exposure patterns (Neuman 1991). Thus, content diversity does not necessarily lead to dramatic changes in exposure diversity. Webster (2007) suggests that looking at the number of cable stations a person visits in a time period (what he calls the horizontal diversity of audience exposure) is different from examining how much viewing time audience members spend with individual channels (i.e., vertical diversity). A horizontally diverse exposure pattern might have a typical member of the audience viewing 15 or more channels in a week. This suggests widespread exposure fragmentation of the audience but does not reveal much about the potential for exposure polarization (Webster 2007). If, however, viewing data show that the typical audience member spends most of his or her total viewing time on one or two channels in a week, this would suggest a substantial lack of vertical diversity. If the few channels to which the viewer attends carry segmented content, then polarization is a likely outcome.

Webster (2007) examined the vertical diversity of exposure to cable-television channels by American audiences in one week in February 2003. He found little evidence of vertical exclusivity in the Nielsen-ratings data he studied. He observed, for example, that viewers of popular and relatively specialized cable channels such as MTV, Fox News, and BET (Black Entertainment Television) spent 98 percent, 92 percent, and 97 percent of their viewing time, respectively, on other channels. Thus, there is little evidence that people who viewed channels with segmented content chose only those channels.

Nonetheless, there is some evidence that audiences may select news and information outlets on the basis of their predispositions. In one study of audiences for newspapers, cable-television news channels, talk-radio programs, and internet sites, people appeared to be making choices guided by political partisanship (Stroud 2008; see also Iyengar and Hahn 2009). People who were strong political partisans were particularly likely to select outlets in all four media that supported their ideology.

Of course, given the nature of polarization, audience loyalty to topics, beliefs, and opinions and their loyalty to news outlets likely form a reciprocal process. We assume that people choose outlets and topics on the basis of their predispositions. It could be that cross-sectional studies showing the audience of a cable-television channel becoming more ideologically polarized over time provide evidence of people maximizing the fit between their predispositions and their exposure. It is sometimes hard to distinguish that pattern from one that posits a one-way causal effect of exposure to segmented news.

Polarization in Online News Use

We noted in chapter 5 that the provision of technologies of abundance and choice on the internet has increased both the study and the expected frequency of selective exposure. We reported that a number of studies have observed that some people use the information cues they find online to tailor their news consumption to fit their interests, consciously or not. In chapter 4, we observed that news providers have the ability and often the incentive to tailor their content to match the interests of their audiences. In the online environment, providers have many ways to do this. They track reader interests directly through their behavior and respond with amenable content.

This pattern has been developing for some online news outlets. One study (Thurman 2007) found signs that British news sites with substantial numbers of international visitors might be catering their content to those readers. In the United States, Baum and Groeling (2008) reported a similar trend with respect to the political orientation of readers and sites. They compared the content of two wire services (the Associated Press and Reuters) with that of partisan blogs and Fox News online. They found that both left-leaning (dailykos.com) and right-leaning blog sites (freerepublic.com and foxnews.com) present more polarized content than the wire-service sites. Over time, we would expect that the interests (topical and ideological) of audiences and sites would converge.

One way for audiences to become polarized in their news exposure is through the application of technologies of customization. Over the past two decades, the online news media have developed ways for audiences to preselect the news topics they want to receive. We described some of those in chapter 3. Some are customizable news feeds (through an RSS news feed or a customizable news site such as iGoogle), subscriptions to Twitter, news-headline feeds to mobile devices such as cell phones, and news links on social-network sites. If a good number of people are using these systems to specialize their news consumption, then polarization of use may be well under way.

The spring 2010 media-use survey by the Pew Research Center included questions about some of these technologies. The responses may shed light on developing patterns. The survey asked people to report how often they used specific customization methods for obtaining news headlines. Table 7.1 presents the percentages of people who said they used the methods "regularly" or "sometimes" (the question about email messages from journalists required a "yes" or "no" response to whether they get news that way). These data are drawn from the entire sample of 3,006 Americans, not just internet users (see Pew Research Center 2010 for more information about the sample). Among people with internet access, of course, the percentages would be much higher.

On the whole, a fair number of Americans receive news through these channels. For example, more than a quarter of Americans read blogs about politics or current events at least sometimes (about one-third of that group does so regularly). Other technologies are less regularly used. Twitter, surprisingly, sees little use for news and headlines, contrary to what one might assume on the basis of news reports about this service (Miller 2010). Summing the use of these technologies reveals that about half of the sample of Americans used at least one of these six news-specialization methods. Among those who used at least one, 24 percent used at least three. Less than one percent used all six.

Table 7.1. AMERICANS' USE OF FOCUSED OR CUSTOMIZED
NEWS TECHNOLOGIES

Use News Technologies Regularly or Sometimes	
Read blogs about politics or current events	29%
Receive news or news headlines on a cell phone	15%
Receive news or news headlines by email from news organizations or journalists*	14%
Receive news or news headlines through customizable Web page or an RSS reader	20%
Receive news or news headlines through Twitter	1%
Receive news or news headlines though social-networking site	19%

N = 3,006
* Responses to this question were "yes" and "no" only; "yes" responses are shown.
Source: Pew Research Center 2010.

Exposure polarization also seems likely to be facilitated by technologies that support common news exposure by people who share some feature or attribute. The most obvious form of this is the influence of news recommendations by friends in Facebook and other social media. People can "like" specific news stories, indicating to others that the stories may be of interest to them. To the extent that online social networks develop around common social attributes, the shared media exposure that may develop from the recommendation process may produce a form of polarization.

Polarization of Public-affairs Knowledge

In theory, one likely result of people attending to a small number of sources on a few topics or perspectives is that awareness and knowledge about issues, events, and people will become more one-sided. Our earlier comments about the distribution of knowledge in a fragmented society also apply here. If there is widespread fragmentation, fewer people will know about a great many things. The focus on polarization adds a different dimension to this picture. Fewer people may know a lot about what happens in society, but some segments will know more. This does not sound so surprising, of course. The people who want to know more about a topic will come to do so. That sounds like a rather functional relationship between demand and supply.

What makes polarization interesting, from a normative point of view, is how this pattern differs from what was the norm in the mass-audience system of the 20th-century media. Media outlets trying to maximize their audience size had little incentive to provide specialized content for audience segments. They sought to provide content for everyone. Naturally, resource constraints drove them to supply a little bit of content on a broad range of topics. The economic and technical boundaries of television and radio through the 1970s limited audience access to multiple sources, practically ensuring exposure to the relatively broad topical diversity provided by the press (Prior 2007). As a result, most people knew something (but often not too much; see Delli Carpini and Keeter 1996) about many things, including public affairs.

With polarization of exposure, fewer people will follow a broad range of topics in the news; consequently, they will come to believe different things about the world around them. One way to investigate whether this has been occurring is to look at whether use of customization technologies is associated with polarized attention to events in the news. Data for examining this relationship are available in the 2010 Pew survey results discussed earlier. We looked at the technologies that seem most likely to allow the selection of news along personal political lines. We asked whether a substantial reliance on those technologies, relative to those that might encourage broad exposure to topics, might facilitate partisan cleavages in attention to news topics. The polarization thesis suggests that it would.

Again, the data come from a national survey of 3,006 Americans in spring 2010. We constructed a very rough variable to represent reliance on customized news media relative to general news media. We used responses to questions about news use on the day before each respondent's survey experience. This is a relatively valid, if somewhat limited, measure of recent news exposure to media (Converse and Presser 1986). We summed affirmative responses to whether people received news by email from journalists, through a customized Web page or an RSS feed, through Twitter, or through a social-networking site. To this number we added the number of affirmative responses to whether people had read a newspaper, listened to radio news, watched television news, or read online news other than an online newspaper in the previous day. This overall sum represented their total news breadth on the previous day.[1] People with no news use at all were excluded from analysis. We then divided each respondent's use of customized news by his or her total news use. The resulting number had a range between 0 (no customized news use) and 1 (news use was entirely customized). Obviously, a value of .5 indicated that half of the use was customized.

Our goal was to determine whether the topics that people followed in the news would be more extensively determined by political predispositions when they relied on customized news than when they did not. Naturally, quite a few things can determine whether people follow specific topics and events in the news. To account for some of those variables, our analyses applied statistical controls for the respondents' age, sex, education, regular frequency of exposure to online news, breadth of the previous day's general news exposure, and enjoyment of following the news. We expected that the respondents' political-party identification might affect how closely they followed specific news events and topics and that the impact of party would depend on their level of customization reliance (no, low, or high). Party should matter less for people not customizing and more for those strongly relying on it.

For this analysis, we compared self-identified Democrats' and Republicans' responses to questions about whether they had been following news about the war in Afghanistan, the 2010 congressional elections, and the U.S. economy. These are all political topics about which we might expect Democrats and Republicans to express different levels of interest. The results of our analysis can be found in figure 7.1.[2]

The figure shows that there are very few differences between Democrats and Republicans when they do not use customized news. Some differences emerge when they rely, at least somewhat, on the customized news sources.[3] This is particularly the case with respect to news about the election. Reliance on customized sources appears to have increased partisan divisions in attention to a political news topic. An effect of customized news reliance is less visible in the other cases.

Another way to determine whether widespread adoption of the internet for news gathering might be causing polarization of political attention and knowledge would be to see whether attention to politics has dropped or become segmented among the public over time. An analysis of Pew Research Center surveys from 1996 through 2002 shed some light on this (Bennett, Rhine, and Flickinger 2004). The researchers in this case looked at surveyed Americans' self-reported attention to political-news topics in 1996, 1998, 2000, and 2002, a period of rapid adoption of the internet. Self-reports of attention showed very stable values over that period, so Bennett and colleagues examined whether demographic predictors (such as age, ethnicity, race, education, and strength of partisanship) showed changing relationships with attention over time. The polarization approach would have predicted that some variables would become stronger and others weaker over time, as some segments in society used the internet to focus more attention on politics and others used it to focus less. In essence, the predictive power of demographics

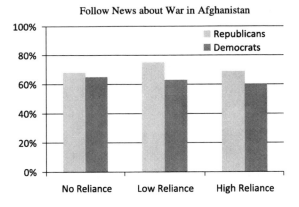

Follow News about War in Afghanistan

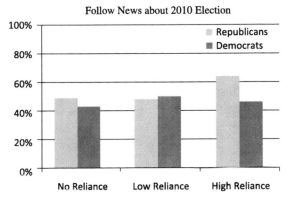

Follow News about 2010 Election

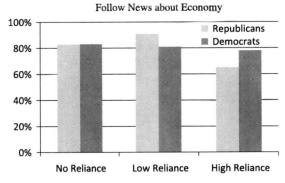

Follow News about Economy

Figure 7.1. Percentage of Americans following specific topics by party identification and reliance on individualized news delivery.

would change over time. There was no clear pattern; the researchers found no evidence of polarization.

In sum, it appears that there is only limited, very mixed evidence of topical attention and knowledge polarization. Absent any direct studies of knowledge effects, very preliminary analyses of news attention presented here showed some effects but not consistently. Once again, this is an area in need of further research. Longitudinal studies of the distribution of knowledge in society might provide a meaningful test of polarization effects.

Polarization of Opinion

In the process of polarization of opinion, people consuming different segments of the news develop divergent opinions about public-affairs issues, events, and people. Of course, different people have different opinions. Whites and blacks in America may see affirmative action differently, and men and women may see abortion differently. This is no surprise. Polarization is consequential when natural divisions between segments of society become exaggerated through divided attention to news and commentary (Sunstein 2001). Content catering to different groups may provide fodder for more deeply ensconced opinion. It might even motivate social and political behavior that further separates groups within society.

There is some evidence of developing political polarization tied to use of the internet for the gathering of news and information. The study by Nie and colleagues (2010), described earlier, examined the ideological extremity of news audiences. For some time, people have been arguing that television news has specialized along partisan political lines. The authors reasoned that the incentives and capacity to specialize news content in the multichannel environment of cable television should be even stronger online. They compared the level of ideological commitment of viewers of Fox News and CNN with the commitment of visitors to those organizations' online news sites. They found that people who watched the Fox News cable channel and visited the online site were more politically conservative than those who only watched the cable channel. Similarly, audiences of CNN on television and on the internet were more politically liberal than the television-only viewers.

A second survey study points to a potential polarization effect of online news exposure (Stroud 2010). Analyzing responses to a series of surveys over the course of the 2004 American presidential election, Stroud tested whether partisans using partisan media develop more polarized political attitudes. The results show that conservatives listening to conservative talk radio, watching the Fox News Channel, reading newspapers that endorsed President Bush in the election, and visiting conservative websites exhibited more conservative attitudes than did other conservatives. Likewise, liberals using liberal media, including liberal websites, expressed more liberal attitudes than did other liberals. The use of a panel design in this study allowed Stroud to determine that people using partisan outlets became more polarized over the course of the election. It is not merely that they began their exposure to partisan media already polarized. They changed over time. Unfortunately for our discussion, the study's combination of website exposure with the use of other partisan outlets means that it is not clear how much of the polarization effect can be attributed to the online content.

To address more directly the question of whether the use of customized-news delivery content contributes to polarization, we return to the data available from the 2010 Pew survey. A question included in the study asked people to report their support for government activism. This question is very similar to one that has been used in the past as a litmus test for ideological attachment (Converse 1964). The question asked people to choose which of two statements came closer to their own opinion. The statements were "Government should do more to solve problems" and "Government is doing many things better left to businesses and individuals." We used selection of the first option as the dependent variable in an analysis that featured party identification and reliance on customized news as the independent variables (the statistical controls mentioned before were also used here).

Figure 7.2 shows the results of the analysis. There is a statistically significant interaction of party identification and reliance.[4] Democrats and Republicans who did not rely on customized news had a 41-point gap in agreement. Those with low reliance had a 54-point gap, and those with high reliance had a 64-point gap. This suggests that partisans who use customized online news are more ideologically polarized than partisans who do not rely on these outlets. This analysis controls for the partisans' general media exposure, general online news exposure, enjoyment of following the news, and demographic characteristics. With these controls in place, these data point to a possible effect of online news consumption on ideological polarization.[5]

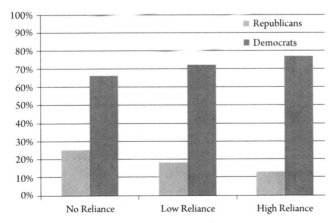

Figure 7.2. Support for government policies by party identification and reliance on individualized news delivery.

CONCLUSIONS

In this chapter, we have described the conditions that might facilitate the fragmentation and polarization of news audiences. We noted that both phenomena can occur when online news outlets specialize their content, providing a relatively narrow set of topics (as opposed to a broad treatment of the events and issues of the day). They might occur also when audiences focus their news exposure on a few sites and areas to the exclusion of a broad consumption of topics and perspectives. The latter might happen in the absence of the former, particularly when there is an abundance of news content available online, but fragmentation and polarization are obviously much more likely to occur when both conditions are met.

Fragmentation of news exposure, public-affairs knowledge, and public opinion represents a reduction in the likelihood that a variety of people within some population will know and feel similarly about a public-affairs event or issue. Ultimately, "fragmentation" is a societal-level term used to describe deviation from a past or desired state of shared knowledge and opinion. In a nonfragmented society, most people follow the same news topics, know roughly the same things about events, and form opinions based on this shared knowledge. In a fragmented society, what is known and felt about political life is more or less randomly distributed among the populace. The concept of fragmentation has an almost anarchic tenor to it. What people know and feel about politics is essentially idiosyncratic. In a fragmented society, the public agenda and mass political behavior are unpredictable (Katz 1996).

In contrast, the process and effects of polarization are relatively predictable. When news outlets engage in audience segmentation, they tailor their offerings with the hope of attracting and holding a reliable audience. If people respond to this approach and limit their news consumption to specific outlets and topics, they may be dividing themselves into clusters of knowledge and opinion. People with shared characteristics (e.g., similar geographic location, educational background, or political ideology) consume a shared diet of information and opinion. They believe what others in their group believe and form attitudes and behaviors on the basis of those beliefs. In a polarized society, people have not just random bits of information and opinion (that would be fragmentation) but information and opinion in opposition. For example, Democrats, Republicans, Libertarians, and Greens in the United States might have knowledge that is consistent with their predispositions but know little about what informs and motivates their political rivals. Political life in that circumstance is very predictable in its conflicts and debates.

Fragmentation and polarization are ideas, still, more than observable realities. There is ample evidence that many people are specializing their news consumption in ways that might lead to either or both outcomes. There is less evidence that knowledge and opinion are fragmenting and/or polarizing. Most of the uncertainty about the operation of these phenomena stems from a lack of research; it rarely lies with disconfirming studies. What is more, much of the evidence—although not all—that we have seen so far is based on cross-sectional survey research that provides few methods for assessing how news exposure, political knowledge, and political opinion develop over time.

A central component in the potential for the development of fragmentation and polarization is the extent to which people are willing to specialize their news consumption. Many online news providers have clearly moved toward segmentation, but their efforts will result in fragmentation and polarization only if people choose to select focused content and opt out of browsing among many outlets and topics. Ultimately, then, audience behavior is very likely the key element to watch as news delivery and consumption develop in the years ahead.

CHAPTER 8
Information Democratization

T he fact that the internet places an unprecedented level of control in the hands of users makes the medium both fascinating and potentially transformative. However, power and technology are both value-neutral (Winner 1985), which is to say that they can be used to either further positive or negative ends. As we discussed in the last chapter, the power of content choice may well facilitate the fragmentation of society, which is generally considered a negative outcome. User control can also lead to more positive outcomes. Chief among these is the internet helping more people to be involved with media than at any point in the last several hundred years. This democratization of public information is only possible because of the content control made possible by the internet.

Defining the likely normative gains from enabling citizens to control content is difficult, just as it is difficult to define the probable negative outcomes of social fragmentation or polarization. This chapter makes a basic assumption for the connection between user control and social good. The premise is that democracy works better as citizens are more responsible for information about government and politics. If we accept this assumption—and there is admittedly room for debate—then we can infer that processes and technologies facilitating citizen responsibility for knowledge are a social positive. The reader will, of course, have to decide whether the benefits of increased citizen involvement outweigh the problems of decreased societal cohesion. This chapter builds the argument that the pros outweigh the cons.

We term the process by which internet use translates to citizen involvement with content creation "information democratization." The primary purpose of this chapter is to define this concept and explore the implications of this process for society. We begin by returning to the role of information in democracy (we gave one perspective on that in chapter 1).

We then discuss the differences between the mass-media system and the media of today. These points will set the stage for a discussion of how the internet strengthens the connections between citizens and political knowledge. We conclude the chapter with a discussion of the forces acting against democratization and a broader discussion of the potential effects of online news for society.

THE ARGUMENT FOR INFORMATION DEMOCRATIZATION

The premise of representative democracy is that government officials are elected by the people. Most scholars accordingly think that at least some level of information is critical to citizens' performance of their civic duties (Berelson 1952). Nonetheless, citizens have not always had good access to—let alone the ability to participate in the creation of—important public information. The result (and to some extent, the cause) of this reality is that elites have long played the key role in controlling public knowledge (Bimber 2003). Information democratization may partially correct this apparent contradiction.

Information and Democracy

The first point about the relationship between information and democracy to consider is the extent to which citizen responsibility for political information is a necessary, or even important, component of democratic government. There are, of course, many versions of democracy (e.g., direct, republic, parliamentary), and observers vary greatly in their opinions about how much information citizens must actually possess (Bennett 2003; Zaller 2003). If we are comfortable with minimal citizen knowledge as the standard for successful democracy, then citizen control of information does not particularly matter. However, if we lean toward the position that democracy functions best when citizens have substantial knowledge of government officials and policies, then involvement with political information is important. The argument for this perspective is that knowledge helps citizens select the correct representation, monitor current government officials, and therefore facilitate the enactment of desirable policies. This is why observers typically assume that some level of knowledge is essential for a properly functioning democracy.

The second point to consider is who bears the responsibility for originating and circulating political information. Citizens are responsible for much of the work themselves. Members of the public cannot be self-reliant, though, if they do not have the means of directly controlling the information themselves. This is the reason many scholars and observers have substantial expectations of officials and journalists (Bennett 2009; McChesney 2008). If these groups do not make political information available or accessible, citizens will not be able to get the information they need to participate effectively in democratic government. This means that while the public is nominally responsible for acquiring necessary political information, government officials, mainstream journalists, and other elites have been able to dictate the extent to which the public can fulfill this responsibility. The problematic nature of this reality most clearly indicates why citizen control of political information should lean toward a social gain.

There is a third point to consider, and that is whether citizens will—or even can—handle an increased responsibility for political information. As discussed earlier, we know that substantial portions of the public do not choose to seek public-affairs content (chapter 5) and that the quality or utility of much news content is somewhat questionable (chapter 3). These problems have long been at the foundation of arguments against expecting citizens to be knowledgeable about politics in the first place (Berelson 1952). To be certain, we should not delude ourselves into thinking that information democratization will mean that all citizens will be actively engaging political content. However, any substantial increase in citizen responsibility for information would bring both a direct improvement in the public and presumably also an indirect one.

Research into second-order media effects (e.g., Katz 1957) has long indicated that many citizens get much of their political information from their peers. This suggests that strengthening the relationship between some citizens X and political information Y will improve democracy not just by a factor of XY but by X^FY, where F is the typical number of friends with which a citizen will share information. In short, even if most people never substantially increase their role in political media, society as a whole may still reap benefits from the actions of a relative few.

Defining Information Democratization

If we are willing to accept that increased citizen responsibility for political information is important for society, then we should examine the process that can bring about this improvement. Information democratization is a term that has been generically applied to any trend toward information being available to the public (e.g., Berthon, Holbrook, and Hulbert 2000; Schiller 1978). However, this general usage insufficiently captures the full range of involvement that the internet facilitates. A clear discussion of the benefits of internet news therefore requires more precise description. We define information democratization as *the increasing involvement of private citizens in the creation, distribution, exhibition, and curation of civically relevant information.* This more precise definition better reflects the fact that the public can now exercise substantial control over content without even writing a word.

Additional clarity may be achieved by breaking the definition of information democratization into its component parts. Involvement can refer to a variety of actions, ranging from writing stories to reposting links or archiving articles. For example, a person who is watching a televised news story is passive, but a person who is commenting on a news article is involved. We refer to private citizens to indicate that the concept applies to regular individuals—not traditional media journalists and not government officials.

Creation signifies the production of news content, and citizens can be involved with this by posting original work or supplying other writers with ideas or information. This is the most commonly considered form of information democratization and is generally what people are referring to when they discuss citizen journalism. Distribution is the process of getting the information from source to receiver, and on the internet, this essentially means the service being used to spread the message. For example, a person could be involved in distribution by linking an article to a blog (mass audience), by sending an email message (close contacts), or by posting a message to a social-networking service (social circle). Exhibition refers to how additional audiences encounter or experience the message, which is often closely tied to distribution. Citizens can also influence the exhibition of a message by, for example, deciding whether to post a mere link, a comment and a link, or a summary and a reference. Curation is essentially the preservation of messages, which citizens can do by storing information themselves.

Finally, the definition applies these terms specifically to civically relevant information, which covers all topics that are related to government. This may include, but is not limited to, candidate positions, pending legislation procedures, government regulation, and policy alternatives. In sum, the concept of information democratization clearly illustrates the possibility of a powerful role of citizens in society.

DEMOCRATIC INFORMATION AND MEDIA RESEARCH

Meaningful information democratization accelerated with the rise of the World Wide Web in the 1990s. The novelty and significance of information democratization can be brought into sharper focus through comparison of its elements with the characteristics of the mass media of the 20th century. We review the mass public model of political communication research before discussing the innovations of the contemporary structure of information.

The Mass Public Model of Political Communication Research

The mass public model of political communication research refers to the observations and assumptions established by media and politics scholars during the dominance of traditional media. The chief characteristic of the mass public model is that the public—or the audience—is assumed to be heavily concentrated in very few locations. This concentration was somewhat necessitated by the media environment, which offered comparatively few options before the rise of satellite and cable television. American broadcast television, for example, originally offered ABC, CBS, or NBC; PBS, Fox, and the CW all came later. By the second half of the 20th century, most towns in America were already down to one newspaper, leaving little option on that front. Furthermore, radio offered little news content apart from a few news-talk outlets. The American media environment limited public news exposure to a few newspapers and the three broadcast-television networks. A single message could therefore reach a substantial portion of the public relatively easily. This had several important implications for the structure of political communication.

The first implication of high levels of media content concentration is that political messages primarily flow from the top down to audiences in the mass public model of communication. If we conceptualize political power as a pyramid with a few elites at the top and the mass public at the bottom, then the top-down communication flow means that elites almost exclusively create and send messages. Concentration contributes to this power structure by making media outlets expensive and fairly inaccessible. When a single newspaper or television station commands a near-exclusive hold on the audience, then opportunities to use the medium are limited and the cost of advertising is very high. Few people have the ability to use the media to reach the audience. Indeed, the mass public model of communication primarily affords traditional journalists and government officials the opportunity to create messages that will reach the public. A top-down flow of information stems, in no small part, from the concentration of the audience among a few news sources.

The second implication of concentration is that audiences are relatively weak in the mass public model. As noted above, concentration contributes to a media system through few opportunities for message creation and a top-down flow of communication. By definition, the audience has little ability to send messages back up the political power structure and is effectively weak. Much of the scholarship about the mass-public model assumes that audiences will passively receive the media under most circumstances. The few exceptions to this rule still did not define a very strong or capable audience. The two-step flow of communication (Katz 1957) suggested that a few attentive viewers share information with peers, and media-selection models (Rubin 2002; Klapper 1960) stipulated that individuals would deliberately choose content from their (few) available sources. While these conceptualizations do depict a somewhat active audience, the masses are not using media to send messages or contribute significantly to the public's store of political information. Overall, the mass public model defines individuals as having little power in the face of a concentrated media system.

The mass public model clearly defines political communication as a top-down process where the elites control information, and the public can, at best, choose whether to receive or ignore incoming messages. This model is heavily influenced by the dominance of the traditional media—particularly newspapers and broadcast television—that existed during the majority of the 20th century. This media system offered little choice, and the concentration of audiences facilitated the elite-centric power structure. However, the traditional media are much less dominant now than they were a few decades ago. Changes in the media system have corresponded with changes in opportunities for audiences. These changes, in turn, cause concern for the continued validity of the mass public model. It is therefore important to consider alternative models of political communication.

Moving Beyond the Mass Public Model

A current scholar of media and politics needs to assess the degree to which the assumptions of the mass public model continue to fit political communication. In fact, many of the assumptions are questionable (Chaffee and Metzger 2001). This problem exists because of a change to what we defined as the chief characteristic of the mass public model, which was the concentrated audience. Current media choices not only include broadcast television (with at least six channels in most markets) and newspapers but also cable and satellite news (as many as 14 news channels on some services), talk radio, and, of course, the internet. These additional options, combined with an increasing ability of the audience to choose among sources deliberately, have deteriorated the mass public almost beyond recognition. Instead of concentration, bits of audiences are now spread across a great many sources. The description sounds graphic, and to a political campaign or a news organization, it is. A distributed audience means that content creators need to work much harder to get their messages to a large number of individuals (see Howard 2006). The change in the nature of audiences causes problems for several of the assumptions made by the mass public model of political communication.

One implied change to the mass public model is that political communication is no longer top-down but also bottom-up and even cuts across social structures. This means that messages are increasingly created by the public (e.g., citizen journalism), either to be sent up the power hierarchy to political elites or to be sent across to other sectors of the public. The increasing fragmentation of the media structures makes outlets less expensive and easier to utilize. Becoming a news anchor requires experience (and perhaps connections), but creating a news channel on YouTube requires merely a video camera and an internet connection. The lower costs and increased access mean that it is harder for elites to dominate the process of message creation.

Of course, many messages—and perhaps the majority of those encountered by most of the public—will be created by the same political elites as before. For example, online video struggles to compare to broadcast television. The December 2010 audiences for the American nightly news broadcasts were 6 million to 10 million viewers (Seidman 2010). The number of unique viewers of videos on Google (YouTube) during an entire day was 4.7 million (comScore 2011a). Many YouTube videos are, of course, professionally produced, as are the vast majority of videos found on other popular video platforms, such as Viacom Digital (MTV, Comedy Central; 1.5 million) or Hulu (primarily NBC and Fox; 0.9 million). These numbers for online video demonstrate that whereas it is easy to become excited about the potential of citizen journalism, the reality is that many types of messages coexist in the current media system. The important point is that the presence of diversity is what alters the mass public model's assumptions about the diffusion of political information.

A second change that distributed audiences imply for the mass public model concerns the role of the audience. As our description suggests, the dispersion of media outlets and audiences affords a stronger conceptualization of the audience than was reasonable under the mass public model. The previous definition of an active citizen was a person who either thought about his or her media choices or received a message from the media and then discussed the information with friends or family. The prevalence of choices today dictates that most people will have to select their media outlets consciously. The most-involved citizens can both share information and use the media to create their own political messages that can either provide feedback to elites or reach a substantial audience. This significantly changes the audience roles assumed by the mass public model of political communication.

The fragmented structure of media today has changed the operation of political communication as defined by the mass public model. Specifically, the improved availability of media outlets has limited the message dominance of political elites and expanded the role of public audiences. Such changes directly contribute to information democratization by providing the opportunities for citizen involvement with political information. However, breaking academic assumptions of media is not the only consequence of the shift from mass to fragmented audiences. The changing relationships among media, elites, and citizens also bear important implications for society.

Opportunity or Hazard?

The shift from the mass public model to a more fragmented model of political communication does not just change the relative power of elites and individuals. Communication is a critical component of society, and any significant change to a communication system will necessarily affect society as a whole. Knowing to look for change is easy, but recognizing and evaluating the shifts are a challenge. We may be inclined to say that citizen involvement is a social good, but the reality may be more complex. It is therefore necessary to give greater consideration to the influence of information democratization for society.

On the surface, citizen involvement with content does seem to offer clear benefits. Increased political knowledge among the public may be one of the positive outcomes. Knowledge could be increased in at least two ways. One route could be that individuals who become involved with political communication take it upon themselves to conduct the research or investigation necessary to produce informed messages. This possibility represents the highest hopes of those encouraging citizen journalism. A second route could be that citizen-produced information would appeal to people who never made regular use of traditional reporting, much in the same way as the two-step political information studies found that nonviewers of news become informed by friends (Katz 1957).

Improved attention to government operations may be another positive outcome. As citizens become increasingly involved with political information, their likelihood of viewing and evaluating officials should increase, which would, in turn, put more pressure on those officials to be responsive to constituents. It is still too early to say whether knowledge and attention are reasonable outcomes of information democratization. Chapters 6 and 7 pointed to research that offered some positive and some negative perspectives on the relationship between online news and audiences' political knowledge and participation. Whether and how involvement—over and above simple news exposure—makes a difference will have to be answered at a later time.

A clearer implication of the evolving system is increased societal fragmentation. American media developed such that a primary contributor to citizen involvement was the division of audiences, as discussed above. Contemporary critics of society must recognize that involvement and fragmentation appear to operate hand-in-hand. This observation leads to two conclusions regarding societal fragmentation. First, it is possible that attempts to unify (or reconcentrate) the news media—if this were even possible—would come at the cost of reducing citizen involvement. Just as the dispersion of platforms and audiences creates opportunities for citizens to shape media, eliminating sources may simultaneously increase the size of audiences and decrease their political opportunities.

Second, it is possible that attempts to expand the role of citizens in the media could increase the level of societal fragmentation. This could occur if individuals focus their contributions on a niche area, and this process could facilitate polarization—the extreme form of fragmentation (see chapter 7). A potential example of this can be seen in most citizen journalism projects, which tend to focus on hyperlocal reporting, leaving other issues for larger outlets. These conclusions suggest that to the extent that we value information democratization, we may also have to accept societal fragmentation.

Information democratization describes the current trend of increased citizen creation, distribution, exhibition, and curation of political information. This trend has its roots in the ongoing transition of the media system. As society has moved from a mass public model of political communication to a more fragmented model, the message dominance of elites and the relative power of private citizens have shifted. The full repercussions of these changes in the media will not be known for years, but the early signs point to citizen involvement, public knowledge, and societal fragmentation as plausible long-term outcomes. Assessing the significance of citizen involvement next requires moving beyond just the changing media system to consider also the changing role of information in democratic societies.

DEMOCRATIZATION OF INFORMATION ONLINE

To this point, we have emphasized two facts. First, information creation, distribution, exhibition, and curation are increasingly accomplished by private citizens. Second, the internet has facilitated this democratization. The next points to consider are the how and why of this transformation. The internet has driven public involvement with the news where other media have been unsuccessful. The reasons for this success rest, in no small part, with the openness of the medium, which has contributed to a new context for citizen involvement with content and facilitated exposure to (and effects from) information.

The Context for Citizen Involvement with Content

The context for involvement with content refers to the factors that influence whether and how often individuals will participate in any component of public information. If we equate the decision to participate in content with the decision to participate in any economic market, we can more readily identify the factors that are relevant to making the choice. The first factor is whether the costs are acceptably low to justify participation. The second factor is the likelihood that participation will yield a satisfying effect. In short, people will want to participate with public information when they can afford to do so and when they think that their efforts will matter. The calculations for assessing the context for participation have changed dramatically in the past two decades, because digital media have changed both the costs and the effects of information creation.

The internet has affected the costs of participation with information in many ways. Among the most important are free or cheap access to government records, corporate documents, secondary sources, and publishing tools. With these components available for the cost of internet access alone, the cost of participation is reduced to almost nothing. As the cost of participation in any market is reduced, the likelihood that more people or companies will get involved in the market increases. The effect of lowered costs in the area of public information is particularly pronounced, because the costs have fallen from such a great height. Newspapers, magazines, and television are all expensive ventures, but the internet and its corresponding platforms enable citizens to produce comparable content on relatively meager budgets. Lower costs for participation with information typically lead to democratization, because more people are able to be involved.

The internet has also increased the likelihood that participation with information will yield some tangible measure of effect. Without online publishing platforms, citizen-produced content would likely be seen only by the author and, perhaps, a few friends. Such a limited potential sphere of effect has always been sufficiently satisfying for a significant number of people. However, most would-be information authors or curators will get serious about their involvement with content only if they think that their efforts will reach others. Beyond the vanity factor, an audience is a necessary component of moving the activity from the realm of hobby to profession. Without readers, most new producers will be limited to creating content in their spare time. Although the internet does not guarantee an audience, the medium does increase the likelihood that any citizen can have his or her content read by numerous others. More important, then, is that the internet increases the likelihood that a person can make a living at writing. For this reason, the internet helps with the social context of news production.

Citizens as Content Providers

Millions of Americans have engaged with public information in some manner, most with no obvious effect. Major papers and channels continue to produce much of the most visible content on the internet. Pulling apart the apparent contradiction between information democratization and corporate dominance requires a closer inspection of the effects of citizen involvement with information. Specifically, we need to look at both direct and indirect routes through which citizens can affect the broader realm of public knowledge.

Public involvement with content has a direct effect when citizen creation, distribution, exhibition, or curation influences the information that is seen and experienced by others. Citizens most often directly affect public knowledge through blogs and social networks, although we can also include wikis, link recommendation systems, and other formats. Blogs and wikis are primarily vehicles for content creation, exhibition, and curation. Participants can use these platforms to add their knowledge for public consumption or use these sites as repositories for the "best word" on a given subject. Traffic to such sites is fairly small (they attract fewer than one in five internet users on a daily basis, according to the Pew Internet and American Life Project 2010b), but the direct influence on exposure for those audiences is meaningful. On the other hand, social-networking sites (and particularly Facebook, as of 2010) are among the most popular platforms on the Web (Pew Internet and American Life

Project 2010b), and they are the biggest driver of online news traffic (Hopkins 2010). When citizens repost or retweet links, they are distributing news content and becoming directly involved in the exposure of others. Through any and all of these venues, the internet has created a significant space for direct channels of citizen influence on information exposure.

Indirect channels of information influence garner less attention than direct channels, but they are at least as significant for the overall quality of a democratic public. The most common forms of indirect citizen participation are those that change how mainstream media operate. Audience behavior in its many aspects is the clearest of these forms. The traffic of visitors through a site influences the position of stories and the "most read" bar—both of which are important predictors of story exposure for subsequent visitors (Knobloch-Westerwick et al. 2005). Off-site participation can also influence mainstream news by indicating what stories citizens find important. For example, blog attention to a political story can have an agenda setting influence on broader news coverage. These indirect channels of citizen influence do not require individuals to see the involvement of their peers directly, and yet the information experiences of these later audiences are altered—often substantially.

In sum, the internet has been a force for information democratization because of its structure. It is not just the connections among computers (servers) but also the openness of those connections that has spurred change. There is no guarantee that a different structural framework would enable the internet to continue to facilitate citizen involvement with political information.

IMPEDIMENTS TO INFORMATION DEMOCRATIZATION

Information democratization is not a necessary consequence of the internet. The current trend in media evolution certainly appears headed toward meaningful citizen involvement with political information, but there are significant factors working against this evolution. Much of the effort against this involvement comes from the traditional media structure in the form of economic barriers, regulatory reform, and advertising precedence. However, citizens are not being restricted entirely by outside forces. Social cleavages and inertia are also contributing factors in this tension. This section explores the nature and implications of the trends that are currently limiting information democratization.

At this point in the book, the importance of money to media should be evident to the reader. However, whereas other parts of the book (e.g., chapter 2) have more often noted the damage digital media have wrought for traditional-media economics, we must now make nearly the opposite point here. Whereas digital media are damaging the bottom lines of old-media corporations, the financial structures of these corporations pose a more fundamental challenge to the continued openness of the internet. The lingering economic imperatives of the mass media system are working against a higher level of citizen involvement with information.

The clearest evidence of this threat is the continued presence—and dominance—of traditional-media companies on the Web. Microsoft (which only partly counts), Warner, CBS, Viacom, Apple, New York Times Co., Fox, Vevo, and Comcast are all among the top 20 internet properties (comScore 2011b). These companies continue to have success in part because of their name recognition, in part because of the quality of their offline offerings, and in part because of their ability to create, copy, or co-opt internet content. One example of this was nytimes.com's purchase of the popular and successful blog FiveThirtyEight ahead of the 2010 elections. Most of these companies are (understandably) resistant to full citizen involvement with media, because that end typically threatens their business models. As a consequence, the success of these companies online is generally a barrier to expanded information democratization.

The more substantial threat posed by the financial structure of old-media companies is the transfer of the profit motive for content creation. To a contemporary audience, this complaint may sound grounded in socialist ideology, but there is actually no reason to assume that the primary purpose of media content—and particularly news media content—would be profit. Whereas the best news content for a democratic society is likely a story that can detail a significant political event and provide sufficient background and outcomes, this content is not likely to attract the largest audiences. The profit motive can be problematic for quality, and again, this is particularly true for news media (Parenti 1993).

Evidence in support of this argument can be seen in the example of New York Times Digital and Demand Media. The *New York Times* is one of the best sources of political content in the traditional media, but the company ranks 15th in terms of internet news audience (comScore 2011b) and operates about.com—a largely entertainment-filled, ad-oriented site—to help improve the company's profitability. Demand Media is a content mill, a company built on the premise that content only serves to space ads and bait search engines, but it was just one rank behind New

York Times Digital in early 2011 and was arguably worth more. This example may seem to fit awkwardly for the overall point, because Demand Media operates by letting common citizens produce their content. However, the form of citizen involvement with content available through Demand Media is thoroughly diluted by the lack of emphasis on either quality or topics of public concern. The case therefore demonstrates that the profit motive for new(ish) content has corrupted—if not stymied— the further evolution of information democratization.

Regulatory Forces—Network Neutrality

Both corporate ownership and profit motivations play a significant role in how regulation may damage information democratization. We stated earlier that the openness of the internet was a key factor in facilitating citizen involvement with information. To illustrate this point, imagine that there are two internets. One provides for unrestricted access to any content that other people or companies have made publicly available. The other internet restricts access to that content. Which one is more likely to facilitate innovation and citizen involvement with information? The answer is the former.

Unfortunately, this two-internets exercise may not be a hypothetical point for long. The notion that internet service providers (ISPs) should respect the neutral architecture of the internet is nearly a thing of the past. Rather than charge you a certain amount per month for access to the internet, ISPs are arguing that they should be able to charge you the same amount for only a portion of the internet. The disagreement—at least on their end—is whether that portion is measured by amount of content (e.g., download caps), type of content (e.g., limited to video), or by site (e.g., no access to Hulu by Comcast subscribers). This type of data discrimination is not built into the internet, but the Federal Communications Commission and the U.S. Congress seem poised to change that.

Setting aside the arguments about whether these changes should or should not be allowed, we should consider how a new approach to managing the internet might affect information democratization. At the very least, citizen involvement with video-based information would probably be curtailed, because almost every form of proposed ISP involvement with traffic would effectively raise the price of online video. Most extensive challenges to information democratization could arise if ISPs move to restrict broader categories of content (e.g., Facebook for premium accounts only) or change internet access plans from monthly access to metered access (e.g., pay by the megabyte of content accessed), and these are some of the most frequently discussed proposals. Any of these changes in the nature of the internet would likely increase costs and reduce audiences, and these are the two factors that particularly enabled the internet to foster information democratization.

Social Factors

Blaming media corporations and ISPs for threatening citizen involvement with information is legitimate, but they do not merit all of the attention. One of the most significant forces working against any movement—literal or figurative, actually—is inertia. A social change of the magnitude we are discussing here requires a lot of work, both physical and mental. People need to create, read, display, and share content. They must change their news consumption habits and perceptions. This is no small matter.

The reason these physical and mental patterns must change for information democratization to develop further is that most people are currently predisposed toward traditional media. No matter how many times CNN, Fox News, or any other major outlet gets a story wrong, audiences will continue to turn to those providers. If a small-time blogger reports a story incorrectly, most of us would probably stop reading—or at least trusting—that writer's content. Even the citizen content producers themselves are far more likely to link to mainstream sources than to other citizen sources (Project for Excellence in Journalism 2010b). Inertia is easier—and the status quo may seem reasonable—but it appears that information democratization will have a ceiling until social norms about journalism change.

CONCLUSIONS

Democracy, by definition, relies on a public that bears at least partial, direct responsibility for the selection and operation of government. This would seem to suggest that the public should have some political knowledge. The realities of elite control and mass-media systems in the 19th and 20th centuries made information difficult to acquire, and the content that was accessible was often released to the public by the very people—or at least types of people—who were involved with the political process. The inefficiencies and potential for abuses of this system are evident.

Information democratization is defined here as the increasing involvement of private citizens in the creation, distribution, exhibition, and curation of civically relevant information. In other words, common individuals are more often the people who are writing stories, sharing articles, displaying content, or archiving resources. Empowering citizens leads to a more equitable information environment than anything that existed during the mass media era. That system featured concentrated audiences whose members were mostly uninvolved recipients of messages generated by socioeconomic elites. The new reality provides many different types of content to a comparatively active audience.

This is not to say that society necessarily will be better. Much of the public could continue to ignore political content, and opportunities to have a regular, widespread voice could remain relatively rare. More significantly, economic, regulatory, and social forces may all work to undermine even the qualified successes of information democratization as it currently stands.

The internet provides audiences with a great deal of control. Information democratization is ultimately significant for understanding online news, because it defines a process by which that control is turned not just into citizen activity—which is also more or less true of fragmentation—but also into a form of activity that actively contributes to democratic society. However, because fragmentation, polarization, and democratization all seem to operate hand-in-hand, the ultimate gain or loss for society is actually rather difficult to evaluate objectively.

CHAPTER 9

Conclusion: Online News and Public Affairs

P eople create the news. That has always been the case, of course. Before the birth of formal media organizations, the human hand was clearly visible. News and other information spread from person to person, moving through populations with alacrity, if not always accuracy. The institutionalization of news in media organizations in the 19th and 20th centuries hid that hand within layers of professionalization, hierarchy, and technology. News on the internet is returning the clear face of individual creation to some of the news while it adds a layer of mechanization to the rest. The result is a novel mix of news and information about public affairs, one that gives everyday individuals a stronger hand in the creation of the news. It also gives them more opportunities to choose the news they prefer and even to avoid it altogether. It is that mix of opportunities that embodies the seeming contradictions of online news today.

Our assessment of the online news environment and audience has identified a number of forces acting on the creation and consumption of the news. Likewise, we have discussed how the dynamics of news technologies and audiences may be affecting people and social systems. Ultimately, the technology of the news may be facilitating change in the nature of citizens and politics in democratic systems. In this chapter, we try to sort through apparent contradictions and balancing forces to build some predictions and questions about how the online news environment will evolve and how it will interact with other social institutions and phenomena.

First, we review some of the larger patterns we discussed above. We highlight how the news business operates online and how internet audiences influence, create, and consume the news. This review sets the stage for a discussion of a core set of seeming contradictions and conflicts in how online news operates. These conflicts are tied to some of the most important potential consequences of the evolution of news on the internet. We finish with a consideration of where the news is going. We look at some ways in which news may develop online and offline and consider how these developments will interact with one another.

PEOPLE CREATING AND USING ONLINE NEWS

Recall that technologies such as the internet very rarely cause social, political, and economic change. Most often, they allow people and institutions to make changes that they already desired, or they open opportunities for new designs and developments to occur. We have tried to keep people at the center of our discussion of online news. In this summary and review of the ways in which internet technology, people, and news messages interact, we try to focus on how human activities and desires have shaped the news system and vice versa.

News-audience Activity

It seems rather obvious at times, but we still need to remark that the news is a product of human activity. Creating news messages is an active process. News professionals very intentionally gather, produce, and disseminate information. In the 20th-century model of news media—one built on newspapers, film newsreels, radio, and television—news creation largely ended there. But that is no longer the entire story.

Communication researchers have acknowledged for some time that audiences are active, too. They choose among news outlets and stories, so they influence news messages and organizations through their consumption (and its connection to ratings, subscriptions numbers, etc.). Internet news audiences have grown dramatically since news went online after 1993. This growth has affected the size and nature of audiences for the traditional news media, but the exact relationship between online and offline news is not entirely hydraulic. Most people use both online and offline news, others use one or the other, and some use neither.

Audience activity is also seen in how people bring their individual goals, feelings, and cognitions to their news consumption. People actively interpret the news. Beliefs, attitudes, and behaviors that emerge from news consumption are joint products of the news messages and the audience's interpretations. Thus, today, as in the last century, audiences play a role in their own interpretations of the news.

Finally, online audiences are active in a way that we did not see with 20th-century news media. Internet audiences are feeding content into the news (both through the news produced by traditional press organizations and via blogs, video file sharing, and other means). Thus, news audiences seem particularly active. They create content, influence the behavior of others online, and translate the content of news messages through their preferences and other predispositions.

Transition from Offline to Online Presentation of News Content

A sizable portion of the news that appears on the internet originates with organizations that create content in the traditional media. Major originators such as the Associated Press, the *New York Times*, and CNN create news stories that can appear online and in other media. The late 1990s and early 2000s saw many of the traditional news organizations limiting their online news to what they had created for their offline outlets. The subsequent years have seen more original-content creation and presentation for the internet and mobile technologies. The major media are taking advantage of the capacity of the internet for information storage and for audience interaction with journalists and the news.

Perhaps more important is that the internet hosts a number of news outlets that lack an offline component. These internet-only outlets are often more focused than the major outlets. They carry news about a particular geography or topic, and they are often free of the traditions—such as the objective-news form—of the offline news media. Ultimately, the distinction between online and offline outlets will disappear as the media evolve. As the technologies of the various media merge, the characteristics of the news industry, as a whole, will outweigh issues particular to any one medium.

As the content of the news online develops, so does the public agenda that sites present. One of the most powerful social and political functions of 20th-century news was the projection of a relatively uniform agenda of issues facing a nation or other entity. This gave the news media significant political power and often resulted in substantial public uniformity of perception. Some observers of the online news environment suggest that news on the internet is changing the political functions of the press. They claim that the volume and diversity of news online and the control that the technology provides the audience member reduce the uniformity of the agenda that people receive. There is some empirical evidence to support this claim, but a full unraveling of the agenda setting function of the news media will take time. It might still be in development.

Audiences Create the News Online

Among the most important developments in the meaning and future of news in this century has been the widespread growth of audience interaction with the news. From the beginning of news service on the internet, some outlets have tried to build audiences through two-way communication systems. In this century, the interaction of people with the news has moved from the original community forums to systems of citizen origination of content. One step in this direction of origination is the access that contemporary audiences have to the inner workings of journalism. Journalist blogs and behind-the-scenes views of the news online (e.g., via the provision of raw video footage or reporting notes online) allow people to see how the news is constructed.

The more consequential development is the capacity that everyday internet users have for creating their own content online. Blogs are perhaps the most visible of the online systems that encourage citizen involvement in the news. Individuals, small organizations, nonprofits, and others who had been outside the traditional elite-originated news stream have substantial power to control the flow of information in contemporary societies.

The development of online news provision and audience interactivity has put online news in something of a leadership position for the industry. The online format provides a space for journalists to work with novel news formats and structures, and the lessons that news organizations learn about their audiences can influence the provision of news offline.

News-site Specialization and Segmentation

In some ways, contemporary development of news technologies and systems online are predictable extensions of how media seem to evolve naturally. The media that came before the internet had, at one point, focused their efforts on mass audiences. Most newspapers, radio stations, and television networks provided content intended to attract large, heterogeneous audiences. What is more, economic and technological boundaries around these media often limited the number of options available to audiences, effectively forcing some members of the audience to consume general-interest fare. These media changed, however, as outside pressures from other media encouraged attention to more focused, homogeneous audiences. Today, the offline news business is increasingly dominated by more specialized content.

The internet essentially skipped the mass audience phase of media evolution. Online news providers are focused on specialized audiences via two routes. First, the technologies of the internet allow news outlets to offer their audiences very personalized experiences with the news. People can customize news sites, from the outlets of major news providers to news aggregators, to provide news and opinion on preselected topics. As a result, people can sample from a relatively narrow set of topics online if they wish.

News sites can also encourage audience segmentation in their content provision. That is, some news sites will see the efficiencies of news production and provision that are found in attracting only a select group of people. By tailoring their content to specific segments of the audiences, sites can package audiences for advertisers. Sharing characteristics such as age, sex, political predispositions, and income, these homogeneous audiences may be attractive to specific advertisers. Part of such a segmentation strategy by online news providers is the diversification of the overall news diet. That is, the provision of novel kinds of news—infotainment is one such type—under the banner of news can allow news providers to divide audiences further into distinct segments.

Research on the development of site segmentation shows some limited trends in this direction. Too little research examines how specific news sites differ in their news content, but there are signs that sites are specializing. One development that followed the collapse of print newspapers in 2008 and 2009 was the creation of a number of news sites that focused on the local news for specific geographical areas. Ongoing research will assess whether news site specialization becomes a widespread phenomenon.

Audience Selectivity and News Specialization

To observe that some sites are specializing their content with the hope of attracting a homogeneous audience begs the question of whether news audiences will take the proffered bait. Online news segmentation is facilitated by audiences whose members are willing to specialize their news consumption around specific topics and perspectives. The evidence gathered thus far tends to suggest that people can be quite selective with the news. Of course, some news exposure happens accidentally, through well-developed habit, or as a by-product of other media activity. Nonetheless, research results point to a number of ways in which people select news online.

Audience selection of the news online is typically a multistep process. People first must choose whether to consume news at all. Increasingly, the wide variety of content online provides many options beyond the news. In such an environment, some people appear willing to forgo the news entirely. If audiences do opt for news content, they have many types of information from which to choose. They can find traditional news assembled and packaged in much the same way as it was throughout the 20th century, news that reflects entertainment-based values, and news and information initiated by other members of the audience. Similarly, they must select from sites that carry specific topics and news formats and those that carry a range of topics and a wide variety of information.

Selective exposure to the news also occurs within sites at the level of story topic. Much as one might expect, people will follow story-importance cues—such as story prominence, story length, and visual graphics and photographs—in their decisions to consume news. In this way, online users behave as news audiences have done for some time. There is also mounting evidence that people use the apparent topics of news stories as guides. Political partisanship, ideology, and race are some of the factors that can influence what topics people select.

Nonetheless, the full extent of audience selectivity online is not yet entirely clear. Some research has suggested that people encounter a fair amount of news incidentally, as a by-product of some other activity. Intentional news audiences appear to contain people who focus their news consumption on a small number of topics, others who sample very broadly from the news, and still others who choose a mixture of both over time. In sum, not everyone is highly selective and intensely focused. The overall news audience is likely to be rather heterogeneous in its orientation to the news. What remains to be seen is whether news audiences exhibit more selectivity as they mature within the internet environment. It might be that selectivity is a learned habit that takes time to develop. Right now, it may have been acquired by only the steadiest and most fully immersed internet audiences. If so, increasing reliance on the internet in developed countries might be accompanied by strengthened patterns of selectivity.

Learning from the News

Under most circumstances, we think that news consumption is consequential largely because people learn from the news. That is, attending to the news affects what people know about public affairs. The integration of the internet into the media that people can consume could change preexisting patterns of how people learn about the political world. So, naturally, we wonder what people learn when they use the internet.

There is ample evidence that people are able to acquire information from the news that appears online. Studies of manipulated and naturally occurring news flows suggest that people can learn from the news. In many ways, learning from the news online largely mirrors what happens offline. Some studies have shown that audience control of news selection online determines what stories they encounter. Obviously, that affects what people learn. Studies that directly compare learning from news online with other media find some differences, but few effects of medium difference are large.

The presence of hyperlinks in news stories online can help audiences navigate between and within news stories. Thus, they are a core element of audience interaction with news sites. There is some evidence, though, that the presence of too many links can create a burdensome cognitive load on audiences. The load can overwhelm audiences, potentially interfering with their mental processing of the information they encounter. Perhaps more important is that some research has suggested that hyperlinks among concepts in the news can suggest ways that concepts are connected with one another. As a result, online audiences might develop more intricate mental models of issues and events in news than other audiences might.

If people can acquire different information, and perhaps even more of it, from the internet than from other media, online audiences may experience advantages that separate them from people who do not have access to the internet. The presence of a digital divide in a population might result in gaps between what different segments of a society know about public affairs. Such knowledge gaps can affect how people think, feel, and behave with respect to the political system. These gaps could serve to reinforce preexisting social and economic inequalities.

Fragmentation of Knowledge in the Online Environment

Unification and division are major, inherent themes in any discussion of the social and political role of the internet. Within the context of the news, observers have suggested that the internet may serve to raise the level of information that citizens have about their societies. Certainly, the diversity of views and sources that pervades the online environment supports that conclusion. Information and source diversity have a possible downside, though. Some observers raise the possibility that the internet might fragment knowledge, affecting the depth and uniformity of information holding in societies. This could affect the character of citizenship.

As we have tried to emphasize in this book, effects that derive from the diffusion of the internet in democratic societies are a joint outcome of what internet technologies provide, what audiences want, and what media elites do. None of these factors acts fully alone. If people take advantage of what the internet offers in terms of news selection and specialization, they might focus their news gathering on some topics to the exclusion of others. Such focused news gathering might fragment people across the news landscape. Few people will be exposed to a cross section of events and issues in the news. A fragmented populace is one in which little information is widely shared, overall levels of political knowledge are relatively low, and there is relatively little public agreement on a common political agenda. If, as we suggest in the introduction to this book, citizens benefit from information about public affairs, fragmentation could damage the quality of democracy.

Researchers have uncovered ample evidence that people can be quite selective online. Many people seem willing to focus on specific outlets and topics. What is more, when faced with an array of content options online, some members of news audiences seem perfectly willing to make choices, favoring some news content over others. Nonetheless, the research record has not produced evidence of pervasive knowledge and agenda fragmentation effects of this audience selectivity. It might be that in practice, the number of highly selective, focused members of the audience is still rather small. It might also be that citizens have many information sources beyond the internet, and sources tend to disseminate information widely. Clearly, we need more research in this area.

Knowledge and Ideological Polarization

Audiences seem unlikely to choose news randomly. Rather, they follow their interests, and they develop routines for online behavior that repeatedly bring them to specific sites and content areas. To the extent that their news preferences are born out of interests and group memberships that others in a society share, online news consumption can facilitate the development of segments in society—distinct in their characteristics—that share specific knowledge, beliefs, and attitudes. The result could be a polarized society, with relatively deep cleavages between segments.

The evidence amassed thus far suggests that many people engage in systematically selective exposure to the news. News audiences for ideologically driven news are relatively distinct from one another. Very clearly, the American audience for news with a liberal inflection is largely made up of Democrats; likewise, the audience for news with a conservative cast is largely Republican. Similarly, survey research reveals that a good many people adopt technologies (such as Twitter feeds and email lists) that direct news to them from specific sources with specific agendas. Thus, some news consumption patterns suggest the possibility of polarization.

There is some evidence, though not a lot, that public beliefs and attitudes are becoming polarized. People appear to follow their partisan political interests a bit more extensively when they use technologies that permit substantial specialization. What is more, one tentative look at the attitudes of online news audiences showed an association with news specialization. When people relied on customized news sources, they exhibited more ideologically distinct opinions. Thus, there is some evidence of polarization in American news audiences. It is not overwhelming, though.

Information Democratization

Whether we're speaking of audiences on the right, on the left, or in any other location on the political spectrum, people are united in the sense that they are offering unprecedented contributions to society's political discussion. Knowledge has historically been primarily under the jurisdiction of socioeconomic elites, and the expense of mass media production afforded common citizens few legitimate chances to be heard. Digital media have facilitated a form of information democratization, or a transition toward public involvement with political knowledge. Citizens can use their computers and other devices to write news, archive facts, and publicize content as never before.

Some people will be tempted to lump the idea of information democratization with earlier thinking that the internet would bring about a new world order, but this is not exactly the claim we are making. The effects of citizen journalism and other involvement with content are difficult to measure, and it is unclear whether the difficulty arises from the challenges of internet research or from the lack of a measurable phenomenon. On the one hand, citizen content can be measured by the hundreds of millions of Facebook pages, the tens of millions of blogs, the thousands of Wikipedia pages, or the hundreds of comments on hot-button news stories. On the other hand, it is highly unlikely that more than a small fraction of these items will ever rise to the level of a measurable media influence. Why, then, do we care about citizens being able to directly handle political media?

The easy answer is that even a small percentage of millions is likely to be meaningful, but we can aim higher than that. The best way to answer this question is to look at an influential study published more than 50 years ago (Katz 1957). The study suggested that the media did not have a measurable direct effect on politics, because most people experienced mediated messages through a friend or a family member who was one of a small group of directly affected individuals. This study on the indirect "two-step flow of communication" was a key contributor to several decades of scholars thinking that the media barely mattered to society at all.

With the internet as it currently stands, that line between direct and indirect media effect is irrevocably blurred in a number of ways. One's friends might now have blogs and therefore be part of the media themselves. Instead of hearing about the news from a friend, one may now get a link directly to the news from a friend. A person who becomes interested in the news is not stuck researching microfiche in a library basement, because he or she can now search online archives or read a few Wikipedia entries. The answer to the question, then, is that information democratization does not simply mean that citizens are more involved with political knowledge than in the past; it means that we have to reconsider many aspects of politics, information, news, media, and communication. There may not be a new world order—media corporations and political elites will likely always garner the lion's share of the audience—but important components of mass society will change (and have changed already).

CONTRADICTIONS AND POSSIBILITIES

We have said that the internet is all media together and at once. The phrase suggests the potential for the internet to change quite a bit about how media and audiences interact. At the same time, it points to the fact that the internet often carries content and perpetuates interaction patterns that characterize the older media. If that is so, how new is the medium? This is an example of the contradictions that seem unusually common regarding the internet. Other media have potentially conflicting effects and social roles, but the size, speed, and ubiquity of the internet seem to render its issues and questions larger than those raised by other media. In this section, we discuss some of the contradictions inherent in news delivery and consumption on the internet. We try to offer some resolutions to the contradictions, when possible. We hope, in the process, to highlight some of the things about online news that make it a challenging and exciting area of study and engagement.

Proliferation and Exclusion

The technologies of the internet simultaneously facilitate a proliferation of content options and the narrowing of content selection by audiences. There is perhaps more irony than contradiction in this situation. We have described how the amount of news content has increased with the growth of the internet. The major news sites that dominated online news in the late 1990s (e.g., CNN, MSNBC, or ABC News) continue to do so and have been joined by blogs, news aggregators, content mills, and other online-centric news providers. At the same time, the internet offers contemporary audiences a number of ways to limit and control their news exposure. Customized news sites, email news subscriptions, and other technologies allow people to avoid news, if they wish, more effectively than ever before. So, at a time when the marketplace of ideas has approached an almost ideal level of information inclusion, people are perhaps uniquely able to sidestep and limit their exposure to that marketplace.

On further reflection, there is less contradiction in this situation than meets the eye. User control is at the heart of both content proliferation and tightened focus. Internet users exert a level of control over the flow of information online that puts almost everyone in the position of adding to an abundance of content. This is at the heart of information democratization. At the same time, sites on the internet allow people to control their online experiences. Site-customization options and other filters provide people with tools to manage the excess of information.

The apparent contradiction of abundance and control raises an interesting question about the concept of diminishing returns. In the traditional meaning of the term, a quantity of something new in a relationship has an effect related to the quantity of what had been present. In the realm of news, we could say, for example, that 10 news stories on a page help readers learn a certain set of facts. We may assume that more of that thing would result in a proportionally larger effect. More news stories on a page means that news readers learn proportionally more facts. Larger quantities do not always have that effect, though. More of something can diminish the impact of any one thing. A good example of this was observed in American households that adopted cable television (Heeter and Greenberg 1985). When households changed from five channels to 15, for example, people would increase the number of channels that they watched. But when a system would add many more channels to an already sizable number, people would not add many more channels to their active repertoire. Ultimately, each new bundle of channels added fewer channels to households' actual consumption.

In the context of online news, we might be tempted to assume that the excess of content would follow a pattern of diminishing returns. But what if it went beyond diminishing? What if adding more news online resulted in negative returns? Perhaps when people had a limited number of news options, they were willing to wade through a broad set of news topics in search of content. But, when faced with an excess of content, people might opt for streamlined information-management solutions at a greater rate. This was the hope of content mills, which attempted to provide "news" that would feature prominently in search results. A more regular concern in the fragmentation literature is that users will automate their news searches by employing customization features. In so doing, people would dramatically limit the breadth of news that they might encounter, perhaps below what they might have seen with a more constrained media system. People might react to a proliferation of options by limiting the number of choices they are forced to make. In the end, some people in a high-choice environment might opt to stop making choices entirely. This is a pattern of negative returns that could bode ill for political systems predicated on broad citizen access to information.

Knowledge Fragmentation and Depth

In chapter 7, we described how the dispersion of news audiences across a wide range of news sources might reduce the level of public exposure to individual items of political information. Some people may come to know more about specific issues and events, but the number of people in a population with shared knowledge about specific information will shrink. This fragmentation of knowledge is widely predicted to be harmful to the quality of democracy (e.g., Katz 1996). That prediction is based on the assumption that citizens need to acquire information so they can make well-reasoned decisions about issues and people (Berelson 1952). What is more, in a fragmented populace, there is relatively little agreement about the issues and problems that require collective or government action. When they disagree about fundamental social and political conditions, people are less likely to agree on political leaders and policies (Sunstein 2001). In short, fragmentation is an undesirable state of affairs for a democracy, according to this perspective.

Despite this, there are some reasons to be a little sanguine about the state of affairs in online news. Whereas fragmentation and polarization facilitated by the internet might inhibit large-scale awareness and agreement about specific political issues, the technologies of online news might have very positive effects on how individual people learn about politics.

One basis for that claim can be found in the concept of issue publics (Converse 1964). An enduring truism in public-opinion research is that the American population is made up of people who have little interest in most political issues and topics. Amid this seeming sea of indifference are islands of people with an intense interest in and knowledge of individual topics. Each of these pockets is an issue public. They likely follow news reports about their focal issue and develop a substantial store of information about it. Kim (2007) has shown that issue publics use specialized news sources online to gather information relevant to their issue. For example, people with an interest in abortion regulation might visit websites of political groups active in abortion policy or search news sites for information about it. The internet appears to be a near-ideal environment for members of issue publics to develop their knowledge about an issue or topic. From a pluralist perspective on politics, the action of issue publics and other groups might adequately represent the diverse interests in a population.

We might also think about learning about politics in terms of the development of audience members' knowledge structures. As noted in chapter 6, hyperlinked news stories can suggest to audiences the presence of specific connections among concepts and issues. People appear to process and store information in this linked fashion. As a result, the knowledge structures they develop about issues in online news stories appear to be particularly dense (Eveland, Marton, and Seo 2004). These dense structures should help them process new information about topics, thereby improving the efficiency and breadth of their overall body of knowledge.

Thus, on an atomistic level, the provision and consumption of online news look like a boon to individual citizens. They have an opportunity to learn about a broader rage of topics than they might find in other media, and the excess of information about most political topics means that interested people can acquire substantial depth in individual topics. Moreover, the structure of some online news presentations might help people develop more useful bodies of knowledge about the subjects they encounter.

Technological Convergence and Agenda Fragmentation

Another seeming contradiction is the development of audience fragmentation via a technology that brings disparate forms and content—and, therefore, audiences—into one place. Technology scholars have been suggesting that media are converging into a shared platform (e.g., Negroponte 1995). This convergence process promises to unite content from previously distinct technologies into a unified format—the internet. A good example of this is the movement of video content online. Over the span of a few short years in the 21st century, entertainment-television content has moved from its exclusive location on broadcast or cable to the internet. There it joins text that migrated from newspapers and magazines and audio content from the radio industry. This convergence on the internet has not yet eliminated the market for the other media, but it has brought multiple media formats into a shared environment. It has given site providers and audiences the chance to combine content from previously different media in unique ways.

On its surface, convergence sounds like a unifying force, both a process and an outcome that promises to bring distinct ideas and people into a common arena of interaction. There is some reality to that promise, of course. We noted in chapter 4 that a number of websites attract substantial portions of the internet audience. The sites that reach these broad audiences are often the ones that combine a number of content areas into one place. For example, Google and Yahoo!—two of the most popular sites in America (Nielsenwire 2010)—feature search engines and a broad range of news and entertainment content. The growing audience penetration of these sites (e.g., Google is used by more than 80 percent of American internet users in a typical month; Nielsenwire 2010) suggests that sites that can be one-stop convergence points can attract large heterogeneous audiences.

We should not overstate the unifying potential of sites such as Google and Facebook (another of the most popular sites in America; Nielsenwire 2010). The 10 most popular sites may account for quite a bit of traffic, but the average American visits more than 50 sites in a typical month (Nielsenwire 2010). There is plenty of online activity beyond the use of general-content sites. That other activity can easily consist of the consumption of highly idiosyncratic diets of news and entertainment. Thus, a fully converged media environment can easily be a highly fragmented one.

THE FUTURE OF THE NEWS

Some early observers of networked computer technology regarded the internet's potential for improving democratic discourse and participation with something approaching awe and wonder (e.g., Corrado 1996). Many of the assumptions supporting the predictions that they made were reasonable then and are reasonable now. Media content and audiences are converging in one place. The media industries appear to be in the midst of a transition from a mass to a specialized model of communication. Disruptions accompanying this transition and the worldwide economic downturn that started in 2007 have hit the news business with particular force. Some newspapers have gone into bankruptcy, and others have dropped some or all of their print operations. In all sectors of the news business, writing and editorial staffs have been reduced. These developments have some wondering about the future of the news. We offer here some comments on what seem to be likely or plausible developments in the industry. We focus first on the long-term prospects of news outlets that predate the internet. We then turn to a discussion of the future of the online news business.

Old Media and the Future

The economic problems facing old-media outlets stem largely from a loss of advertising revenue. Some advertisers scaled back all of their advertising during the recession of 2007 to 2009, and some made particularly significant cuts in newspaper advertising budgets. The online media picked up some advertising expenditures during this period, largely in niche markets. Whereas the transition of advertising dollars to niche outlets online may be a plus for people seeking analysis-based news on particular topics, it is not an encouraging sign for the overall news environment. The fact that advertisements have not only decreased for traditional sources but have also moved to new venues suggests that the plight of old media is likely to be long-term. The problematic aspect of this is that blogs and similar niche outlets are typically not generating original reporting. If the traditional media fall away and nothing steps in to fill the function of generating the news, then the consequences are likely to be severe across the news spectrum. The necessary solution for all parties is a paradigm shift for American news that will likely alter the responsibility of story production and include at least one new business model for news outlets. This is an imposing proposition, but so is the problem. Although it is beyond the scope or purpose of this chapter to explore fully all plausible business models, a few options are worth noting as they relate to news development.

Something must fill the void created as traditional news media decrease their reporting. One possibility is that the importance of wire services (companies that create and distribute freelance news articles) will increase dramatically. This is already occurring to some extent, as we have noted, as papers have become increasingly reliant on the Associated Press (AP), Reuters, and syndication services. The main strike against this potential solution is that as demand for such services increases, so should the price. Indeed, smaller newspapers in the United States are already fighting with the AP over prices and publication policies (Perez-Pena 2008). Reuters and Bloomberg, traditionally smaller wires, may have another solution: becoming news services in their own right. Whereas the traditional wire model has always been to provide content to news outlets—and therefore only indirectly to the reader—these two organizations have been hiring high-profile writers and moving toward providing news more directly to consumers. Whether a direct or an indirect model is chosen, it seems likely that a strengthened wire service could meet much of the reporting shortage.

A second option would be government support of news creation. This could entail any number of solutions, although the most mentioned are bailout, tax breaks, and public news (McChesney and Nichols 2010). Many Americans—including journalists—seem uncomfortable with such solutions, because it is difficult to imagine a state-supported information system devoid of bias. This is a legitimate concern but perhaps overblown. The tax-break proposal would actually give news organizations the same tax status as churches, meaning that they could avoid taxes in exchange for avoiding direct political endorsements. Furthermore, other countries, such as England, have a well-developed public-broadcasting system with excellent news services. The American commitment to public broadcasting has always been weak, as PBS traditionally receives little governmental support and is nonetheless regularly under partisan attack (McChesney 2008). We may see some sort of government support for news organizations in the near future, but it seems unlikely that this would be on a sufficient scale truly to rescue the reporting provided by traditional media.

A third solution would be for traditional outlets, many of which are owned by larger corporations (see www.cjr.org/resources) to risk operating at a loss in the pursuit of a product that is of high quality and good for the public. This option may seem radical—increase costs in the face of declining revenue—but might be the key to success for the traditional news media. None of the other likely solutions to this problem will preserve interest in the traditional media brands. The cost-cutting options so far employed by media organizations have not rescued those companies from their economic plight. Perhaps the key to solvency for old media is to re-create a high-quality product that audiences may find worth reading or watching.

The fourth and final potential solution we will discuss is increasing the emphasis on citizen journalism. Organizations such as New Voices and J-Lab view this phenomenon (Witt 2004) as a capable (and solvent) alternative to mainstream sources. Under this paradigm, the people are responsible for reporting on events in their locality. Individual stories might not be highly polished, but the range of stories covered could be broader than when the news collection is conducted by companies. Critics concerned about the bias of such reporting should consider that all modes of journalism contain some sort of bias (Bennett 2009), that partisan reporting appears to be on the rise in traditional media (Project for Excellence in Journalism 2007), and that Americans used to—and much of the world still does—rely on advocacy journalism (Hamilton 2004). Admittedly, the transition from professional to citizen journalism would be quite a change for our conceptualization of news production, but it might be the best way to harness the strengths of the new media environment.

The Future of News Online

The internet will certainly continue to drive change in news across the board, but the face of online news itself is far from settled. Many years into the popular availability of the internet, two fundamental aspects of online news remain open questions: how online audiences will consume political news and how online news will become financially viable. Answering these questions is imperative in order for online news to play a significant, lasting role in society.

Determining how audiences will consume the news really requires dealing with several prerequisite issues. One of these is where news will show up next. Google News, Facebook, and Twitter are all services that (1) very rapidly became popular channels for news, (2) changed at least one core aspect of news consumption (e.g., customization, source, speed), and (3) will quickly become outdated. Online news first reached audiences through desktop computers, then laptops, and now mobile phones and tablets.

This brings us to a second concern, which is how audiences will respond to changes in the news environment. Twitter—which can offer instant news, mobile access, and content customization—may seem like a perfect vehicle for online news, but only a fraction of the public will ever really use this service, and only another fraction of those people will use Twitter for news. The same can be said for mobile devices or Second Life (Reuters paid to have a "building" with this service) or whatever the "next thing" in digital content will be. It is not enough to see what forms online news might take, largely because the history of media choice suggests that having more choices actually leads to a smaller overall news audience (Prior 2007). Observers need to decipher which forms of news might be actually utilized by significant audiences.

Addressing the question of how online news will become financially viable is literally a million-dollar task. One obvious choice is charging for content through paywalls (systems that require people to pay for access to news stories). These were relatively popular in the 1990s, but they gave way to ad-based models, and now the news industry is turning to them again. Of course, the reason news companies are vacillating on this point is that no solution has yet provided a level of revenue that can sustain a quality news product online. The challenge that confronts news producers is that their content is worth vastly different amounts to different audiences. Several examples illustrate the challenge.

Imagine that Juan, a frequent consumer of online news, has preferred national (e.g., the *New York Times*), local (e.g., the *News-Gazette*), and specialty (e.g., It's All Politics and Bloomberg News) news sources and then also reads articles from other sources when he comes across an interesting link. It is highly unlikely that he would be willing to pay for all of these sources—and this is particularly true of the circumstantial sources. If each of these sites introduces a blanket paywall, then the two or three sources that make the cut will earn some revenue. The other sources will not only lose out on the subscription fee, but they also will lose out on ad revenue.

This calculus becomes even rougher for online news providers when considering audiences who are from higher socioeconomic classes and already have established offline consumption patterns. A study of 2006 Pew internet data suggests that these audiences are particularly unlikely to use—let alone purchase—online news content (Chyi and Yang 2009). These results do predate much of the development in smartphones, e-readers, and tablets, but it is still easy to see how this may be the case.

Imagine that Lisa, a fairly wealthy white-collar worker, watches CNBC while getting ready for work, reads the *Wall Street Journal* while drinking a morning coffee, listens to talk radio during her commute, and browses a few online financial news sources (Bloomberg News and the business section of the *New York Times*) while at work. The online news is clearly functioning as a supplement to a broader news habit. If any one of those sources puts up a paywall, then she seems particularly likely just to switch to a different, open outlet.

The financial challenge to news producers is evident in each of these examples, but see what happens if we put them together. The *New York Times* might make the cut for Juan, but it has now lost the ad revenue for Lisa. Whether the decision to use a blanket paywall makes sense depends on whether Juan's subscription makes the company enough money to offset the lost ad revenue from Lisa (and all of the other people like her). Actually, this is the simplistic version of the calculation that a company must make. In reality, if it is true that wealthier people have a particularly low tolerance for paying for online content, then losing Lisa will not only cost the company in terms of ad revenue. The company will also have a smaller, less affluent audience, which means that future ads will actually be worth less. Meanwhile, if Bloomberg News applied a paywall in our examples, then both people would be likely to switch to other sites. That calculation is much easier.

The solution to this problem is somewhat obvious: Online news producers will have to develop methods of implementing multiple business models simultaneously. For example, heavy users, who are likely to subscribe, will be asked to pay. Casual users will be forced to see ads (or fill out surveys; data are valuable). Audience members who forward content to a specified number of friends will be able to bypass a site's paywall. Users entering a site from a content partner will get free access to that article only. Sports articles will always cost something—except for premium subscribers.

All of these options could be implemented for one site, and that company would be doing an excellent job of maximizing revenue. At least, this would be true if—and this is a big *if*—the simultaneous options could be implemented effectively from a technological and public-relations standpoint. Only time will tell whether this type of solution is viable. Either way, content providers will have to find some means of financial stability. If they do not, then the future of online news content (and possibly all news content) will be in serious jeopardy.

CONCLUSIONS

For the average visitor to news websites, the internet is much the same from day to day. This veneer of continuity belies the very rapid change roiling the news business in the 21st century. Big changes are afoot, to be sure. The power of the traditional news providers is weakening. A proliferation of news sources has undermined the easy supremacy enjoyed by print and broadcast news through much of the 20th century. Citizen-driven news, entertainment-oriented news, and just plain entertainment all are vying with traditional news product for audience attention.

The upshot of this competition and change in the news business is a developing tension between the provision of news and the quality of democratic participation. By some standards—fragmentation and polarization are prominent examples—changes in the landscape of information mean that citizens will be ill prepared to debate and act on the important issues facing a nation. By other standards—for example, the diversity of content and contributors—online news presents a vibrant and rich set of resources for active and involved citizenship. Both of these standards are appropriately applied to the online news environment.

Running through predictions of change, utopian and dystopian, should also be a measure of caution and even disinterest. Democracies have proven to be resilient in the face of changes in the relationship between information and citizenship. The intermediaries between government and the governed may change, but many of the core institutions and social practices that underlie democratic systems appear resistant to change. As usual, whether their resilience is good or bad depends on one's perspective. And time.

NOTES

CHAPTER 3

1. *HTML*, the basic language of websites, stands for "hypertext markup language."

CHAPTER 4

1. The sample of internet users was recruited and maintained by Nielsen//NetRatings (now part of the Nielsen Company). In 2000, the company had recruited more than 50,000 people to participate in the panel and claimed that it represented American at-home and at-work internet users. The company recorded the uniform resource locator (URL) address for every page viewed by a member of the panel. In response to author request, the company provided the URL for view pages of a select set of news sites in March and May 2000. With each URL was included basic demographic information about the site visitor and the date and time of the page view.

CHAPTER 5

1. Data for this study were taken from the Pew Research Center's Biennial Media Consumption Surveys from 2002, 2004, and 2006. The dependent variable in each analysis was whether the respondent voted in the preceding presidential election. The independent variables of interest were cable access, internet access (for both, 1 = access, 0 = no access), and relative preference for societal news. This last variable is related to the relative entertainment-preference measure introduced by Prior (2007), which essentially measures entertainment-media consumption as a ratio of overall media consumption. This study modified that concept by measuring users' attention to crime, community, and health news (4 = very closely, 3 = somewhat closely, 2 = not very closely, 1 = not at all closely) as a ratio of their attention to these categories plus political figures, international affairs, and local government. Controls included in the analysis were news exposure, political interest, and a thorough set of demographics. The statistical analysis was conducted with a binary logistic regression model.
2. A binary logistic regression model was estimated with source number as the dependent variable (1 = "get news from many different sources," 0 = "mostly rely on a few sources"). The model included control variables for respondent age, sex, education level, and frequency of news exposure with television, newspaper, and radio (these were measured in terms of exposure on the day before the survey interview, with responses coded 4 = 1 hour or more of use, 3 = 30–59 minutes, 2 = 15–29 minutes, 1 = less than 15 minutes, and 0 = no use). The two variables of interest in the analysis are questions about the internet. The first asked whether and how often the respondents got news online (5 = "yes, every day," 4 = "yes, 3–5 days per week," 3 = "yes, 1–2 days per week," 2 = "yes, once every few weeks," 1 = "yes, less often," and 0 = "no, never"). The other question asked

which medium people used most over the course of an average weekday to obtain news (1 = internet, 0 = other; 18 percent of the sample reported using primarily the internet for news).

3. Nielsen//NetRatings provided the URL for each page visited on 13 selected national and local news sites (ABC News, CNN, *New York Times*, *USA Today*, *Chicago Sun-Times*, *Dallas News*, *Detroit News*, *Louisville Courier-Journal*, *Oregonian*, *San Diego Union-Tribune*, *San Jose Mercury-News*, BBC, Nando Net). These sites covered national and local news and included outlets of mainstream television and newspaper organizations. They were selected for analysis on the basis of their audience size and geographical diversity and how well their URLs facilitated topic identification.

4. The URLs identified the general topic for each news story. A classification of the URLs grouped them into site home-page views and views of one of 21 major news topics.

CHAPTER 7

1. We offer this variable with some hesitation. We recognize that the use of some media that we call general includes some specialized exposure (e.g., watching CNBC on cable television), whereas the use of some customizable services can be rather general (e.g., receiving email updates from the *New York Times* national news feed). Nonetheless, we believe that the bulk of the use of each type of outlet matches our conceptualization.

2. All group figures are the percentage of people saying that they follow the topic fairly or very closely. A demographic weight supplied by Pew has been applied to all analyses.

3. For attention to Afghanistan, the interaction of party identification and level of reliance in a logistic regression model is statistically significant, $p < .001$. It is not significant in the other two topics.

4. The interaction of party identification and level of reliance in a logistic regression model is statistically significant, $p < .001$.

5. Of course, the reverse is also possible. It might be that people with more polarized attitudes seek more specialized content. If that is the correct interpretation, it would still suggest an important connection between specialized content and audience beliefs, but the implications for a polarization effect would be less clear.

REFERENCES

Abelson, R. P. 1981. The psychological status of the script concept. *American Psychologist* 36: 715–729.

Adam, P.G., S. Quinn, and R. Edmunds. 2007. *Eyetracking the News: A Study of Print and Online Reading*. St. Petersburg, Fla.: Poynter Institute.

Adamic, L. A., and N. Glance. 2005. The political blogosphere and the 2004 U.S. election: Divided they blog. Paper presented at the Annual Workshop on the Weblogging Ecosystem, Chiba, Japan.

Adegoke, Y. 2008. Comcast to limit customers' broadband usage. Reuters, August 28. http://www.reuters.com/article/internetNews/idUSN2833325220080829.

Ahlers, D. 2006. News consumption and the new electronic media. *Harvard International Journal of Press/Politics* 11: 29–52.

Althaus, S. L. 2002. American news consumption during times of national crisis. *PS: Political Science and Politics* 35: 517–521.

Althaus, S. L., and D. Tewksbury. 2000. Patterns of internet and traditional news media use in a networked community. *Political Communication* 17: 21–45.

———. 2002. Agenda setting and the "new" news: Patterns of issue importance among readers of the paper and online versions of the *New York Times*. *Communication Research* 29: 180–207.

Anderson, C. 2004. The long tail. *Wired* 12. http://www.wired.com/wired/archive/12.10/tail.html.

Anderson, J. Q., and L. Rainie. 2008. The future of the internet III. Pew Internet and American Life Project. http://www.pewinternet.org/~/media/Files/Reports/2008/PIP_Future-Internet3.pdf.

Appiah, O. 2004. Effects of ethnic identification on Web browsers' attitudes toward and navigational patterns on race-targeted sites. *Communication Research* 31: 312–337.

Aviles, J. A. G., and M. Carvajal. 2008. Integrated and cross-media newsroom convergence: Two models of multimedia news production. *Convergence* 14: 221–239.

Baker, C. E. 2002. *Media, Markets, and Democracy*. New York: Cambridge University Press.

Baker, P., and J. M. Broder. 2008. Obama pledges public works on a vast scale. *New York Times*, December 6. http://www.nytimes.com/2008/12/07/us/politics/07radio.html?ref=us.

Baker, W. E., and R. J. Lutz. 2000. An empirical test of an updated relevance-accessibility model of advertising effectiveness. *Journal of Advertising* 29: 1–14.

Bartels, L. M. 1993. Messages received: The political impact of media exposure. *American Political Science Review* 87: 267–285.

Basil, M. D. 1990. Primary news source changes: Question wording, availability, and cohort effects. *Journalism Quarterly* 67: 708–722.

Bauder, D. 2010. Broadcast audience aging faster than population. *Boston Globe,* August 16. http://www.boston.com/ae/tv/articles/2010/08/16/broadcast_audience_aging_faster_than_population.

Baum, M. A., and T. Groeling. 2008. New media and the polarization of American political discourse. *Political Communication* 25: 345–365.

Baumgartner, J., and J. S. Morris. 2006. The *Daily Show* effect: Candidate evaluations, efficacy, and American youth. *American Politics Research* 34: 341–367.

Becker, L. B., and K. Schoenbach, eds. 1989. *Audience Responses to Media Diversification: Coping with Plenty.* Hillsdale, N.J.: Erlbaum.

Bennett, S. B., S. L. Rhine, and R. S. Flickinger. 2004. The things they cared about: Change and continuity in Americans' attention to different news stories, 1989–2002. *Press/Politics* 9: 75–99.

Bennett, W. L. 1996. *News: The Politics of Illusion,* 3rd ed. White Plains, N.Y.: Longman.

———. 2003. The burglar alarm that just keeps ringing: A response to Zaller. *Political Communication* 20: 131–138.

———. 2009. *News: The Politics of Illusion,* 8th ed. White Plains, N.Y.: Longman.

Benoit, P. J., and W. L. Benoit. 2005. Criteria for evaluating political campaign webpages. *Southern Communication Journal* 70: 230–247.

Berelson, B. 1952. Democratic theory and public opinion. *Public Opinion Quarterly* 16: 313–330.

Berthon, P., M. B. Holbrook, and J. M. Hulbert. 2000. Beyond market orientation: A conceptualization of market evolution. *Journal of Interactive Marketing* 14, no. 3: 50–66.

Bimber, B. 2003. *Information and American Democracy: Technology in the Evolution of Political Power.* New York: Cambridge University Press.

Boczkowski, P. 2004. The processes of adopting multimedia and interactivity in three online newsrooms. *Journal of Communication* 54: 197–213.

———. 2009. Technology, monitoring, and imitation in contemporary news work. *Communication, Culture and Critique* 2: 39–59.

Bogart, L. 1989. *Press and Public: Who Reads What, When, Where, and Why in American Newspapers,* 2nd ed. Hillsdale, N.J.: Erlbaum.

Bolter, J. D., and R. Grusin. 2000. *Remediation: Understanding New Media.* Cambridge, Mass.: MIT Press.

Brainard, C. 2008. CNN cuts entire science, tech team. *Columbia Journalism Review,* December 4. http://www.cjr.org/the_observatory/cnn_cuts_entire_science_tech_t.php

Bucy, E. P. 2004. The interactivity paradox: Closer to the news but confused. In E. P. Bucy and J. E. Newhagen, eds., *Media Access: Social and Psychological Dimensions of New Technology Use,* pp. 47–72. Mahwah, N.J.: Erlbaum.

Bucy, E. P., and C.-C. Tao. 2007. The mediated moderation model of interactivity. *Media Psychology* 9: 647–672.

Butler, J. K., and K. E. M. Kent. 1983. Potential impact of videotext on newspapers. *Newspaper Research Journal* 5: 3–12.

Campbell, R., C. R. Martin, and B. Fabos. 2010. *Media and Culture: An Introduction to Mass Communication,* 7th ed. Boston: St. Martin's.

Carlson, N. 2010. AOL to launch "hundreds" of local news sites in 2010. Silicon Alley Insider, February 17. http://www.businessinsider.com/aol-plans-to-launch-hundreds-of-local-news-sites-in-2010-2010-2?utm_source=Triggermail&utm_medium=email&utm_campaign=SAI_Select_021810.

Cassidy, W. P. 2005. Variations on a theme: The professional role conceptions of print and online newspaper journalists. *Journalism & and Mass Communication Quarterly* 82: 264–281.

Catledge, L. D., and J. E. Pitkow. 1995. Characterizing browsing strategies in the World Wide Web. *Computer Networks and ISDN Systems* 27: 1065–1073.

Chadwick, A. In press. Recent shifts in the relationship between the internet and democratic engagement in Britain and the United States: Granularity, informational exuberance, and political learning. In E. Anduiza, M. Jensen, and L. Jorba, eds., *Comparing Digital Politics: Digital Media and Political Engagement around the World.* Cambridge, U.K.: Cambridge University Press.

Chaffee, S. H., and S. F. Kanihan. 1997. Learning about politics from the mass media. *Political Communication* 14: 421–430.

Chaffee, S. H., and M. J. Metzger. 2001. The end of mass communication? *Mass Communication and Society* 4: 365–379.

Cho, J., and D. M. McLeod. 2007. Structural antecedents of knowledge and participation: Extending the knowledge gap concept to participation. *Journal of Communication* 57: 205–228.

Chyi, H. I., and D. Lasorsa. 2002. An explorative study on the market relation between online and print newspapers. *Journal of Media Economics* 15: 91–106.

Chyi, H. I., and G. Sylvie. 2001. The medium is global, the content is not: The role of geography in online newspaper markets. *Journal of Media Economics* 14, no. 4: 231–248.

Chyi, H. I., and M. J. Yang. 2009. Is online news an inferior good? Examining the economic nature of online news among users. *Journalism & Mass Communication Quarterly* 86: 594–612.

Cohen, E. L. 2002. Online journalism as market-driven journalism. *Journal of Broadcasting & Electronic Media* 46: 532–548.

Coleman, R. and M. McCombs. 2007. The young and agenda-less? Exploring age-related differences in agenda-setting on the youngest generation, baby boomers, and the civic generation. *Journalism & Mass Communication Quarterly* 84: 495–508.

ComScore. 2011a. December 2010 U.S. online video rankings. http://www.comscore.com/Press_Events/Press_Releases/2011/1/comScore_Releases_December_2010_U.S._Online_Video_Rankings/%28language%29/eng-US.

———. 2011b. Media Metrix ranks top 50 U.S. Web properties for December 2010. http://www.comscore.com/content/download/7241/125317/file/comScore%20Media%20Metrix%20Ranks%20Top%2050%20U.S.%20Web%20Properties%20for%20December%202010.pdf.

Converse, J. M., and S. Presser. 1986. *Survey Questions: Handcrafting the Standardized Questionnaire.* Newbury Park, Calif.: Sage.

Converse, P. E. 1964. The nature of belief systems in mass publics. In D. A. Apter, ed., *Ideology and Discontent,* pp. 206–261. New York: Free Press.

Cook, K. 2008. Learning on the go. *Nursing Standard* 23: 61.

Cooke, L. 2005. A visual convergence of print, television, and the internet: Charting 40 years of design change in news presentation. *New Media & Society* 7: 22–46.

Corrado, A. 1996. Elections in cyberspace: Prospects and problems. In A. Corrado and C. M. Firestone, eds., *Elections in Cyberspace: Toward a New Era in American Politics,* pp. 1–31. Washington, D.C.: Aspen Institute.

Dahlberg, L. 2007. Rethinking fragmentation of the cyberpublic: From consensus to contestation. *New Media & Society* 9: 827–847.

D'Alessio, D., and M. Allen. 2007. The selective exposure hypothesis and media choice processes. In R. W. Preiss, B. M. Gayle, N. Burrell, M. Allen, and J. Bryant, eds., *Mass Media Effects Research: Advances through Meta-analysis,* pp. 103–118. New York: Erlbaum.

December, J. 2002. The World Wide Web unleashed. In E. P. Bucy, ed., *Living in the Information Age: A New Media Reader,* pp. 187–193. Belmont, Calif.: Wadsworth/Thompson.

DeFleur, M. L., and S. Ball-Rokeach. 1989. *Theories of Mass Communication,* 5th ed. New York: Longman.

Delia, J. G. 1987. Communication research: A history. In C. R. Berger and S. H. Chaffee, eds., *Handbook of Communication Science,* pp. 20–98. Newbury Park, Calif.: Sage.

Delli Carpini, M. X., and S. Keeter. 1996. *What Americans Know about Politics and Why It Matters.* New Haven, Conn.: Yale University Press.

Dessauer, C. 2004. New media, internet news, and the news habit. In P. N. Howard and S. Jones, eds., *Society Online: The Internet in Context,* pp. 121–136. Thousand Oaks, Calif.: Sage.

D'Haenens, L., N. Jankowski, and A. Heuvelman. 2004. News in online and print newspapers: Differences in reader consumption and recall. *New Media and Society* 6: 363–382.

Diddi, A., and R. LaRose. 2006. Getting hooked on news: Uses and gratifications and the formation of news habits among college students in an internet environment. *Journal of Broadcasting & Electronic Media* 50: 193–210.

Dimmick, J., Y. Chen, and Z. Li. 2004. Competition between the internet and traditional news media: The gratification-opportunities niche dimension. *Journal of Media Economics* 17: 19–33.

Dover, M. 2007. Web news: Conjuring trick or brave news world? *Econtent,* July/August 2007: 48–53.

Drew, D., and D. Weaver. 1998. Voter learning in the 1996 presidential election: Did the media matter? *Journalism & Mass Communication Quarterly* 67: 740–748.

Dutta-Bergman, M. J. 2004. Complementarity in consumption of news types across traditional and new media. *Journal of Broadcasting & Electronic Media* 48: 41–60.

Edwardson, M., K. Kent, and M. McConnell. 1985. Television news information gain: Videotex versus a talking head. *Journal of Broadcasting & Electronic Media* 29: 367–378.

Elmer, G., Z. Devereaux, and D. Skinner. 2006. Disaggregating online news: The Canadian federal election, 2005–2006. *SCAN: Journal of Media Arts Culture* 3. http://scan.net.au/scan/journal/display.php?journal_id=72.

Enquiro. 2005. Enquiro eye tracking report I: Google. http://www.enquiro.com/whitepapers/pdf/enquiro-eye-tracking-report-I-google.pdf

Eveland, W. P. Jr. 2002. News information processing as a mediator of the relationship between motivations and political knowledge. *Journalism & Mass Communication Quarterly* 79: 26–40.

———. 2003. A "mix of attributes" approach to the study of media effects and new communication technologies. *Journal of Communication* 53: 395–410.

Eveland, W. P., Jr., J. Cortese, H. Park, and S. Dunwoody. 2004. How Web site organization influences free recall, factual knowledge, and knowledge structure. *Human Communication Research* 30: 208–233.

Eveland, W. P. Jr., and S. Dunwoody. 1998. Users and navigation patterns of a science World Wide Web site for the public. *Public Understanding of Science* 7: 285–311.

———. 2001a. Applying research on the uses and cognitive effects of hypermedia to the study of the World Wide Web. *Communication Yearbook* 25: 79–113.

———. 2001b. User control and structural isomorphism or disorientation and cognitive load? Learning from the Web versus print. *Communication Research* 28: 48–78.

Eveland, W. P. Jr., K. Marton, and M. Seo. 2004. Moving beyond "just the facts": The influence of online news on the content and structure of public affairs knowledge. *Communication Research* 31: 82–108.

Eveland, W. P. Jr., M. Seo, and K. Marton. 2002. Learning from the news in campaign 2000: An experimental comparison of TV news, newspapers and online news. *Media Psychology* 4: 352–378.

Farivar, C. 2008. Wi-Fi has hit the streets—mostly in places you've never heard of. *Wired,* February 25: 1603. http://www.wired.com/special_multimedia/2008/st_atlas_1603.

Festinger, L. 1957. *A Theory of Cognitive Dissonance.* Stanford, Calif.: Stanford University Press.

Fico, F., C. Heeter, S. Soffin, and C. Stanley. 1987. New wave gatekeeping: Electronic indexing effects on newspaper reading. *Communication Research* 14: 335–351.

Frey, D. 1986. Recent research on selective exposure. *Advances in Experimental Social Psychology* 19: 41–80.

Gans, H. 1979. *Deciding What's News.* New York: Pantheon.

Gasher, M., and S. Gabriele. 2004. Increasing circulation? A comparative news-flow study of *Montreal Gazette*'s hard-copy and on-line editions. *Journalism Studies* 5: 311–323.

Gomery, D. 1991. Who killed Hollywood? *Wilson Quarterly* 15: 106–112.

Graber, D. 1988. *Processing the News: How People Tame the Information Tide,* 2nd ed. New York: Longman.

———. 1997. *Mass Media and American Politics,* 5th ed. Washington, D.C.: Congressional Quarterly.

———. 2001. *Processing Politics: Learning from Television in the Internet Age.* Chicago: University of Chicago Press.

Gross, G. 2008. FCC rules against Comcast P-to-P throttling. *PC World,* August 1. http://www.pcworld.com/businesscenter/article/149260/fcc_rules_against_comcast_ptop_throttling.html.

Hamilton, J. T. 2004. *All the News That's Fit to Sell: How Market Transforms Information into News.* Princeton, N.J.: Princeton University Press.

Hargittai, E. 2002. Beyond logs and surveys: In-depth measures of people's Web use skills. *Journal of the American Society for Information Science and Technology* 53: 1239–1244.

Hargittai, E., and A. Hinnant. 2008. Digital inequality: Differences in young adults' use of the internet. *Communication Research* 35: 602–621.

Hayes, C., and P. Avesani. 2007. Using tags and clustering to identify topic-relevant blogs. In Proceedings of the International Conference on Weblog and Social Media, Boulder, Colo.

Heeter, C., N. Brown, S. Soffin, C. Stanley, and M. Salwen. 1989. Agenda-setting by electronic text news. *Journalism Quarterly* 66: 101–106.

Heeter, C., and B. Greenberg. 1985. Cable and program choice. In D. Zillmann and J. Bryant, eds., *Selective Exposure to Communication,* pp. 203–224. Hillsdale, N.J.: Erlbaum.

Higgins, E. T. 1996. Knowledge activation: Accessibility, applicability, and salience. In E. T. Higgins and A. W. Kruglanski, eds., *Social Psychology: Handbook of Basic Principles,* pp. 133–168. New York: Guilford.

Hindman, M. 2007. A mile wide and an inch deep: Measuring media diversity online and offline. In Philip M. Napoli, ed., *Media Diversity and Localism: Meaning and Metrics,* pp. 327–347. Mahwah, N.J.: Erlbaum.

Hollander, B. A. 2008. Tuning out or tuning elsewhere? Partisanship, polarization, and media migration from 1998 to 2006. *Journalism & Mass Communication Quarterly* 85: 23–40.

Hopkins, H. 2010. Facebook largest news reader? Hitwise Intelligence, February 3. http://weblogs.hitwise.com/us-heather-hopkins/2010/02/facebook_largest_news_reader_1.html.

Horrigan, J. B. 2008. Home broadband adoption 2008. Pew Internet and American Life Project, July. http://www.pewinternet.org/~/media//Files/Reports/2008/PIP_Broadband_2008.pdf.

Hotelling, H. 1929. Stability in competition. *Economic Journal* 39: 41–57.

Houston, F. 1999. What I saw in the digital sea. *Columbia Journalism Review* (July/August): 34–37.

Howard, P. N. 2006. *New Media Campaigns and the Managed Citizen.* Cambridge, U.K.: Cambridge University Press.

Huang, E., L. Rademakers, M. A. Fayemiwo, and L. Dunlap. 2004. Converged journalism and quality: A case study of the *Tampa Tribune* news stories. *Convergence* 10: 73–91.

Hughes, T. P. 1997. The technological torrent. In A. H. Teich, ed., *Technology and the Future,* 7th ed., pp. 42–54. New York: St. Martin's.

Hurley, R. J., A. Sangalang, and A. Muddiman. 2009. Googling cancer: News aggregation's impact on article overlap, medical frame, and fear in internet-based cancer news. Paper presented at the 59th annual International Communication Association Conference, Chicago, May. http://www.allacademic.com/meta/p299376_index.html.

Imfeld, C., and G. W. Scott. 2005. Under construction: Measures of community building at newspaper Web sites. In M. B. Salwen, B. Garrison, and P. D. Driscoll, eds., *Online News and the Public,* pp. 205–220. Mahwah, N.J.: Erlbaum.

Iyengar, S., and K. S. Hahn. 2009. Red media, blue media: Evidence of ideological selectivity in media use. *Journal of Communication* 59: 19–39.

Iyengar, S., and D. Kinder. 1987. *News That Matters: Television and American Opinion.* Chicago: University of Chicago Press.

Jennings, M. K., and V. Zeitner. 2003. Internet use and civic engagement: A longitudinal analysis. *Public Opinion Quarterly* 67: 311–333.

Jerit, J., J. Barabas, and T. Bolsen. 2006. Citizens, knowledge, and the information environment. *American Journal of Political Science* 50, no. 2: 266–282.

Katz, E. 1957. The two-step flow of communication: An up-to-date report on a hypothesis. *Public Opinion Quarterly* 21: 61–78.

———. 1996. And deliver us from segmentation. *Annals of the American Academy of Political and Social Science* 546 (July): 22–33.

Katz, E., J. G. Blumler, and M. Gurevitch. 1974. Utilization of mass communication by the individual. In J. G. Blumler and E. Katz, eds., *The Uses of Mass Communications: Current Perspectives on Gratifications Research,* pp. 19–32. Beverly Hills, Calif.: Sage.

Katz, E., M. Gurevitch, and H. Hass. 1973. On the use of the media for important things. *American Sociological Review* 38: 164–181.

Kaye, B. K., and T. J. Johnson. 2002. Online and in the know: Uses and gratifications of the Web for political information. *Journal of Broadcasting & Electronic Media* 46: 54–71.

Kaynay, J. M., and P. Yelsma. 2000. Displacement effects of online media in the socio-technical contexts of households. *Journal of Broadcasting & Electronic Media* 44: 215–229.

Kennedy, R. S. 2004. Weblogs, social software, and new interactivity on the Web. *Psychiatric Services* 55: 247–249.

Kenski, K. K., and N. J. Stroud. 2006. Connections between internet use and political efficacy, knowledge, and participation. *Journal of Broadcasting & Electronic Media* 50: 173–192.

Kim, K. S., and Y.-C. Kim. 2007. New and old media uses and political engagement among Korean adolescents. *Asian Journal of Communication* 17: 342–361.

Kim, S. H. 2008. Testing the knowledge gap hypothesis in South Korea: Traditional news media, the internet, and political learning. *International Journal of Public Opinion Research* 20: 193–210.

Kim, Y. M. 2007. How intrinsic and extrinsic motivations interact in selectivity: Investigating the moderating effects of situational information processing goals in issue publics' Web behavior. *Communication Research* 34: 185–211.

Kiousis, S. 2002. Interactivity: A concept explication. *New Media & Society* 4: 355–383.

Klapper, J. T. 1960. *The Effects of Mass Communication.* New York: Free Press.

Knobloch, S., F. D. Carpentier, and D. Zillmann, D. 2003. Effects of salience dimensions of informational utility on selective exposure to online news. *Journalism & Mass Communication Quarterly* 80: 91–108.

Knobloch, S., M. Hastall, D. Zillmann, and C. Callison. 2003. Imagery effects on the selective reading of internet newsmagazines. *Communication Research* 30: 3–29.

Knobloch-Westerwick, S., and J. Meng. 2009. Looking the other way: Selective exposure to attitude-consistent and counterattitudinal political information. *Communication Research* 36: 426–448.

Knobloch-Westerwick, S., N. Sharma, D. L. Hansen, and A. Alter. 2005. Impact of popularity indications on readers' selective exposure to online news. *Journal of Broadcasting & Electronic Media* 49: 296–313.

Krosnick, J., and D. Kinder. 1990. Altering the foundations of support for the president through priming. *American Political Science Review* 84: 497–512.

Kwak, N., N. Poor, and M. M. Skoric. 2006. Honey, I shrunk the world! The relations between internet use and international engagement. *Mass Communication and Society* 9: 189–213.

Labaton, S. 2001. New F.C.C. chief would curb agency reach. *New York Times*, February 7. http://query.nytimes.com/gst/fullpage.html?res=9C01E3D61F3EF934A35751C0A9 679C8B63&scp=1&sq=New%20F.C.C.%20chief%20would%20curb%20agency%20 reach&st=cse.

Lang, A. 2000. The limited capacity model of motivated mediated message processing. *Journal of Communication* 50, no. 1: 46–70.

Leccese, M. 2009. Online information sources of political blogs. *Journalism & Mass Communication Quarterly* 86: 578–593.

Lee, J. H. 2008. Effects of news deviance and personal involvement on audience story selection: A Web-tracking analysis. *Journalism & Mass Communication Quarterly* 85: 41–60.

Lee, J. K. 2007. The effect of the internet on homogeneity of the media agenda: A test of the fragmentation thesis. *Journalism & Mass Communication Quarterly* 84: 745–760.

Leighley, J. E., and J. Nagler. 2007. Unions, voter turnout, and class bias in the U.S. electorate, 1964–2004. *Journal of Politics* 69: 430–441.

Levy, M., and S. Windahl. 1984. Audience activity and gratifications: A conceptual clarification and exploration. *Communication Research* 11: 51–78.

Li, X. 1998. Web page design and graphic use of three U.S. newspapers. *Journalism & Mass Communication Quarterly* 75: 353–365.

Lim, J. 2006. A cross-lagged analysis of agenda setting among online news media. *Journalism & Mass Communication Quarterly* 83: 298–312.

Lin, J., and A. Halavais. 2006. Geographical distribution of blogs in the United States. *Webology* 3, no. 4. http://www.webology.ir/2006/v3n4/a30.html.

Lowrey, W. 2006. Mapping the journalism-blogging relationship. *Journalism* 7: 477–500.

Lynch, M. 2005. *Voices of the New Arab Public: Iraq, al-Jazeera, and Middle East Politics Today.* New York: Columbia University Press.

MacGregor, P. 2007. Tracking the online audience: Metric data start a subtle revolution. *Journalism Studies* 8: 280–298.

Macht, J. 2001. New medium, old rules: The on-line editor comes of age. *Harvard International Journal of Press/Politics* 6: 128–131.

MacKenzie, D., and J. Wajcman, eds. 1985. *The Social Shaping of Technology.* Milton Keynes, U.K.: Open University Press.

Maisel, R. 1973. The decline of mass media. *Public Opinion Quarterly* 37: 159–170.

Mangani, A. 2003. Profit and audience maximization in broadcasting markets. *Information Economics and Policy* 15: 305–315.

Manovich, L. 2001. *The Language of New Media.* Cambridge, Mass.: MIT Press.

Margolis, M., and D. Resnick. 2000. *Politics as Usual: The Cyberspace "Revolution."* Thousand Oaks, Calif.: Sage.

McChesney, R. W. 2004. *The Problem of the Media: U.S. Communication Politics in the 21st Century.* New York: Monthly Review.

———. 2008. *The Political Economy of Media: Enduring Issues, Emerging Dilemmas.* New York: Monthly Review.

McChesney, R. W., and J. Nichols. 2010. *The Death and Life of American Journalism: The Media Revolution That Will Begin the World Again.* Philadelphia: Nation.

McCombs, M. E. 1972. Mass media in the marketplace. *Journalism Monographs* 24.

———. 2004. *Setting the Agenda: The Mass Media and Public Opinion.* Cambridge, U.K.: Polity.

———. 2005. A look at agenda-setting: Past, present and future. *Journalism Studies* 6: 543–557.

McCombs, M. E., and J. Nolan. 1992. The relative constancy approach to consumer spending for media. *Journal of Media Economics* 5, no. 2: 43–52.

McDonald, D. G., and C. J. Glynn. 1984. The stability of media gratifications. *Journalism Quarterly* 61: 542–549, 741.

McDonald, M. P. 2008. Voter turnout. *United States Election Project.* http://elections.gmu.edu/voter_turnout.htm.

McGerr, M. E. 1986. *The Decline of Popular Politics.* New York: Oxford University Press.

McLeod, D. M., G. M. Kosicki, and J. M. McLeod. 2008. Political communication effects. In J. Bryant and M. B. Oliver, eds., *Media Effects: Advances in Theory and Research,* pp. 228–251. New York: Erlbaum.

McLeod, J., C. Bybee, and J. Durall. 1982. Evaluating media performance by gratifications sought and received. *Journalism Quarterly* 59: 3–12.

McQuail, D. 1997. *Audience Analysis.* Thousand Oaks, Calif.: Sage.

———. 2010. *McQuail's Mass Communication Theory.* London: Sage.

Merrill, J. C., and R. L. Lowenstein. 1979. *Media, Men, and Messages: New Perspectives in Communication,* 2nd ed. New York: Longman.

Miller, C. C. 2010. Twitter makes itself more useful. *New York Times,* April 14. http://bits.blogs.nytimes.com/2010/04/14/twitter-makes-itself-more-useful/?emc=eta1.

Miniwatts Marketing Group. 2010. Internet world stats. http://www.internetworldstats.com/stats.htm.

Mutz, D. C. 2006. *Hearing the Other Side: Deliberative versus Participatory Democracy.* New York: Cambridge University Press.

National Telecommunications Information Administration. 1995. Falling through the net: A survey of the "have nots" in rural and urban America (report).

Negroponte, N. 1995. *Being Digital.* New York: Knopf.

Neuman, W. R. 1976. Patterns of recall among television news viewers. *Public Opinion Quarterly* 40: 115–123.

———. 1986. *The Paradox of Mass Politics: Knowledge and Opinion in the American Electorate.* Cambridge, Mass.: Harvard University Press.

———. 1991. *The Future of the Mass Audience.* Cambridge, U.K.: Cambridge University Press.

Neuman, W. R., M. R. Just, and A. N. Crigler. 1992. *Common Knowledge: News and the Construction of Political Meaning.* Chicago: University of Chicago Press.

Nguyen, A., and M. Western. 2006. The complementary relationship between the internet and traditional mass media: The case of online news and information. *Information Research* 11, no. 3. http://informationr.net/ir/11-3/paper259.html.

Nie, N. H., D. W. Miller III, S. Golde, D. M. Butler, K. Winneg. 2010. The World Wide Web and the U.S. political news market. *American Journal of Political Science* 54: 428–439.

Nielsen Company. 2010a. Americans using TV and internet together 35% more than a year ago. http://blog.nielsen.com/nielsenwire/online_mobile/three-screen-report-q409.

———. 2010b. June 2010: Over 10B videos streamed in U.S. http://blog.nielsen.com/nielsenwire/online_mobile/june-2010-more-than-10b-videos-streamed-in-u-s.

Nielsen, J., and K. Pernice. 2010. *Eyetracking Web Usability.* Berkeley, Calif.: New Riders.

Nielsen//NetRatings 1999. Top 25 Web properties for the month of August 1999. http://www.clickz.com/clickz/stats/1705034/top-web-properties-august-1999.

Nielsenwire. 2010. June 2010: Top online sites and brands in the U.S. http://blog.nielsen.com/nielsenwire/online_mobile/june-2010-top-online-sites-and-brands-in-the-u-s/#.

Noh, G.-Y., and A. E. Grant. 1997. Media functionality and the principle of relative constancy: An explanation of the VCR aberration. *Journal of Media Economics* 10, no. 3: 17–31.

Online Publishers Association. 2004. Multi-channel media brands: Attitudinal and usage study. http://onlinepubs.ehclients.com/images/pdf/140_W_opa_multichannel_media_brand_study_nov03.pdf.

Palser, B. 2006. Hype or the real deal? *American Journalism Review* (February/March): 65.

Parenti, M. 1993. *Inventing Reality: The Politics of News Media.* New York: St. Martin's.

PC Magazine. 2006. Web applications: Blogs, podcasts, and photo sharing hit their stride. *PC Magazine* (January): 110.

Peiser, W. 2000. Cohort trends in the media use in the United States. *Mass Communication and Society* 3: 185–205.

Perez-Pena, R. 2008. Some papers in financial trouble are leaving the A.P. to cut costs. *New York Times,* October 20. http://www.nytimes.com/2008/10/20/business/media/20ap.html.

Perloff, R. M. 2007. *The Dynamics of Persuasion: Communication and Attitudes in the 21st Century.* Mahwah, N.J.: Erlbaum.

Pew Internet and American Life Project. 2010a. Report: Internet, broadband, and cell phone statistics. http://www.pewinternet.org/Reports/2010/Internet-broadband-and-cell-phone-statistics.aspx?r=1.

———. 2010b. Trend data: What internet users do on an average day. http://www.pewinternet.org/Static-Pages/Trend-Data/Online-Activities-Daily.aspx.

Pew Research Center for the People and the Press. 1998. Event-driven news audiences: Internet news takes off. http://people-press.org/1998/06/08/internet-news-takes-off.

———. 2004. News audiences increasingly politicized. http://people-press.org/2004/06/08/news-audiences-increasingly-politicized.

———. 2006. Online papers modestly boost newspaper readership. http://people-press.org/2006/07/30/online-papers-modestly-boost-newspaper-readership.

———. 2007. Public knowledge of current affairs little changed by news and information revolutions: What Americans know, 1989–2007. http://people-press.org/report/319/public-knowledge-of-current-affairs-little-changed-by-news-and-information-revolutions.

———. 2008a. Internet's broader role in Campaign 2008: Social networking and online videos take off. Washington, D.C.

———. 2008b. Key news audiences now blend online and traditional sources: Audience segments in a changing news environment. http://people-press.org/report/444/news-media.

———. 2010. Americans spending more time following the news: Ideological news sources: Who watches and why. http://people-press.org/2010/09/12/americans-spending-more-time-following-the-news.

Poindexter, P. M., and M. E. McCombs. 2001. Revisiting the civic duty to keep informed in the new media environment. *Journalism & Mass Communication Quarterly* 78: 113–126.

Price, V., and J. Zaller. 1993. Who gets the news? Alternative measures of news reception and their implications for research. *Public Opinion Quarterly* 57: 133–164.

Prior, M. 2007. *Post-broadcast Democracy: How Media Choice Increases Inequality in Political Involvement and Polarizes Elections.* New York: Cambridge University Press.

Project for Excellence in Journalism. 2007. The state of the news media 2007: An annual report on American journalism. http://www.stateofthemedia.org/2007.

———. 2008. The state of the news media 2008: An annual report on American journalism. http://www.stateofthemedia.org/2008.

———. 2010a. How news happens: A study of the news ecosystem of one American city. http://www.journalism.org/analysis_report/how_news_happens.

———. 2010b. New media, old media. http://www.journalism.org/analysis_report/new_media_old_media.

———. 2010c. The state of the news media 2010: An annual report on American journalism. http://www.stateofthemedia.org/2010.

Ramsaye, T. 1960. The rise and place of the motion picture. In W. Schramm, ed., *Mass Communications,* pp. 24–38. Urbana: University of Illinois Press.

Reese, S. D., L. Rutigliano, K. Hyun, and J. Jeong. 2007. Mapping the blogosphere: Professional and citizen-based media in the global news arena. *Journalism* 8: 235–261.

Richard, M. 2004. Modeling the impact of internet atmospherics on surfing behavior. *Journal of Business Research* 58: 1632–1642.

Rittenberg, J. L., and D. Tewksbury. 2007. Browsing through the news: Determining predictors of linear behavior on an online news site. Paper presented at the annual meeting of the National Communication Association, Chicago, November.

Rittenberg, J., D. Tewksbury, and S. Casey. 2009. Media preferences and democracy: Refining the "relative entertainment preference" hypothesis. Paper presented at the annual meeting of the International Communication Association, Chicago, May.

Rogers, E. M. 2003. *Diffusion of Innovations,* 5th ed. New York: Free Press.

Rubin, A. M. 1984. Ritualized and instrumental television viewing. *Journal of Communication* 34, no. 3: 67–77.

Rubin, A. M. 2002. The uses and gratifications perspective of media effects. In J. Bryant and D. Zillmann, eds., *Media Effects: Advances in Theory and Research.* Mahwah, N.J.: Erlbaum.

Rubin, A. M., and E. Perse. 1987. Audience activity and television news gratifications. *Communication Research* 14: 58–84.

Salaverria, R. 2005. An immature medium: Strengths and weaknesses of online newspapers on September 11. *Gazette* 67: 69–86.

Salwen, M. B. 1995. News of Hurricane Andrew: The agenda of sources and the sources' agendas. *Journalism & Mass Communication Quarterly* 72: 826–840.

Schatz, A. 2007. U.S. broadband rank: 15th and dropping. Washington Wire. http://blogs.wsj.com/washwire/2007/04/23/us-broadband-rank-15th-and-dropping.

Schiller, H. I. 1978. Decolonization of information: Efforts toward a new international order. *Latin American Perspectives* 5: 35–48.

Schoenbach, K., E. de Waal, and E. Lauf. 2005. Online and print newspapers: Their impact on the extent of the perceived public agenda. *European Journal of Communication* 20: 245–258.

Schramm, W., ed. 1960. *Mass Communications.* Urbana: University of Illinois Press.

Schramm, W., and D. E. White. 1949. Age, education, economic status: Factors in newspaper reading. *Journalism Quarterly* 26: 149–159.

Schudson, M. 1998. *The Good Citizen: A History of American Civic Life.* Cambridge, Mass.: Harvard University Press.

Sears, D. O., and J. L. Freedman. 1967. Selective exposure to information: A critical review. *Public Opinion Quarterly* 31: 194–213.

Seelig, M. I. 2008. An updated look at trends in content and Web page design in news web sites. *Electronic News* 2: 86–101.

Seidman, R. 2008. Cable news ratings for October 31. http://tvbythenumbers.com/2008/11/03/cable-news-ratings-for-october-31/7471.

———. 2010. "NBC Nightly News with Brian Williams" closes out America's number one evening newscast. TV by the Numbers. http://tvbythenumbers.zap2it.com/2010/12/29/nbc-nightly-news-with-brian-williams-closes-out-2010-as-americas-number-one-evening-newscast/76793.

Shah, D. V., J. Cho, W. P. Eveland Jr., and N. Kwak. 2005. Information and expression in a digital age: Modeling internet effects on civic participation. *Communication Research* 32: 531–567.

Shoemaker, P. J., and S. D. Reese. 1996. *Mediating the Message,* 2nd ed. White Plains, N.Y.: Longman.

Siapara, E. 2004. From couch potatoes to cybernauts? The expanding notion of the audience on TV channels' websites. *New Media & Society* 6: 155–172.

Singer, J. B. 2001. The metro wide web: Changes in newspapers' gatekeeping role online. *Journalism & Mass Communication Quarterly* 78: 65–80.

———. 2003. Campaign contributions: Online newspaper coverage of Election 2000. *Journalism & Mass Communication Quarterly* 80: 39–56.

————. 2005. The political j-blogger: "Normalizing" a new media form to fit old norms and practices. *Journalism* 6: 173–198.

————. 2006. Stepping back from the gate: Online newspaper editors and the co-production of content in campaign 2004. *Journalism & Mass Communication Quarterly* 83: 265–280.

Singer, J. B., and M. Gonzalez-Velez. 2003. Envisioning the caucus community: Online newspaper editors conceptualize their political roles. *Political Communication* 20: 433–452.

Smith, A. 2010. Home broadband 2010. Pew Internet and American Life Project. http://www.pewinternet.org/~/media//Files/Reports/2010/Home%20broadband%202010.pdf.

Son, J., and M. E. McCombs. 1993. A look at the constancy principle under changing market conditions. *Journal of Media Economics* 6, no. 2: 24–36.

Stelter, B. 2008. Mainstream news outlets start linking to other sites. *New York Times,* October 13. http://www.nytimes.com/2008/10/13/business/media/13reach.html?_r=1&scp=1&sq=Mainstream%20News%20Outlets%20Start%20Linking%20to%20Other%20Sites&st=cse.

Stempel, G. H., T. Hargrove, and J. P. Bernt. 2000. Relation of growth of use of the internet to changes in media use from 1995 to 1999. *Journalism & Mass Communication Quarterly* 77: 71–79.

Sterling, C. H., and J. M. Kittross. 2002. *Stay Tuned: A History of American Broadcasting,* 3rd ed. Mahwah, N.J.: Erlbaum.

Stroud, N. J. 2008. Media use and political predispositions: Revisiting the concept of selective exposure. *Political Behavior* 30: 341–366.

————. 2010. Polarization and partisan selective exposure. *Journal of Communication* 60: 556–576.

Sundar, S. S. 2000. Multimedia effects on processing and perception of online news: A study of picture, audio, and video downloads. *Journalism & Mass Communication Quarterly* 77: 480–499.

Sundar, S. S., S. Kalyanaraman, and J. Brown. 2003. Explicating web site interactivity: Impression formation effects in political campaign sites. *Communication Research* 30: 30–29.

Sunstein, C. R. 2001. *Republic.com*. Princeton, N.J.: Princeton University Press.

Tedesco, J. C. 2007. Examining internet interactivity effects on young adult political information efficacy. *American Behavioral Scientist* 50: 1183–1194.

Tewksbury, D. 1999. Differences in how we watch the news: The impact of processing goals and expertise on evaluations of political actors. *Communication Research* 26: 4–29.

————. 2003. What do Americans really want to know? Tracking the behavior of news readers on the internet. *Journal of Communication* 53: 694–710.

————. 2005. The seeds of audience fragmentation: Specialization in the use of online news sites. *Journal of Broadcasting & Electronic Media.* 49: 332–340.

————. 2006. Exposure to the newer media in a presidential primary campaign. *Political Communication* 23: 313–332.

Tewksbury, D., and S. L. Althaus. 2000a. Differences in knowledge acquisition among readers of the paper and online versions of a national newspaper. *Journalism and Mass Communication Quarterly* 77: 457–479.

————. 2000b. An examination of motivations for using the World Wide Web. *Communication Research Reports* 17: 127–138.

Tewksbury, D., M. L. Hals, and A. Bibart. 2008. The efficacy of news browsing: The relationship of news consumption style to social and political efficacy. *Journalism & Mass Communication Quarterly* 85: 257–272.

Tewksbury, D., A. Weaver, and B. Maddex. 2001. Accidentally informed: Incidental news exposure on the World Wide Web. *Journalism & Mass Communication Quarterly* 78: 533–554.

Thelwall, M., and D. Stuart. 2007. RUOK? Blogging communication technologies during crises. *Journal of Computer-Mediated Communication* 12: 189–214.

Thurman, N. 2007. The globalization of journalism online: A transatlantic study of news websites and their international readers. *Journalism* 8: 285–307.

Thurman, N., and B. Lupton. 2008. Convergence calls: Multimedia storytelling at British news websites. *Convergence* 14: 439–455.

Tuchman, G. 1978. *Making News: A Study in the Construction of Reality.* New York: Free Press.

U.S. Census Bureau. 2006. America's families and living arrangements: 2006. http://www.census.gov/population/www/socdemo/hh-fam/cps2006.html.

Valentino, N. A., V. L. Hutchings, and D. Williams. 2004. The impact of political advertising on knowledge, internet information seeking, and candidate preference. *Journal of Communication* 54: 337–354.

Walker, D. 2006. Blog commenting: A new political information space. Poster presented at the annual meeting of the American Society of Information Science and Technology, Austin, Texas.

Wallsten, K. 2007. Agenda setting and the blogosphere: An analysis of the relationship between mainstream media and political blogs. *Review of Policy Research* 24: 567–587.

Webster, J. G. 2005. Beneath the veneer of fragmentation: Television audience polarization in a multichannel world. *Journal of Communication* 55: 366–382.

———. 2007. Diversity of exposure. In Philip M. Napoli, ed., *Media Diversity and Localism: Meaning and Metrics,* pp. 309–325. Mahwah, N.J.: Erlbaum.

Webster, J. G., and P. F. Phalen. 1997. *The Mass Audience: Rediscovering the Dominant Model.* Mahwah, N.J.: Erlbaum.

White, D. M. 1964. The gatekeeper: A case study in the selection of news. In L. A. Dexter and D. M. White, eds., *People, Society, and Mass Communications,* pp. 160–171. New York: Free Press.

White, L. 1960. The growth of American radio. In W. Schramm, ed., *Mass Communications,* pp. 39–42. Urbana: University of Illinois Press.

Whitney, D. 2008. 119: Adverteasing. This Week in Media. http://www.pixelcorps.tv/twim119.

Williams, R. 1974. *Television: Technology and Cultural Form.* New York: Schocken.

Wilson, J. R., and S. R. Wilson. 2001. *Mass Media/Mass Culture,* 5th ed. St. Louis: McGraw-Hill.

Winner, L. 1985. Do artifacts have politics? In D. MacKenzie and J. Wajcman, eds., *The Social Shaping of Technology,* pp. 26–38. Milton Keynes, U.K.: Open University Press.

Wise, K., P. D. Bolls, and S. R. Schaefer. 2008. Choosing and reading online news: How available choice affects cognitive processing. *Journal of Broadcasting & Electronic Media* 52: 69–85.

Witt, L. 2004. Is public journalism morphing into the public's journalism? *National Civic Review* (Fall): 49–57.

Zaller, J. 2003. A new standard of news quality: Burglar alarms for the monitorial citizen. *Political Communication* 20: 109–130.

Zetter, K. 2008. Six-year-old news story causes United Airlines stock to plummet. *Wired,* September 8. http://www.wired.com/threatlevel/2008/09/six-year-old-st/.

Zhou, Y., and P. Moy. 2007. Parsing framing processes: The interplay between online public opinion and media coverage. *Journal of Communication* 57: 79–98.

Zillmann, D., L. Chen, S. Knobloch, and C. Callison. 2004. Effects of lead framing on selective exposure to internet news reports. *Communication Research* 31: 58–81.

INDEX

journalism and, 11, 150–152; costs of participation and, 153; definition of, 146–147; economic forces and, 156–157; efficacy and, 154; impediments to, 155–159; indirect channels of information influence and, 155; news creation and, 147, 154; news curation and, 147, 154; news distribution and, 147, 154; news exhibition and, 147, 154; regulatory forces and, 157–158; social factors and, 158; social networking sites and, 154–155; societal fragmentation and, 152; versus mass-public model of political communication, 148–152

Instapundit, 60

interactivity, 8, 42–43, 59, 84, 107, 114, 163

international news, 60, 75–77, 100, 113, 128, 133, 165

internet. See online news.

internet protocol (IP) addresses, 70

internet service providers (ISPs), 38–39, 157–158

internet video, 45, 47, 110, 150, 157, 172–173

issue publics, 171–172

J-Lab, 175

Jankowski, Nicholas, 113

Kenski, Kate, 112

Knobloch-Westerwick, Silvia, 86

knowledge gap, 115–118, 166

Kwak, Nojin, 112

learned media, 91

Leccese, Mark, 60

liberal pluralism, 19–20

Life, 26

long tail, 10, 36, 78

Look, 26

Lott, Trent, 57, 78

MacGregor, Phil, 71

magazines, 3, 25–27, 34, 35, 153

mass public model of political communication, 148–152

McCombs, Maxwell, 27–28, 60, 129

media ownership, 41, 49, 61, 157

media replacement, 27–29, 32–33, 40

media effects approach, 9–10, 23, 39

media system dependency, 85

Meng, Jingbo, 86

Microsoft, 61, 125, 156

mobile devices, 4, 22, 38, 50, 70, 135, 162, 176

movies, 25, 26

MSNBC, 60, 67, 75–76, 81, 170

MTV, 134

Napster, 48

National Enquirer, 77

National Public Radio (NPR), 49

naturally occurring news, 113, 166

NBC, 26, 61, 65, 124, 148. See also CNBC; MSNBC

Netherlands, 113, 129

network neutrality, 39, 157–158

Neuman, W. Russell, 14, 80–81, 124

New Voices, 175

New York Times, 49, 60–61, 72–76, 93, 125, 156–157, 162

news agenda: audience and, 57–59, 162–163; fragmentation of, 123, 128–130, 167, 172–173; homogeneity of, 57, 61; offline news sources and, 54–57, 61, 128–129; online news sources and 54, 57–62, 128–130, 162–163; setting of, 54, 56–57, 128–129, 162–163

news aggregators, 18, 47, 52–53, 59, 81, 122, 125–126, 164, 170

news popularity rankings, 58–59

news tickers, 45–46

newspapers: audiences of, 56, 64, 125, 133; compared to online news, 106, 113, 116; decline of, 3–4, 26, 30–34, 79, 121, 124, 148, 164, 173; fragmentation and, 125, 128–129; history of, 25–26; learning and, 113, 116, 129; mass media model and, 20; news agenda and, 54, 56; online presence of, 11, 33, 42–44, 79, 125

Nie, Norman, 99, 129, 140

Nielsen//NetRatings data, 101, 179n4.1, 180n5.3

nonreplacement of media, 28–29, 32–33

O'Reilly Factor, 35

objectivity, 3, 19–20, 162

online news, impact of: advertising and, 174, 177; audience activity and, 161–165; citizen journalism and, 168,

style-based, 77–79; topic-based, 4, 71–77, 82, 100–102, 121, 126, 139. *See also* specialization

selective exposure, 24, 86, 91, 165

selectivity: advertisers and, 85; audience demography and, 90–91; audience desires and, 84–86, 103; audience ideology and, 98–99; credibility and, 92–93; deliberate story selection and, 93; diversity of news sources and, 97–99; incidental exposure and, 89–90; interactivity and, 84; learned media use and, 91; news formats and, 90–91; news versus nonnews choice, 87–91; personal preference and, 88; popularity and, 92, 94; reputation and, 91–92, 98; serendipitous story selection and, 93–95; topic selection and, 100–104; web page layout and, 94–96

serendipitous story selection, 93–95

Shah, Dhavan, 51

Skoric, Mario, 112

Slate, 49, 61

social media, 41, 46, 52, 59, 71, 136. *See also* Facebook, Twitter.

soft news, 64, 77–79, 81, 90–91, 106

South Korea, 61, 112

specialization: advertisers and, 67–68; distribution and, 70; EPS cycle and, 64–67, 69, 81; internet and, 66–68; large news sites, 69–70, 81; limits of 80–81; mobile devices and, 70; news blogs and, 68–69; radio and, 65. *See also* segmentation.

story prominence, 55, 165

story repetition, 55–56

Stroud, Natalie Jomini, 112, 140

technological determinism, 8

Technorati, 50

techPresident, 68

television: adoption of, 8, 30; decline of, 12, 31, 32; expansion of, 26–27, 28–29, 65, 124; learning from, 106, 116, 118;

mass-public model of communication and, 148–149, 163; news on, 3, 20, 32, 34, 109–110; news agenda and, 54–55; news format and, 55, 77–78, 109–110; specialization and, 35; websites and, 42, 44–48. *See also* cable television

Tewksbury, David, 113

Thurmond, Strom, 57, 78

Time Warner, 61, 156

Time, 61, 91

topic tags, 50

Twitter, 11, 38, 50, 52, 76, 135–136, 137, 168, 176

U.S. Congress, 157

U.S. elections: 2000, 113; 2004, 61, 112, 140–141; 2008, 35, 46; 2010, 138–139

United Airlines, 53

USA Today, 72–74, 92

uses-and-gratifications perspective, 24, 28, 88, 91, 93, 108–109

Vevo, 156

Viacom, 150, 156

videocassette recorders (VCRs), 28

videotex, 31, 107

visual convergence, 45–46

Walker, Dana, 51

Wall Street Journal, 125

Washington Post, 22, 49, 60, 61, 125

Washington Times, 125

web browsers, 31, 66, 70

web logs. See blogs

Webster, James, 120–121, 134

Wikipedia, 168, 169

wikis, 47, 154

wire services, 34, 43–44, 135, 174–175

Wired, 22

Yahoo! News, 53, 61, 75–76, 81, 92, 103, 125

YouTube, 150

CPSIA information can be obtained at www.ICGtesting.com
Printed in the USA
BVOW041217191012

303391BV00003B/1/P